The

University

in a

Corporate

Culture

——————————

THE

UNIVERSITY

IN A

CORPORATE

CULTURE

Eric Gould

Yale University Press   *New Haven & London*

For Diane

Published with assistance from the foundation established in memory of
Philip Hamilton McMillan of the Class of 1894, Yale College.

Printed in the United States of America.

Library of Congress Cataloging-in-Publication Data
Gould, Eric, 1943–
The university in a corporate culture / Eric Gould.
  p.   cm.
Includes bibliographical references and index.
ISBN 0-300-08706-3 (alk. paper)
1. Education, Higher—Economic aspects—United States. 2. Industry
and education—United States. 3. Education, Higher—Aims and
objectives—United States.   I. Title.
LC67 .62 .G68 2003
338.4'3378—dc21   2002014242

A catalogue record for this book is available from the British Library.

The paper in this book meets the guidelines for permanence and durability of the
Committee on Production Guidelines for Book Longevity of the Council on Library
Resources.

10   9   8   7   6   5   4   3   2   1

Contents

Preface   vii

CHAPTER 1. A Complex Mission in a Market Culture   1

CHAPTER 2. The Consumerist Culture of the University   38

CHAPTER 3. A Corporate Ethos   79

CHAPTER 4. Faculty and the Division of Labor   113

CHAPTER 5. The Ideal of a Liberal Education   143

CHAPTER 6. Knowledge, Modernity, and Pragmatism   174

CHAPTER 7. Democratic Education   208

Notes   227

Index   239

Preface

For more than a hundred years, following the rise of the new industrial economy in the late nineteenth century, higher education in the United States has developed an increasingly complex capitalist market in its own right. How that educational marketplace has served to shape democratic educational ideals and the development of knowledge is the subject of this book. The scope is more modest than this preamble might suggest, since I do not focus on the impact of technology, the development of technoscience, and the intricate politics of sponsored research in the university, which have all been well covered elsewhere.[1] But I do go into detail about how the university has become, as Thorstein Veblen rather presciently noted in 1918, a "corporation of learning." I am especially interested in the way the economics, politics, and bureaucratic structures of the university shape the nature of knowledge and how the market has had an extraordinary influence on what is valued in teaching and learning.

The politics of corporate and government connections to the university through the funding of research and other special two-way relations allow for a relatively objective analysis. More intangible, yet equally important, is the impact of the market on the way we define knowledge in the liberal arts and sciences, especially as it is developed in undergraduate studies. For a long time this definition has been in the domain of liberal education. If universities promote a general, introductory "sampler" education in the disciplines of the arts and sciences along with a liberal dose of literacy training and humanist theory to bind it all together, it is assumed that all will be well. Perhaps, but the days when we can safely leave a liberal education to course distribution requirements are probably over. This book does not assume any natural hegemony for liberal studies in the modern university or any easy definition of a liberal or general education. Much of the book is given over, then, to a discussion of how the market economy of the American university has strongly challenged the power of the liberal arts disciplines. It also argues for how we might revise the basic principles of liberal learning to develop a stronger and more coherent *democratic liberal education* at the undergraduate level. My study aims to provide a detailed account of the market effects on university culture and their impact on the development of knowledge, along with a close look at the philosophy of liberal education and how it has developed over the years. The book also differs from more radical critiques of the university in that it aims to work with the realpolitik of higher education and not assume that the market nature of U.S. university culture is going to change.

A complex and remarkably ambitious public mission has evolved from the diversified market culture of higher education in the past century, and education policymakers are still seeking ways to prioritize and focus that mission. The closest we can come today, perhaps, is to talk about the social mission of the university: its oft-stated belief that all its activities—from research to general education to civic education to professional education—are anchored in a sense of public duty, a concern for the common good. Faculty in the arts and sciences participate in some version of a democratic education, the business of replicating and transmitting the social, intellectual, cultural, and political ideals that inform a liberal democracy. This for me is the starting point, the place from which one might develop an idea of the university that links the best of what we have to offer in the arts and sciences with the power of our social idealism and concern for social justice.

For a number of reasons that have as much to do with the development of knowledge inside the university as with the pressures from without, the modern university in the United States is an institution with an intensely contradictory culture. It is one in which even the word *culture* is problematic. It is a corporation of learning that has developed pervasively influential, corporate-styled efficiencies in management, public relations, and the development of knowledge itself. It is a professional training institution as well as a place dedicated to nurturing the intellect. It is home to many of the world's great researchers, scholars, and teachers. The sheer complexity of the modern American university is daunting; its power to shape social ideals and to generate new knowledge is extraordinary. Yet its market culture is in many ways problematic because it strongly favors knowledge with exchange value over knowledge with symbolic and cultural value. It is supportive of competition and entrepreneurial thinking, but it does not allow easy access to a high quality education. The economic future of higher education, of both its institutions and its clientele, is troubling. In addition, Americans are floundering about with no integrative social and intellectual ideal as the mission for higher education. We do not possess a definitive idea of the contemporary university. We have taken a more entrepreneurial than theoretical route to self-definition in relation to the other, larger, commercial marketplace. And we speak rather too easily of service to society without including a strong rationale for what we mean by service, what kind of society we are trying to shape, or what our mission is in mediating liberal capitalism's discontents.

The central challenge facing the contemporary American university is the need to be particularly innovative in responding to market pressures in the arts, humanities, social and natural sciences.

Of course other writers have said this too, proposing even that we go beyond the corporate university or that we dismantle it and create true higher learning.[2] But universities are going to continue functioning in a market culture. The search for important knowledge in technoscience is not going to slow down. University bureaucracies are not going to look less like corporate bureaucracies in the future. Students are not going to cease the search for credentials for the workplace. Neither are they going to have fewer problems financing their education. Discipline-based knowledge in the arts and sciences is not going to become less professionalized. The old ideal of a liberal education as something that is pursued for its own sake is most unlikely to have a revival in a marketplace in which the exchange value of knowledge is regarded as being of higher account than its symbolic value. The role of the university in mediating what are increasingly obvious contradictions in our democratic and market cultures is not going to become less demanding. But all this is not to say that we cannot find a more cogent idea for the university within this culture or that we cannot rethink what we mean by a liberal and a democratic education. My argument is that if we do not prioritize the mission and establish a firm understanding of what a democratic education is, the university will implode under the weight of its own entrepreneurial instincts.

This book, then, is about the interplay between educational ideals and market forces in defining the modern American university, with a special focus on that most theorized of all educational enterprises, undergraduate general education. The argument of the book develops as follows. The first chapter sets up the issue: the complex mission of the university, the need to prioritize it, the problems of liberal education in the attempt to do so, and the power of the market to shape educational values. Chapter 2 details the market culture of higher education: its credentialism, its finances and business practices, its undemocratic public effects, and its impact on student learning. Chapter 3 explains the development of the modern American university as a corporation of learning, exploring the history and rhetoric of its business-styled culture and how that has shaped the contradictory nature of knowledge as commodity and capital. The fourth chapter is about the impact of the university's corporate culture on faculty: the threat to academic freedom and the radical division of labor that has occurred in the modern university, which not only defines faculty work but has evoked much anxiety. Against this backdrop of market thinking that propels modern university politics, chapter 5 explores the ideal of a liberal education from the ancient Greek academies to the present day in search of a theory of how intellectual and humanistic learning can be valorized in a market culture. I take into account various traditional concepts for dealing with knowledge itself, the importance of argument and rhetoric, and concerns for knowledge for its own sake. Then, in chapter 6, I build on the history of ideas about liberal education to define a *pragmatic humanism,* starting with John Dewey and ending with spokespeople for the "knowledge economy," considering how pragmatism might address ways of linking concepts of culture and society, enlightenment and modernity, utilitarian and humanist knowledge. Chapter 7, "Democratic Education," summarizes the argument. It explores how liberal learning in the corporate university is concerned with negotiations between power and knowledge, which is also precisely what a democratic education is about.

The book deals with two basic cultural conditions that have long been in place in the American university. The first is that its complex mission has evolved within and has been sustained by a market system. Universities are in competition one with another for students and funding. State and federal governments step in to help and to make some few academic demands, but there are no thoroughgoing national controls, no common set of standards for intellectual achievement, degree quality, accreditation, or assessment of learning. There are many first-rate institutions of higher learning, and the system has a remarkable way of sustaining itself with some measure of self-regulation. But higher education is always under negotiation. As in all markets, even standards and values are relative, a fact which strongly challenges the principle of a democratic education in the full sense of the term: providing an education for democracy and an education available to all who want it and are qualified for it.

The second cultural condition that shapes the argument of this book is the sheer complexity of the social mission of higher education. American higher education may be deeply corporatized in its management systems and preoccupied with developing knowledge primarily for its exchange value. But higher education is equally concerned to do the right public thing, and that right thing is about sustaining the American way of life, educating a broad section of the community, and insisting on the search for new knowledge. All this is part of the rhetoric of the university's best intent. But are we really cultivating democracy the best we can in our university system? It is easy to argue, as I will, that the cultural contradictions of academe develop from the same contradictions that drive any capitalist-styled democracy—the tension between culture and society, between modernity and tradition, between free-market thinking and social justice, between divided labor and happily productive workers. But how can those contradictions be resolved, if at all?

Any book like this must be political, for the simple reason that there is no full agreement about what the American university should look like, even while the American public expects it to serve society at large. Many theorists and public intellectuals deliver messages about how the university is connected to democratic agendas and to taxonomies of learning. Many humanists tell us what humanity is really like and what it needs to know. Universities are social institutions entrusted with the role of mediation and reproduction, with synthesizing important public knowledge. But the problem is that the academy has trouble mediating its own contradictions, let alone anyone else's. And there is no indication that faculty are having much effect as public intellectuals. Nonetheless, we have to engage the problem, which is that the culture of higher education has evolved from a rich but conflicting history of ideas, from complex and often contradictory structures of organizational power, from academic professionalism as much as corporate management strategies, from a contentious relation to society and the world of politics, and from a positively Darwinian market culture. How does one make sense of all that?

In approaching this broad cultural dilemma, I still find the university, at its best, too well intentioned and idealistic to be in the ruined state that some writers claim it is in.[3] It certainly is in trouble, and much that I will describe—from corporatism to faculty professionalism—has sad implications if left to run unchecked. Besides, if one defines *trouble* by uncertain community relations and unclear strategic planning, then the American university has been in trouble for more than a hundred years, as have universities all over the world. The cultural value of the university is down one moment and up the next, and it has been both overvalued and undervalued with the best and the worst intentions. It is also without question the most overtheorized of all social institutions, and every bit as undercapitalized as any of them. The only way it can be defined as ruined is if in a bygone age it was quite different and considerably better— but no study has been able to show that convincingly. On the contrary, I will argue that the current university system not only has close affiliations with the pragmatic ideals of liberal education that began long before Dewey, but also has evolved into an institution that could still reflect with great effect on what it is like to live in a capitalist democracy, with all the attendant responsibilities, delights, and perplexities that entails.

Of course, one could argue that one shouldn't be living in a capitalist democracy, as a number of educational critics imply, or that if one must, then higher education, at least, should not be a capitalist enterprise. This latter thought has crossed my mind more than once. But I take it as a given that because Americans live in a capitalist democracy and like it that way and also because they like the fact that their universities can in principle contribute to the achievements of liberal democracy and mediate the discontents of capitalism, so higher education is a capitalist enterprise. That it will have to modify its capitalism in the future in order to survive is another issue. But I am not assuming that ideally we should be inhabiting another world, nor is my message a dystopian one. We have the educational system we seem to want and deserve. But I also think that academe must more consciously, thoughtfully, and outspokenly mediate the contradictions of its own culture as well as the problems of society at large by rethinking the curriculum and its working philosophy. Some fine studies notwithstanding, the theorizing of academic culture is not as widespread as it might be and certainly is not institutionalized in the curriculum itself. At times we barely show we have understood the historical origins of the university or its philosophical underpinnings.

Instead, universities pursue a utilitarian rationality coupled with a rousing rhetoric of entrepreneurial brilliance to convince the public that they are responsible and competitive business entities and that the knowledge they sell is cutting edge. They often act as though cultural values and cognitive rationality are not the real focus of undergraduate education; getting ahead in life is. Thus disputes over what should be in the curriculum continue, and the culture wars are not over. University politics tend to be noisy and disconcerting to a public for whom the political give and take in American society at large rarely reveals deep ideological differences. In many ways, the only place where ideology actually has a home today is in higher edu-

cation, for we are erasing all boundaries elsewhere in our multimediated culture, and some would say we are doing our best to erase them
in the university too. Serious political differences lie at the heart of
higher education in a complicated way, for universities are by necessity wedded to capitalism, the pursuit of knowledge, and agendas for
sustaining social justice and academic freedom all at once.

My argument, then, aims to go beyond Left and Right. Arguments about the contemporary university seem to make most
sense when they put aside concern over who sits at the left hand of
the king or queen and who at the right and concentrate rather on
whether he or she is doing a good job or not—and who is counting
the votes. Not fully trusting the monarch, after all, is the American
way; lack of trust in educational policy and practices is something
we all have in common. Very few critics or scholars today are willing
to oppose the democratic impulse deeply inherent in the American
educational agenda, and rightly so. Some notion of the egalitarian
mission of higher education seems shared by almost all commenta-
tors. Democracy and constitutional rights are invoked with equal
passion by both Left and Right, even if we still have a long way to go
before all university communities reflect a full range of diversity
based on social background, race, gender, political views, and economic advantage.

There are many published critiques of the university from the
Left and from the Right, and they usually concern exactly the same
issues—the academy's social failures, its narrow professionalism, its
inability to provide a democratic education—but from different perspectives. The social failures for the Left tend to result from allegations of egregious academic profit motives and market-driven
thinking; for the Right, they result from social engineering through
liberal multiculturalist agendas and political correctness. And once
one has waded through the rhetoric and lived the academic culture,
one finds there is reason on both sides. There is also a complicating

politics of nostalgia inside the university, for academics readily dream of a past time when students were smarter and liberal learning was lord over all. So there is a good deal of eloquent humanist discourse available—the kind that insists that the humanities have to do with being human and therefore must be central. I feel much sympathy for this view, but, as a humanist, I interpret being human, rather like being creative or even being aesthetic, as having wide ownership in the community. A number of academic disciplines, for example, many not in the arts and humanities, have very useful insights into what being human involves. So too do many public intellectuals and people who do not work in academe but who sustain the humanities through their appreciation of the arts and sciences. So I do not want to propose a narrow "cultivating humanity in the humanities" solution, however important it is, because humanism is not an exclusively academic enterprise confined to one or two departments; indeed, at its best, it is not an academic enterprise at all. Neither do I long for a return to a time when knowledge was somehow free of contradictions and not corporate because no such time has ever existed for the American university.

If this book is to be different, useful, and fresh on the subject of the contemporary American university, then it needs to be more existential and contextualist than discussions of liberal learning usually are. It needs first to explore the economics and politics of the university as the context for the curriculum; it cannot see liberal learning as a separate peace faculty make with themselves and their students somewhere distant from the business school. It needs to make sense of the contradictory culture of academe, trying to capture the influences on education from all major campus perspectives and not merely that of the radical or the professional sensitive. And it needs to be able to argue that citizenship (whose Greek word is the origin of our term *politics*) is always political and a work in progress. For the curriculum is not pure and unadulterated; it is itself intensely rhetorical in its efforts to define what makes us human. The business of the university is political, then, not simply because it is a place of Machiavellian intrigue, self-serving negotiation, passive aggression, devious alliances, and mind-numbing committee discussions—all of which it is—but because it is a place where citizens critique knowledge in the service of defining happiness and a democratic community.

The problem for me in writing this book, apart from all the theoretical issues listed above, is that the debate about the mission and accomplishments of American higher education has had a life of its own in an immigrant body. I am not sure this book solves my mind-body problem, but it does at least try to be honest about the thorny but necessary work of seeing both sides of the question: the difficulty of playing off idealism against market thinking, American against European and postcolonial habits. It is written from the perspective of someone who had wonderful experiences growing up and being academically trained elsewhere, in New Zealand and the United Kingdom, places that were not then market systems of learning. Yet I have a real affection for the remarkable energy and egalitarian hopes of American higher education, an admiration born of thirty years' experience as an English professor and university administrator in this country. This is, in the end, a very personal book, one in which I debate with myself the pros and cons of what is still for me a somewhat foreign and yet familiar system of higher education—one that I never cease to find provocative and enticing.

Of course, those not indigenously cultural never quite get it right, we are often told these days. But I hope I have come close. And if that is the case, then I want to thank those good friends and colleagues over the years, especially at the University of Denver, who have educated me in the ways of a market-driven democratic education. There have been times when the contradictions of such a culture appeared sharp indeed, and the reader will notice that, I expect. There have been moments when one can only marvel at the collective good will and intelligence of people who, with an un-characteristic lack of academic hubris, have wanted to make higher education work better for the good of the academic community as well as the public and have put their reputations and their re-sources on the line in this effort. But I won't mention by name those friends and colleagues who have helped me—faculty, students, and administrators—because I'm not sure whether I would be promot-ing their careers by doing so. They know who they are and they know they are thanked.

But I can publicly thank my parents, Coula and George, who in their peripatetics taught me the importance of looking at things from an international perspective. Theirs was and is a lovely wisdom that grew out of the spirit of place. I thank Gladys Topkis of Yale University Press for her support, advice, and fine editing, even if she is not responsible for the claims of this book. Thanks go to Jonathan Brent and his staff at the press, especially Erin Carter and Lawrence Kenney, for seeing this project through most graciously. And, as she knows, I thank over and over again my wife, Diane, who really has shown me, among so many other things, the best of what an Ameri-can liberal education can be.

The

University

in a

Corporate

Culture

———————————

CHAPTER 1

A Complex Mission in a Market Culture

The years following the American Civil War saw the rise of the "university movement" in the United States through the founding of land-grant institutions under the Morrill Acts of 1862 and 1890. In these years, too, came the development of universities on the German scientific research model. Both land-grant and research universities filled important national needs for new and useful knowledge, but at the same time they challenged the centrality of the liberal arts, which had sustained higher education and its cultural mission since the nine English colonial colleges were founded before the American Revolution. Born of democratic idealism and the fast-growing capitalist economy and accompanying the move of the sprawling agrarian republic to a modern industrialized and urbanized nation, the universities that dominated American higher education by the turn of the century brought a new professionalism to learning. They promoted the development of knowledge in a society that needed strong educational institutions to theorize America's increased power in the world and to mediate the spread of capitalism and democracy within the United States.

Thus developed a remarkably comprehensive university mission for higher education, one whose huge ambitions we are still trying to understand and prioritize. While there never has been a generic mission for American universities, educational histories make it clear that at least four main goals powered their progress by the early years of the twentieth century:[1]

- *General, liberal education* dedicated, as President Charles Eliot of Harvard put it, to "intellectual culture in the development of the breadth, serenity, and solidity of mind, and in the attainment of that complete self-possession which finds expression in character";[2]
- *Research and scholarship* that professionalized the academic disciplines, developed the sciences as the dominant model for research protocols, and encouraged the growth of specialized learning;
- *Support for the economy through the provision of useful knowledge* by developing professional skills for the service of industry, agriculture, the state, and the community and by developing the work competencies of a broad section of the population;
- *Service to society* by providing knowledge in the national interest, transmitting democratic values and helping to shape the national character, creating a social meritocracy, and socializing students into what it meant to be a modern, newly progressive American.

These four basic goals have continued in an alliance to the present day, with different kinds of institutions tending to emphasize different aspects of the educational mission. Public research universities began with a special focus on advanced degrees but soon became multiversities offering a broad range of scholarly and professional specialization. It is estimated that by 1920 only about 25 universities could legitimately claim to have a comprehensive research agenda.[3] But by 2001, just over 150 public and private institutions were listed in the Carnegie classification of doctoral research universities, not a remarkable number considering there are 3,900 institutions of higher education in the United States, but certainly enough to show that research plays a large role in elite university education. The top 50 institutions ranked in federal research-and-development expenditures for 2000 received more than $14 billion in funds.[4] Land-grant universities began as regional schools that offered, as Morrill himself claimed, a professional as well as liberal education for "the industrial classes." But with the decline of agriculture and the move to a postindustrial economy, they now reach beyond state boundaries with strong research programs—a number are included in the top 50 for federal funding—and comprehensive offerings in graduate and undergraduate education. A few specialized institutes and polytechnics have developed science and technology research in highly sophisticated ways. Smaller, private urban universities often function as liberal arts colleges surrounded by professional schools, and they usually offer a range of graduate credentials. For-profit universities have grown rapidly in recent years as professional and vocational training centers. Liberal arts colleges have maintained a primary emphasis on intellectual culture at the undergraduate level but often reach out to professional and nontraditional audiences.

However diversified higher education has become, though, the majority of American universities focus on a broad mission that serves both the individual and society while implicitly seeking to support democratic institutions and a market-driven economy. They serve the growth of knowledge, personal development, social and cultural values, and professional training all at once. Read any contemporary university mission statement and you will most likely find reference to all four major goals cited to justify the rise of the modern American university a hundred years ago. You will probably not find a statement that liberal education is the integrating factor in higher education. But there is broad traditional consensus on the importance of the distinctively American liberal arts model for undergraduate education, one in which students are required to take a broad range of courses in the disciplines of the arts and sciences over four years, even if they are majoring in business or another professional field. Business is by far the biggest undergraduate major in the United States, but a sampler education in the liberal arts at least is assumed to provide the basic rationale for the university's undergraduate mission. Thus universities believe that the so-called outcomes of liberal education—for example, critical and imaginative thinking, a concern for ethics and cultural values, and training in the basic literacies—undergird their strong social idealism.

In describing their mission, universities work with a list of goals and values that tend to repeat themselves from one school to another. Mission statements are designed to set forth major principles for education and their relation to public needs. No one reads them too closely, even if their preparation often requires university-wide committees dedicated to the task, one that has to be regularly repeated. Students do not choose their colleges by comparing mission statements because there is little difference between the various philosophies they contain. Yet the statements are purposefully symbolic of why colleges and universities believe they are in business and reveal how consistent is the broad set of goals driving American higher education in the past one hundred years.

Here is a typical example of how a highly ranked, midsized, urban, private, comprehensive university has recently sought to define its educational mission. This university's intent is "to promote learning by engaging students, advancing scholarly inquiry, cultivating critical thought, and creating knowledge. We empower the lives and futures of students by fostering productive synergies between intellectual and personal development, research and teaching, disciplinary and interdisciplinary perspectives, classroom and experience-based learning, and theoretical knowledge and professional practice. Our engagement with diverse local and global communities contributes to the common good."[5]

All the university mission statements I surveyed in a representative sample are very similar to this one.[6] No one can mistake what the modern university stands for: service to society. No one reading closely can miss what such statements all leave out: how one gets from engaging students to empowering social ideals through learning, multiple perspectives, "productive synergies," and so on. What is left out is the actual process of education, the content of the curriculum, the pedagogy that drives it all—this is not unreasonable given that the mission statement is like an advertisement. It is an enthymeme or argument in which a claim is made with limited explanation: we get the first premise ([a] promote learning by engaging students) and a conclusion ([c] contribute to the common good). The trick, of course, is getting from (a) to (c), and that is what has preoccupied educational theorists for a century and more. It is also what will preoccupy this book.

Frequently, mission statements are accompanied by visions and sets of values. These help a little. But in the main, the real questions—What holds an undergraduate education together as students roam from subject to subject? What educational process actually leads to developing the values and outcomes citizens cherish so much?—are left very open. Few schools leave out mention of striving for and achieving excellence, but excellence, we know, is a highly relative term: one school's excellence is another's mediocrity. Most recognize the importance of technology to assist learning, and ancillary goals often include good stewardship of resources, training in leadership, interdisciplinary studies, experiential and lifelong learning, holistic education, and bold and innovative thought. These are all interesting curricular and ideological add-ons. But basically, any university's mission statement implies that higher education believes in very general terms that there is a connection between knowledge and power in our democratic agenda, that somehow a liberal education contributes to this, that empowerment (intellectual and economic) naturally follows from gaining knowledge, and that knowledge is often needed by and shaped for those who already have power. These hardheaded facts are embedded in an egalitarian, pragmatic humanism, along with a multicultural and even internationalist set of cultural values.

So why not simply say that we prize a liberal education above all, since it has traditionally been assumed to do all these things? For a number of reasons that I want to explore in this book, *liberal education* no longer has the cachet it once had as a way of describing what higher education is really all about. It clearly needs redefinition and not simply the restatement, however eloquent, that it has received in recent years from a number of humanists. Its values remain, perhaps —those virtues of the whole, the inquisitive, and the wise person— but we have (a) an extraordinarily complex mission in the contemporary university, no matter what its size, and the utilitarian value of knowledge is sorely challenging its symbolic value; (b) we rely heavily on exposure to the social sciences and sciences to instill cognitive rationality, and this has plainly a greater value for the public than intuitive or inductive epistemologies; (c) we are wary and somewhat skittish, after the long culture wars, of culture itself and have little agreement over its values; (d) we have thrown higher education to the marketplace to solve our curricular problems, and the university has become more and more like a business in recent years, one that sees theory as an unnecessary complication; and (e) we have never in our educational history had a sustaining idea of what a university undergraduate education consists of, even though we seem to muddle through with great credit in a number of schools. Again, the general goals of higher education focus mainly on a comprehensive social mandate for higher education, one that seems to reflect that we want such an education to offset the consumerist culture that drives our economy, even while we replicate that very same culture in the university.

But not all see consumerism as the enemy. Higher education, after all, is the child of its context; it is driven by social forces of change—technological, social, economic, cultural, and political— that challenge any single integrative *idea* for the university. It is also the child of its market context, which relentlessly organizes both the management and development of knowledge. Universities are allowed the indulgence of pursuing esoteric knowledge, but so often we hear that it is most important for universities to respond quickly to public needs, to be flexible in meeting external demands, and to improve faculty productivity and efficiency in the process. University presidents are quite outspoken about the need for higher education to be more businesslike and effective in supporting public concerns.

As James J. Duderstadt, a recent president of the University of Michigan, says at the conclusion of his study *A University for the 21st Century,*

> We have entered a period of significant change in higher educa-tion as our universities attempt to respond to the challenges, opportunities, and responsibilities before them. This time of great change, of shifting paradigms, provides the context in which we must consider the changing nature of the university.
>
> Much of this change will be driven by market forces—by a limited resource base, changing societal needs, new technologies, and new competitors. But we also must remember that higher education has a public purpose and a public obligation. Those of us in higher education must always keep before us two questions: "Whom do we serve?" and "How can we serve better?" And society must work to shape and form the markets that will in turn reshape our institutions with appropriate civic purpose.
>
> From this perspective, it is important to understand that the most critical challenge facing most institutions will be to de-velop the capacity for change. . . . universities must seek to remove the constraints that prevent them from responding to the needs of a rapidly changing society. They should strive to challenge, excite, and embolden all members of their academic communities to embark on what should be a great adventure for higher education.
>
> While many academics are reluctant to accept the necessity or validity of formal planning activities, woe be it to the institu-tions that turn aside from strategic efforts to determine their futures.[7]

Apart from trying to win us over by arguing for the drama of shifting paradigms, this is, of course, a benign way of saying that the future belongs to the entrepreneurial, which Duderstadt clearly does say in a book that manages not to use the term *liberal education.* "The entrepreneurial university has been remarkably adaptive and resilient throughout the twentieth century," he writes, "but it still faces some major challenges as it moves into the next century. We must find ways to allow our most creative people to drive the future of our institutions rather than simply reacting to the opportunities and challenges of the moment. Our challenge is to tap the great source of creativity and energy associated with our faculty's entrepreneurial activity in a way that preserves our core missions, character, and values."[8]

So public needs are identified as market needs, students are now "active learners," learning takes place mainly in "learning communities," knowledge "is created, sustained, and transformed in 'communities of practice,' " and faculty are no longer teachers but "designers of learning experiences." The thrust of the book, the perceptible hum of annoyance with traditional liberal learning behind the rhetoric of corporate eduspeak, albeit in a study fulsomely praised by a number of leading university presidents, is perhaps understandable. Faculty who insist on traditional paradigms above all and refuse to budge from a narrow professionalism can indeed be infuriating— and to other faculty, too, not just to university presidents. And of course the emphasis on student learning, on a new sensitivity to the fact that students are not passive receptacles of information but learn best when they too can be creative with the information they have, is important as well. But the entrepreneurs of the new university did not invent this. Good teachers have always known it; the oldest form of learning in the Greek academies took place in groups; questions have been part of intelligent answers for more than two thousand years, and some answers have only been intelligent questions. Furthermore, we need more substance to the argument that things must change in the liberal arts—which I am also arguing must happen—and not simply because change is demanded by the market and the "global knowledge and learning industry" inevitably absorbs such change. We need to identify the complexity of our social mission as something more than a market inspiration but as a genuinely democratic enterprise, one that may very well be a gendered epistemology, and a multicultural one too.

The spirit of everything Duderstadt says is in keeping with the longtime mission of the American university, which, in the past one hundred years or so, has been dedicated to actively sustaining a competitive liberal democracy and its knowledge-based economy. It is also not unreasonable that this president finds that liberal learning lacks a certain panache in our age of corporate-styled entrepreneurialism. I think it does too. But it is precisely our deep concern to support democratic institutions and the economy at the same time, and our need to acknowledge the contradictions this can create, that must lead us to substantive ways of preserving knowledge as having something other than mere exchange value. Our passionate pilgrimage into democracy and liberal capitalism through the university, after all, is the key to understanding the remarkable scope of U.S. higher education and its widely publicized discontents in recent years, and not simply the decline of the concept of liberal education. After all, the market-driven flexibility demanded of the university informed its runaway growth in the 1960s and 1970s, its ongoing financial concerns and growing costs, its difficulty in diversifying in order to keep up with demographic changes (or its overdiversification into multicultural correctness, depending on whom one is speaking to), the lack of national standards and a general "dumbing down" of academic expectations, a declining interest in liberal arts degrees, the increasing culture of entitlement among students, the comprehensive spread of corporate culture in managing and generating knowledge, the shrinking job market for specialized PhDs as vocational education takes over, and the slow but steady breakdown of the traditional disciplines. All these issues grow out of a simple, well-known fact of university life in America: universities are of central importance to society because they must reproduce the American way of life for succeeding generations, sustain liberal capitalism with appropriate energy, support research, and do all this within a market-driven culture.

The Discontents of Liberal Education

For some centuries, when there were fewer academic disciplines but not a lesser challenge to understanding the world, the philosophical motives and analytic skills of liberal education were all of learning, both a theoretical and a practical approach to understanding self and society, culture and nature. The disciplines focused on the nature of knowledge itself, and for some in the arts and sciences this has not changed. I am not sure, therefore, that everyone would agree that anything has gone wrong with liberal education because of the way the disciplines have become more specialized. Many faculty especially believe, maybe with good reason, that the social mission of the university is strongly upheld by the cumulative effect of taking courses in the arts and sciences in their particular schools, and that their students have had the experience and not missed the meaning. It is, of course, impossible to generalize the effectiveness of liberal education because it is variously taught and is the most osmotic of learning experiences, turning up in unexpected memories and insights sometimes years after the event. One relies mainly on one's own experience in making such judgments of worth but also on the fact that fewer and fewer degrees are being awarded in liberal arts fields, a trend that both critics and government statistics show has been going on for nearly a century. Of course, there is increasing complaint about the rigid barriers between the traditional disciplines and the decline of liberal learning because faculty in the arts and sciences find it difficult to cooperate on scholarly issues. And one can also refer to some interesting statistics about the puzzling reputation of liberal learning today, which I do below.

My argument is that two things in particular have gone wrong with liberal learning under the influence of enormous market pressures to develop professionism and usable knowledge in all academic fields. If the major thrust of the university's mission is service to society, in all the subtle ways that the mission statement implies, then only an ideal of an integrative education can make sense of this complexity. And a broad liberal education really has the expertise to provide an integrated focus on analytic, ethical, historical, and aesthetic issues. Only through the liberal arts and sciences are a broad number of perspectives on the nature of reality available.

So the first problem—this is not a new argument—is that liberal learning remains relentlessly specialized and discipline centered. The barriers between the disciplines have not fallen, even though the fault lines are clear. Only briefly, here and there, largely through the wisdom of a historian like Eric Hobsbawm or an economist like John Kenneth Galbraith or a scientist like Stephen Jay Gould or Richard Feynman or a poet like John Ashbery or a philosopher like Isaiah Berlin, do we see glimpses of what it is to have a broadly informed grasp of a subject like evolution, a concept of power, a sense of the historical extremes of the past century, the paradoxes of physics, the complexity of time, or the dangers of utopian thinking. This is, of course, a very general observation. Everyone has his or her own favorite thinkers who seem to see experience somewhat if not entirely whole and can argue for a worldview from a close reading of the history of ideas and with persuasive displays of learning. Yet this is, surely, what we hope a lifetime of learning can bring and certainly what four years of liberal learning in college might at least set us up to hope to achieve: the modest but meaningful personal development of an experience-based, open-ended, personal philosophy that might be called a worldview.

This can still be met by effort, but we leave a lot to chance in our vast tour of the disciplines in undergraduate education. Liberal arts and sciences faculty too infrequently cooperate on interdisciplinary themes and integrative topics but believe, understandably, in the professionalism of each of the majors. Faculty are, after all, living proof of the importance of this, for it is the measure of academic reputation and self-respect. But the liberal arts disciplines are more than individual methodologies; they are each part of a group of disciplines that have developed interdisciplinary tentacles over two thousand years in the pursuit of essential knowledge about what it is to be human. It is difficult to study one discipline without realizing the related importance of another. The disciplines need, as nearly as possible, to be studied together for their combined effect in addressing major social, cultural, scientific, and environmental issues. Only this offers us the hope of developing the knowledge necessary to understand the world in an integrated way. Institutes spring up inside and outside academe to bring together people of various perspectives to study special social problems and issues in this way, but undergraduate and graduate education has not emphasized the importance of dramatizing interdisciplinary problem-solving approaches to key social and intellectual issues.

The second problem with liberal education lies in the difficulty of reaching consensus on the meaning of the word *liberal*: its historical meaning is complex, and neither the public nor the academy is quite clear about what a liberal education is. Consider the range of contemporary meanings of the term, for that in itself reveals the problem of opting for this traditional definition of undergraduate general education. *Liberal* derives from the Latin *liberare,* to free. A liberal education, then, has been described as one *for a free mind,* a mind curious to roam where it will, intent on study for its own sake. (But does this imply an elitist education, one only for those who can afford the luxury? Can knowledge ever be free and an end in itself?) A liberal education is also one that *frees the mind,* that proposes to liberate it, to bolster its confidence in dealing with intellectual challenges. (But a mind free to do what, exactly? To serve its self, above all? Will it necessarily arrive at some concept of the common good? And what can we teach that will have such a liberating effect on the mind?) Recently, a liberal education has become for some a liberal as opposed to a conservative education, and the question of the political nature of a moral education comes to the fore. (Does this mean that a liberal education is inevitably politicized, or even a politically correct education?) And although education has no formal place in the Constitution, many would argue that a liberal education, even if not actually free, should at least be affordable. (Is it a democratic society's responsibility to its people to provide an affordable if not a free basic education, and if so, what should that comprise? Should a university education be open to all?)

The public simply does not know; and the academy does not make the meaning clear. In 1997, an extensive survey conducted for Richard Hersh, the president of Hobart and William Smith Colleges, found only 14 percent of high school students and only 27 percent of parents claimed to be very familiar with liberal arts education. Further, only 32 percent of university and specialty school graduates and 54 percent of business executives claimed familiarity with the term *liberal education.* The survey also produced the curious statistic that unlike students and parents, who "overwhelmingly believe the reason to go to college is to prepare for a prosperous career, fewer than 40 percent of business executives agree."[9]

Hersh interpreted the results this way: "As we enter the twenty-first century, the perceived value of a liberal arts education is seriously questioned by prospective college students and their parents, most of whom view higher education almost exclusively as preparation for jobs. . . . [I]n a review of more than 30 public opinion surveys [reported] in the May 12, 1993 *Chronicle of Higher Education*, researchers James Harvey and John Immerwahr found a consistent public belief that higher education was a necessity for employment. Moreover, liberal arts education was generally seen as irrelevant to this purpose." Hersh's own conclusions endorse this finding:

- "Few people still believe in the importance of learning for learning's sake. . . .
- "Parents and high school students have little or no idea what a liberal arts education is. . . .
- "Other than faculty members and liberal arts college graduates, few groups have positive feelings toward liberal arts education [which most people assume meant above all a "broad introduction to a wide variety of academic disciplines/well-rounded education"]. . . .
- "Most people believe you can get a liberal arts education anywhere— it's not unique [to colleges and universities]. . . .
- "On a number of measures, business executives have greater faith in the effectiveness of a liberal arts education than do parents . . . [and these measures include critical thinking, literacy, and problem-solving skills, professional school preparation, appreciation of culture, foreign language skills, self-discipline, global perspective, loyalty, and tolerance]
- "Students and parents overwhelmingly believe the reason to go to college is to prepare for a prosperous career—but fewer than 40 percent of business executives agree. . . .
- "When pushed, most people agree that problem-solving, critical thinking, and writing and oral skills—abilities traditionally imparted by a liberal arts education—are, in fact, career skills, and are the most important goals of higher education. . . .
- "Liberal arts colleges should teach skills for the workplace. . . .
- "No college or university is performing well, say parents and business executives, but small liberal arts colleges excel in certain areas: culture/arts appreciation and foreign language teaching. . . .

- "More than one-third of parents consider liberal arts education a luxury beyond their reach. . . .
- "Belief in the importance of a college education is significantly lower among college and high school faculty and administrators than in society at large."

Not surprisingly, Hersh's conclusions from these findings are the same ones frequently heard from administrators of liberal arts units or schools. Based on the belief that liberal education is a sampler education in the traditional arts and sciences disciplines, Hersh claims that the real importance of a liberal education is that it can satisfy many public needs at once, especially if supplemented by "business internships, international education, higher writing and speaking standards, and computer literacy." A liberal education can answer better than any other the public's "preoccupation with value," "the pursuit of quality-of-life goals," and "movement away from a focus on self." Indeed, this has become the primary justification for a liberal education even among those who most strongly support it: that it assumes importance precisely as the instigator of pragmatic, broadly humanistic values for a commercial culture. As Hersh further explains, "Small liberal arts colleges need to communicate better to their key audiences what the 'liberal arts' they offer mean in today's and tomorrow's world and provide evidence that they do offer important skills for the world of work. They need to demonstrate that small liberal arts colleges are 'places of value' where intellectual prowess, articulate communication, passion for ideas, engagement with others, the creation of meaning, security in the face of cultural, class, and social differences, and joy in new challenges are learned best with caring and dedicated teachers."

These are, of course, solid educational values, and, again, they are frequently invoked in colleges and universities across the country. But as appropriately down-to-earth as Hersh's goals for American liberal education are, the solution he proposes for our educational ills is little more than an argument for the socially therapeutic value of the arts and sciences mysteriously added to some practical skills courses, a formula that has been in place in many urban universities for years already. Our mission statements are mysterious enough about how we fill the gap between learning and the common good, but when liberal educators themselves cling to the mystery, one wonders what the future holds. In short, Hersh, along with other college and university presidents, urges more socialization and vocational training rather than a definition of why a liberal education is itself essential to produce the important list of outcomes he presents. After all, the credibility gap that has opened up between the liberal arts and the public at large derives not from the fact that the public is unconcerned with cultural and personal values, but from its uncertainty as to why pursuing a traditional liberal education will necessarily impart those values. We take a lot on faith in the world of liberal education.

Within faculty ranks, the view of liberal education is not vastly different. The most comprehensive survey of faculty attitudes and beliefs is "The American College Teacher," conducted every three years by the UCLA Institute for Higher Education. The two most recent surveys, in 1995–96 and 1998–99, each canvassed some thirty-four thousand faculty in institutions of all types and produced the following results, among others.[10] In 1995–96, only 53 percent of the faculty felt it important that "Western civilization and culture should be the foundation of the undergraduate curriculum," while only 28 percent of professors find teaching the classics of Western civilization essential or very important. In 1998–99, the number of faculty believing in the foundations of Western civilization had risen to 57 percent, but still only 28 percent wanted to teach the classics. Since 1989, the survey has shown that there has been "an increased commitment [by faculty] to diversity and multiculturalism." But when it comes to the goals of an undergraduate education that faculty think are "essential or very important," the survey does not allow criteria related to the content of the curriculum to be the focus. The issue is not what is taught, but whom it is taught to and to what ends. The two surveys revealed that faculty rank highest among the goals for undergraduate education "develop[ing] the ability to think clearly" (99.4 percent in both surveys). This is followed by "preparing students for employment after college" (69.9 percent in 1995–96, 70.7 percent in 1998–99), "enhanc[ing] students' self-understanding" (61.4 and 61.8 percent), preparing students "for responsible citizenship" (59.5 and 60 percent), and "develop[ing] personal values" (59.5 and 59.7 percent). Yet in each survey just over 62 percent of faculty think it is important that colleges be "actively involved in solving social problems," and, answering a new question in 1998–99, 60 percent of faculty think that an essential goal of undergraduate education is to prepare students for responsible citizenship. The survey, that is, reveals that faculty view the mission of the university as primarily social. Learning skills, civic responsibility, and character enhancement have taken center stage, while any sense of the value of specific knowledge in a liberal education has to a large extent been marginalized.

Surveys, of course, are only as good as the questions they ask, and this particularly broad survey sticks to socially anchored learning outcomes. The problem with this approach is not that clear thinking or socialization are unworthy goals, but that we continue to perpetuate an old problem, one the Harvard "Red Book" Report spelled out at some length in 1945 as our modern educational dilemma. In academe, the report said, we struggle between implementing an undergraduate curriculum that stresses a rationalized body of disciplinary knowledge covering the "nature of reality" *and* one that emphasizes student learning processes in a more pragmatic, inductively based curriculum that favors "learning by doing." We still have not found a successful way of resolving the concerns of the

Harvard Report because the ideal driving the organization of knowledge for faculty is disciplinary, while the ideal driving the university's mission in the public eye is more broadly process-centered, namely, socialization. Perhaps faculty and society are closer together these days in agreeing on pragmatic goals; but disciplinary knowledge and a social education have yet to find a happy blend because we lack a broadly accepted theory of democratic education. We certainly have strong theories of why a pragmatic education itself is important—none more strong than those of John Dewey. But the content of such a curriculum remains an open issue—as it always has and probably always should—yet we constantly need to readdress the following large issues in our public philosophy: What kind of higher education does the United States owe its citizens? What is the relation of a liberal education to good citizenship? To what extent can higher education be expected to solve the cultural contradictions of contemporary capitalist societies? What does it mean to be a citizen of the world? How can learning be more firmly grounded in the experience of democratic practices?

All these questions are difficult, quite as difficult as defining the word *liberal*. But they challenge us more than ever in the United States, and not just because of the millennial moment and the common call to refashion education "for the twenty-first century." That moment is real enough, but so too is the need to face up to our intellectual, cultural, and social responsibilities in higher education, which have been around for more than three hundred years and have rarely been effectively addressed of late by liberal learning as a collection of discrete university disciplines. The point is that no other country has put as much emphasis on linking higher learning to the formation of social values. Yet we entrust those values to an educational *market* and to corporate-styled promotional practices for higher learning. We have never developed in the United States a broadly accepted, comprehensive theory of liberal education linked to the mission—at least not since the old classical/theological college model lost its hegemony over cultural values with the rise of the modern university.

The Exchange Value versus the Symbolic Value of Knowledge

The main challenge to liberal learning now, then, is to renegotiate the relation between its symbolic and its exchange values. Historically, the liberal arts disciplines have promoted primarily their symbolic value: their ethical importance, their constitutive role in developing essential concepts of social justice, beauty, truth, power, and so on. In the absence of liberal learning it is difficult to theorize, with any degree of irony and self-assessment, what it is to be good, happy, just, and powerful; and it is difficult to develop a comprehensive worldview that is not at least skeptical of these options. Of late, even these functions of liberal learning have been given an exchange value in the American university. In exchange for a brief tour of the disciplines and perhaps one or two capstone or interdisciplinary courses, students are supposedly empowered to think clearly, understand the significance of art activity, and be prepared for an ethical professional life. One hardly needs reminding that a small vaccine of liberal learning does not offer very much immunity.

As Pierre Bourdieu, the French sociologist, has pointed out, the field of intellectual work is not very different from the field of art production.[11] Knowledge is both a commodity and a symbolic object. We may want the cultural and commercial values of academic learning to appear integrated in the public eye, but they rarely are, or else liberal studies would not have to argue for their place in the sun. The symbolic values of liberal learning—above all their specialized values—are in a tensional relation, ethically and theoretically, through the commodification of knowledge. The arts and sciences cannot rid themselves of the tension between exchange value and symbolic value because they are often thrust into a service role at the undergraduate level and are often forced to find ways to make themselves useful to professional and vocational interests. And, as I have been saying, they insist on defining their integrity individually, in professionalized disciplines, rather than symbolically, as a superbly rich cooperative major, a way of seeing specific problems or issues whole.

This seems to me to be as much the fault of the liberal arts disciplines at the present time and their failure to cooperate and argue from a position of strength, as it is of any administrative or market strategy. Indeed, it actually seems harder to create the identity of the university by forging relations between the academic disciplines than through large social themes now often related to student life enterprises. That many universities have become vast theme parks of learning by interning, with the added value of exposure to concepts like wellness and leadership, is hardly surprising. Very often this is as worldly as undergraduate education gets. For academically, the university is at best a loose federation of knowledge fiefdoms, supported by student and operations services, overseen by centralized authorities who try to speak for the whole but have little hope of conceptualizing a unified mission beyond the simple tautologies describing responsible behavior, useful knowledge, and service to society. Meanwhile, faculty most often go about their business romantically consumed by the vision of their own disciplines as a kind of superior reality, not reducible to the demands of cultural integration. Until American universities succeed in developing strong priorities for an interdisciplinary liberal education, one that integrates disciplinary learning with the social mission of the university, things will not get much better.

There is a sense of urgency about this. True, crisis has long been the natural state of the academy, especially in the humanities, where many political issues about the value of knowledge have traditionally found a focal point. But there have perhaps never been quite so many willing to tear entrails from the academic carcass, toss them to the winds, briefly scrutinize them where they fall, and consign them to the dustbin of culture. Indeed, scholars often throw up their hands and say that nothing can bind us together in academe. As the historian Christopher Lucas put it recently,

> At the most fundamental level, the question of deciding what the university's aims and priorities ought to be seems insoluble, if only because empirically there is so little agreement at present about them within society and even less prospect for achieving some general consensus among all the protagonists involved. At another level of discourse, the problem of reconciling priorities and objectives is a challenge each academic institution must face on its own, and within each, a question of what stance individuals are prepared to assume. The terms under which seemingly incompatible or contradictory pressures are reconciled amounts to an ongoing challenge, one worked out anew by each successive generation. For the immediate future, it seems unlikely the university will abandon any of its multiple tasks. The real and most meaningful choices, possibly, have to do not with including certain activities at the expense of other involvements, but instead working out and negotiating the terms under which competing but legitimate interests may be honored in appropriate measure.[12]

As widely held as this view is—and as wise as it may be to say that each institution much work things out for itself and that academe must render unto Caesar what is Caesar's and unto Sophia what is hers—there is something sad about Lucas's statement and the position it represents in the politics of academe. Social demands and the university marketplace do shape and implicate liberal learning in ways that are tangible, if not always understood. The subject matter of liberal learning is the social experience of trying to learn about our contexts and environments. Rarely, though, do those who administer or teach in universities examine how academic culture itself shapes almost all our agendas, how knowledge is produced and consumed.

As I want to show in some detail, this is especially disturbing given the unstable and often unreflective relation between democracy and capitalist markets in the world of academe itself, let alone in business, politics, and other social institutions. Any market, after all, has its profit motives and is not in itself democratic, flourishing equally well in open and repressive regimes. Faculty freedoms do not stall market hegemony. Academe, then, must examine how its market culture actually affects the production and consumption of knowledge. Being not-for-profit does not mean that universities are altruistic; it simply means that trustees cannot personally profit from a university's commerce. The university is very much a for-profit institution in actuality, and all aspects of its business are driven by this aim.

On the other hand, public critics of academe's inefficiencies, right as they sometimes are to keep scratching at our scabby sensibility, rarely get to the heart of the matter either. In their concern to improve faculty "productivity" or to return us to curricula promoting the hegemony of Western ideas as a corollary to global capitalism, they do not see how the market system of education actually threatens the development of syncretistic knowledge itself. After all, capitalism, as the economist Lester Thurow has noted, requires "a supportive physical, social, mental, educational and organizational infrastructure, some form of social glue if individuals are not to be constantly battling each other. . . . [C]apitalism isn't about abstract efficiency—inculcating values of honesty so that the system runs at a lower cost. It is about letting everyone maximize their utility by exercising their own individual personal preferences. Wanting to be a criminal is just as legitimate as wanting to be a priest. . . . Values or preferences are the black hole of capitalism. They are what the system exists to serve, but there are no capitalistic theories of good or bad preferences."[13]

One can translate this into the current realpolitik of academic culture. Campus bureaucracies and the organization of knowledge on campus are not about abstract efficiency. They are, with a quite obvious egalitarianism, about letting every service unit, discipline, and department maximize its utility. But they are also about shaping, in their own way, the nature of an education. All vocational outcomes are treated equally in the postmodern university; there are no capitalistic theories of good or bad vocations. But even while values are not exactly the black hole of a university education, and every university claims that general education provides the essential infrastructure to the curriculum, we have yet to convincingly give that education the ingredients it requires to be the glue that binds our capitalist educational enterprise together. We sorely need to reinvent it in freshly conceived ways as the chief negotiator between campus (and even global) capitalism and the knowledge capital of the disciplines. We need, that is, a powerful identity theme for undergraduate general education that can establish with some hope of security a focus on a broadly symbolic education that can withstand market vagaries.

Market Culture

Universities clearly see themselves as players in the commercial market at large, a market whose economy claims to be knowledge-driven. As economists and business journals frequently remind us, universities are in business today to develop the investment of human capital for the knowledge economy. Knowledge in this market becomes decidedly utilitarian, important mainly for its exchange value. Such a knowledge economy is not sustained by hypotheses or concepts of the problematic or political status of knowledge, which is why mission statements do not deal with such things. The knowledge economy is sustained by information that enables us to achieve measurable outcomes, such as a financial profit or a social asset of some kind or a research breakthrough or a credential that has strong importance in the marketplace. It enables us to make claims that higher education is socially relevant, that we can show advances in knowledge development, that we can swell a conceptual scene or two.

The outcome is clear: the academy has difficulty affirming the autonomy of knowledge apart from its market value. We make claims for all kinds of learning as essential and of equal worth—and the we includes not just administrators but faculty promoting their own fields of study. The gap between the intellectual and commodity values of knowledge in the university has therefore widened, with much stronger market value, not surprisingly, assigned to the latter. Rhetorically, of course, we make more claims than ever for the co-existence of both values—and, at its best, academic learning does seem to fuse the two. The contemporary university may not enjoy quite the same power for legislating cultural legitimacy that it once did, but it can still provide very strong constructions of social reality by appearing—as our elite schools do—to link the intellectual and the economic value of a degree as a credential.

It is not surprising, then, that the dominant rhetoric for explaining and promoting higher education today is a mix of entrepreneurial rhetoric and a special fondness for excellence, along with good social intentions about building student character, by which we try to socialize the corporate ethic. That is how we try to establish knowledge as power. The assumption, that is, is that knowledge will bring empowerment in a world in which we are lost without it. It has also been argued with some force by Benjamin Barber that knowledge is just as likely to be appreciated by those in power or at least those who are engaged in political engagement.[14] However we look at it, it is *the relation between knowledge and power* that defines the nature of academe: we empower those without the required knowledge to be a part of a liberal democratic society, and we feed knowledge to those with power who want more of it.

But so byzantine have been the workings of bureaucratic power in academic culture in the past few decades, in response to its changing management styles and in the layering of business management styles on top of faculty governance, that we need a new field of educational anthropology to examine the ways in which universities organize and develop knowledge. If Michel Foucault is right in saying that power exists in reciprocal relations that deconstruct legitimacy and authority as fast as a control point is located, then maybe there is no need for concern because university power structures will inevitably implode or mutate. In coming chapters I will suggest that is a real possibility, largely because of our faith in a market economy for developing knowledge. But perhaps, too, only a multivolumed work of cultural anthropology can find the true pulse of higher education. One can, of course, rely also on the usual discourses of educational power: historical narratives, educational statistics, demographic data, speeches from leaders and scholars, and developing philosophies of education, most of which proceed as though the culture is not in the least bit contradictory and can be easily reshaped by change therapy. All these issues, though, rarely deal with the complex relations among faculty, administrations, trustees, and students, which reveal that power in academe is constantly under negotiation and is never conclusively in anyone's hands, no matter where competing interests have traditionally located the villains and heroes in the academic power games. Universities are communities in which academic priorities shift according to market trends and leadership styles; degrees and courses are dependent on client consumption; hierarchical bureaucracies have inevitably become flatter; control is decentralized; and master narratives of educational theory are remarkably difficult to write.

The key question, then, is how to make sense of all this, especially how to make sense of the culture that is academe. It would seem that any culture is "an ensemble of texts," as the cultural anthropologist Clifford Geertz once put it, a site of competing influences and diverse meanings that can be read and interpreted as if they were always open to interpretation. Culture is plural, several works in progress at once. Its practices are metaphorical in their implications, subtly connected and disconnected in their suggestiveness, loosely binding rituals and beliefs, yet somehow adding up to a whole that is not really a whole, because to sum up a culture as unified is always to radically oversimplify it. In reading cultural texts, many of which compete with and even contradict each other, one has no option but to chart only significant paths of meaning and acknowledge one's own interpretative biases. And I think this is the way to deal sensibly with university culture, with its astonishing array of texts denoting the value of knowledge, its subtle exchange systems, and its complex ways of disaggregating knowledge into educational experiences, especially at the undergraduate level. So in this book, I am trying to look at the "deep play" of different functions of knowledge in the university, their competing power structures—both financial and ideological—and their often contradictory motives, all within the context of dominant market influences.

We know that a traditional liberal education, for example, refers to learning in the arts and sciences, which we value for their ability to develop intellect and sensibility and to give us a working understanding of what self, society, nature, and culture are like. But we also know that the agenda for liberal education has often seemed hopelessly idealistic, especially when we insist, as many have ever since Aristotle, that it exists for its own sake. For one thing, knowledge is never for its own sake: it is always for someone's sake; it always has some personal, functional, or pragmatic value. Thus the modern American university has long looked beyond aesthetic humanism to pragmatic education, never quite content with great books and ideas as ends in themselves, seeking to develop knowledge that is above all useful in preparing people for applied research or the world of work. This in itself is not the problem. The university has usefully become involved in the arenas of politics, public policy making, patent development, and corporate research. It does have a role to play in ameliorating capitalism's social problems. It inevitably will borrow more and more management strategies from the world of business to make its entrepreneurial mission more efficient. But as we fail to give the curriculum integrative power through the arts and sciences, as we resist focusing on the symbolic functions of knowledge—its ability to make meaning in broadly suggestive ways —and as we fail to conceptualize a comprehensive democratic education as the main thrust of our social mission, we will increasingly trust in the blind ambition of the market to set our values and curricular emphases. So then will the power of any kind of disciplinary learning become more difficult to assert. The more abstract and philosophical motives for acquiring a liberal education—especially those of the humanities—frequently rub up against the insatiable needs of global capitalism and the corporate motives of the university itself, and they will lose almost every time.

Market Hegemony

One of the problems in effecting change in the university, though, is that there is little public or internal pressure to review the general mission of higher education and to explain its means as well as its ends. The higher education market has little interest in promoting a liberal or a democratic education as the saving grace for higher education. President Duderstadt is well aware of the fact that such a mission is often far too abstract and even precious. The current entrepreneurial mission of the American university and the energy of its good social intentions, along with its extraordinary ability to drive research and theoretical expertise in a wide range of fields, has made U.S. higher learning the most influential in the modern world, largely because it has allowed a market culture for higher education to flourish and be influential. American universities play principal roles on the international stage, helping to conceptualize the global economy, training professional workers and managers, influencing policy making, developing knowledge through vast research and consulting enterprises, theorizing the arts of persuasion and multiple therapies for the human condition—and exporting the desire for democracy as freedom to accumulate knowledge as capital. And they do so because to the outside world, and to many within, higher education today aims above all to relate free-market thinking and liberal capitalism to the development of new knowledge. If we look closely, that juggling act with social and intellectual values for the edification of the market is really what the comprehensive mission of the university is about. American universities start with a given— the cultural aspiration of the nation; in this case, to empower individuals to be productive citizens—and they develop a structure for organizing knowledge that aims to bring this to fruition. That is not a bad thing, perhaps, but it is not a good one when we ignore the fact that democracy and capitalism do indeed breed their own discontents. The university's ideological claim is to capitalize the human (faculty and students and their intellectual capital) and to humanize capitalism (to mediate and where possible eradicate its contradictions). And that, many have pointed out, pulls us in two directions at once, as we shall explore in the chapters on the economy of the university and the nature of academic freedom.

Yet the market culture for higher education, if one measures the number of institutions in existence, has been very good to academe, so it is unlikely that arguments for the quality and the curriculum are going to make much headway, any more than arguments for better car mileage have impressed either Congress or automakers. In 1950 there were some eighteen hundred American colleges and universities. In the next fifty years, that number doubled.[15] Since 1980, the current-fund revenues of these institutions have increased threefold, from over $65 billion to over $250 billion today, greater than the gross domestic product of Austria, Denmark, Sweden, or Switzerland. In 1900 twenty-nine thousand degrees were awarded; fifty years later the number had reached nearly half a million. In 1995, more than 2 million people received some kind of college or university degree, and in 2000 the number reached 2,265,600.[16]

One result of this expansion is that, except for a handful of flagship colleges and universities offering the most valued credentials, U.S. institutions have developed a decidedly uncompetitive student admissions system to bolster its democratic market activity, one in which the degree itself is a commodity item priced according to need and what the market will bear. So we work hard to find new criteria for judging student talent, even moving away from standardized test scores and taking into account any number of ways that students have made themselves distinctive. We have elaborate admissions scenarios, but few schools out of the thirty-nine hundred can afford to be very selective. From the point of view of promoting an egalitarian ideal for higher education, this is not a problem. Given the vast range of degrees, certificate programs, and other diplomas of varying quality and value that are available to fill almost every public need, about fifteen million student clients are indeed catered to somewhere, somehow every year since the turn of this century. There is a college for everyone. The question of whether everyone should have a college is rarely raised, however, and probably never can be precisely because university degrees are a market-driven credential. A university in possession of a good degree program, any degree program, must be in want of a customer. Of all late-capitalist markets, American higher education is indeed extraordinarily successful because it is highly diversified, flexible, and based on an endless consumer need for degrees in order to enter the general or professional workplace.

Since the turn of the twentieth century, furthermore, colleges and universities have sought to shore up the mass market system of higher education by strongly supporting numerous professional organizations, accrediting agencies, and consulting bodies, all of which try to regulate the educational market even while they promote its importance and play a key role in assessing value, cost, and reputation. Higher education, that is, has theorized itself largely through its professional organizations. Each successful institution hangs its academic reputation on the strength of its competitive market position. This is achieved through strategies that amount to trading in the market of human, conceptual, and financial capital: hiring star faculty, attracting talented students and enlightened philanthropy, and establishing research programs of importance to both national and corporate interests. Universities devise recruiting strategies that play to student and parental needs; they discount cost through subtle financial aid practices and endowment-based grants; they offer a vast range of employment credentials to meet instant market demands, preferably with a postdegree earning potential that might offset the price of tuition. And universities are aided in these activities by accrediting agencies whose primary function is to ask institutions what their mission statements are and whether they have lived up to them. That is an exercise often as vaguely rhetorical as the mission statements themselves, for the market controls both the mission of the university and how it is valued and assessed.

Few would assume, then, that a university can escape the ambiguities of the educational marketplace and survive by simply correcting the rhetoric of its best intentions. A limited number of schools have the endowment capacity or tuition income base to be independent of market trends. Even those schools that do not rely entirely on tuition income have more than enough business savvy to insist that they stay in the traditional market and become its blue chip players, expanding their endowments, building greater plant enhancements and research capabilities, seeking ever more competitive students, buying expensive faculty and their research, and even giving away substantial portions of their earnings in financial aid in order to keep their market niche alive. There is no contradiction, then, for the owners of all universities—be they state boards of regents or independent trustees—in the fact that educational institutions have inevitably become more rather than less entrepreneurial and corporate in their business practices and in their strategies of expansion and profit seeking.

The corporatization of higher education takes many forms but includes the following: quality management criteria and strategies drawn from the world of business; an emphasis on marketing, visibility, and public image promotion; accounting concerns for contribution margins and the perennial cost effectiveness of learning; decentralized power structures with incentives for growth and gain-share revenues; the redistribution of labor—in this case away from tenured to part-time and adjunct faculty; the development of sophisticated ancillary products, patents, and services; a vague rhetoric of excellence that replaces specific details of what an education is about, and, of course, research and other financial collaborations with the corporate world.

It can be easily argued that the corporatization of the modern university has brought many welcome efficiencies to the way academe does business and has attracted some wonderful examples of corporate philanthropy. It has also had a damaging effect on liberal and democratic education, as I shall show. The higher education market propels itself forward blindly, largely in response to the growing public need for credentials and work skills, through the market's inability to assess quality carefully beyond the criteria of supply and demand. Grade inflation, as is well documented of late, is little short of a scandal, even in our best schools, and results in large part from the culture of consumerism, one in which the student client, carefully attuned to the theory of individual talent development that many schools promote, sees good grades as an entitlement. (A report written by an ex-dean of Arts and Sciences at Harvard and published in 2002 by the American Academy of Arts and Sciences cites several causes for grade inflation and uncritical letters of recommendation and includes a discussion of how students count on good transcripts and good grades as a result of "universities operating like businesses for student clients.")[17] Not surprisingly, too, the rhetoric of institutional self-promotion plays to student expectations. Claims of curricular excellence often reach egregious heights and are as widely accepted a public discourse as commercial advertising.

True, the federal government did try to "nationalize" higher education by increasing funding to higher education by a factor of twenty-five during 1940–90,[18] and certainly federal and state education offices have in recent years tried to exert some power over educational standards. But in most states, universities set their own standards through accrediting bodies whose standards, as mentioned, are largely based on claims of fulfilling some kind of generic mission that is scarcely specific enough to warrant close analysis. Accrediting associations certainly do propound worthy values: the importance of general education, the need for creativity, the concern for a sustainable university culture, and so on. No one should mistake the fundamental sincerity of their task. But the major criteria for quality tend to lie in whether an institution is limited or overextended by its ambitions and whether that ambition can in some way partake of the myth of meaningful measurement. Thus universities choose to move closer and closer to the statistical empiricism of corporate quality management, as evidenced by the annual Malcolm Baldridge National Quality Award established by Congress in 1987 to "enhance the competitiveness of US businesses." The businesses given the award by President George W. Bush and Commerce Secretary Don Evans in 2002 were a regional campus of the University of Wisconsin, two school districts, Pal's Sudden Service of Kingsport, Tennessee, and Clarke American Checks of San Antonio. (The University of Wisconsin is a member of the Academic Quality Improvement project of the Higher Learning Commission of the North Central Association.) Thus, in the end, all quality is alike. A fast-food chain, a personalized check manufacturing company, a Catholic school district, and a university can all gather under the tent of what Secretary Evans calls a "passion for excellence."

Market Contradictions

Markets have a large number of advantages. They allow individuals and institutions wide freedom of choice, encourage private initiative, and offer the chance to profit individually. Furthermore, as Giovanni Sartori notes, "The market is (a) the only basis for the calculus of prices and costs; (b) management-costless; (c) flexible and change responsive; (d) the complement of freedom of choice; (e) an enormous information simplifier."[19] Many believe that, because universities and colleges are largely independent corporate entities, the market has been a good fit for higher education, even when it comes to simplifying or commodifying information. We allow our lives to be determined by peer competition, consumer needs, national trends, and so on. We constantly seek to adapt and mediate market influences, whether this concerns a financial aid policy or a new degree offering in digital media studies. But our activities are not without ambiguities that have to be constantly negotiated. The market in higher education has a broad egalitarian motive: to educate everyone who wants postsecondary schooling. But it also serves to define a social meritocracy, one in which merit is determined not simply by intelligence, but by a host of social and economic support factors enabling some students to be better prepared for college life. We have to admit, that is, that the market-supported democracy of learning can be a contradiction in terms because it is quite Darwinian in its functions.

Markets can also create external relations that may have negative effects. They fail when they cannot deliver products at prices that people can afford or at prices that cannot subsidize production, when they offer goods that can be enjoyed without payment and exchange does not take place, or when they provide a benefit that can be duplicated in some way outside the market. Currently the higher education market is troubled by all these problems. It is especially troubled by the problem of cost and by the growing presence of one of its own externalities: for-profit and (to a lesser degree) Internet-based proprietary schools. These may have gained academic accreditation but do not employ regular, tenured faculty. They vend degree programs, largely to adult students, largely based on the mere dissemination of information.

For-profit schools, that is, insist that knowledge is *only* a commodity. There is no ambiguity about this. Knowledge simply has to be packaged and marketed for public consumption. The practices of for-profit schools result from extending and undercutting the traditional market's own development of commodity knowledge by lowering costs, improving efficiencies, and radically simplifying the nature of the product. That is hardly surprising, and there is a good deal of hypocritical outcry from the traditional market at the growing success of proprietary schools when in fact it is the traditional market that invented knowledge as a commodity through its schools of continuing education and its professional schools. The for-profit market has simply found a more efficient way of delivering the goods. Yet if the university assumes, as a number of traditional institutions have, that it can best stay in business and turn a profit by investing even more heavily in nontraditional and professional education or by making knowledge even more of a commodity than it already is or by outsourcing labor needs to adjunct faculty, then it will find itself in difficult competition with for-profit institutions. True, the university can still have the advantage of prestige name recognition, but unless it can radically improve the delivery of degree programs in areas in which information is relatively standardized anyway, it will inevitably be forced to change quite radically its bureaucratic inefficiencies. The new for-profit market is an external benefit of the traditional market but it can also have a negative effect on the traditional academic market if not for society at large.

The commodification of knowledge, then, is both a positive and a negative effect of the market, and one could argue, of course, that it is precisely this competitive tension between symbolic and commodified knowledge that keeps higher education alive and well. Markets thrive on ambiguities and contradictions; culture wars of all kinds are unavoidable; symbolic knowledge will always be elusive. By definition, the American university must serve many clients, and it has become healthy by doing so. It would appear that one cannot integrate a university's mission simply because there is much to do in the name of socialization, and those needs change greatly over time and are inevitably linked to economic power. Perhaps it would be foolhardy to try to achieve any assimilation, for that will release the demons of utopian thinking. In short, it can easily be assumed that the market for higher education is nothing if not contradictory even while it tends to be risk-averse and highly conservative.

Perhaps, too, higher education cannot be expected to mediate society's problems at all if, as Daniel Bell suggests:

Capitalism is an economic-cultural system, organized economically around the institution of property and the production of
commodities and based culturally in the fact of exchange relations, that of buying and selling, which have permeated most of
society. Democracy is a socio-political system in which legitimacy lies in the consent of the governed, where the political
arena is available to various contending groups, and where fundamental liberties are safeguarded.

Though capitalism and democracy historically have risen
together and have been commonly justified by philosophical
liberalism, nothing makes it either theoretically or practically
necessary for the two to be yoked. In modern society, the political order increasingly becomes autonomous, and the management of the techno-economic order, or the democratic planning, or the management of the economy, becomes ever more
independent of capitalism.[20]

But here precisely is the issue that needs to be addressed through
a democratic liberal education. This explanation of a possible or
even necessary divide between capitalism and democracy, between
useful and symbolic knowledge—an explanation that asserts that
capitalism has no theoretical or practical responsibility to democracy or vice versa—is related to our problems with liberal education.
The capitalist market system, to which the university belongs, has a
strong social responsibility to consistently theorize and evaluate its
activities and not simply celebrate its entrepreneurial brilliance. But
when the central contradiction of capitalism—that the economy is
just about buying and selling and is a law unto itself while democracy has much explaining to do and must constantly strive for legitimacy—becomes the central contradiction of how we do business in
academe as well as society at large, then we have a serious problem.

What we must address, then, is not simply the metaphysical
problem of defining the content of the democratic American mind,
as some might have it, but the growing gap between democracy and
capitalism in higher education. Defining the legitimacy of a demo-

cratic education is perfectly in order and a genuine necessity. Much of what goes on in the culture wars, for example, barely touches on the real ambiguities at the heart of the university's social mission. But defining the market itself and its commodification of knowledge is equally important because the two cannot be distanced. The solution is not simply a matter of affirming the value of education as an egalitarian social ritual or an energetic entrepreneurial enterprise. The problem to be addressed is how the postmodern university can be the place where the pursuit of knowledge, a more just society, and a vital economy are yoked for the common good. I am assuming that this can be done only through careful reflection on the cultural contradictions of academe itself. Educational reform should begin by examining the deep social inequalities created by the market culture of academe, for the curriculum will always breed a morally schizophrenic citizenry if it does not involve a critical effort to analyze the way academe itself does business.

CHAPTER 2

The Consumerist Culture of the University

In March 1996, the following personal account by an undergraduate of her experience at a leading American private university appeared in the Sunday *New York Times* "Voices" column—not surprisingly, tucked away in the business section. Throughout the 1990s, the American press, including the *Times* and the *Wall Street Journal*, carried frequent stories dealing with the spiraling costs of college education and its effects on an increasingly large part of the population. Amy Wu, a student planning to graduate with a history degree from New York University, gave this public issue a personal yet not unusual spin:

> I am one of a growing number of young people who are condensing their college education from four years to three. My decision to graduate a year early has much less to do with ambition, however, than with saving a good deal of money.
>
> I decided to graduate a year early even before I entered college. Tuition . . . was about $16,000 my freshman year; yearly increases would far exceed the inflation rate, and room and board and books would add several thousand more. The financial aid office didn't help, so my father considered refinancing the mortgage and I planned to fit a job into my study schedule. . . .
>
> The excitement I felt toward higher education diminished every time my father received the tuition bill, which by my third year had grown to more than $19,000. I felt almost guilty and apologetic for going to college.

In high school, my friends and I couldn't wait to go to college. We had the typically idealistic view of ivy-covered buildings, lifetime friendships, romantic dances. In the early summer before freshman year, we pored over course booklets as if they were J. Crew catalogues. We wanted to take everything, to learn everything. But the thrill faded under the weight of tuition payments that promised to go only higher as financing for higher education declined.

So my friends and I started college bent on cutting corners, and we became ingenious at scrimping and saving. We copied pages from library books instead of spending $500 a semester on our own texts. One classmate took advantage of the college bookstore's two-week refund policy. She would buy the books, read or copy them, then return them before the deadline.

My roommate bought Cliff Notes instead of the real books because Cliff Notes were cheaper and easier to comprehend. Many of us built up our credits with odd electives: I indulged in modern dance and Chinese cooking; others delved into the meaning of Elvis's music and the history of U.F.O.'s.

In the end, the high cost of higher education has created a generation whose determination to cut that cost has drastically altered the college experience. As more students finish their education faster, spend more spare time on jobs to meet tuition bills or choose community colleges they can afford over prestigious universities they cannot, little time is left for the camaraderie of college, for learning free from other pressures, for making the transition to adulthood leisurely. These days young people worry more about debt than the quality of intellectual debate on campus—or how to survive rush week. . . .

Slowly, I have come to see the tragedy in all this. I grew up in a household where education was coveted, where my father believed that "the more you learn, the more you earn." I have learned, but not all that I believe I might have.

The consequences of a generation that has scrimped on its college education may include a less qualified work force and a less knowledgeable adult population. But most unfortunate is the changed perception of higher education. For too many in my generation, higher education has become a bothersome stage of life that must be endured solely to satisfy the market-place with that decorated piece of paper. It is now more a bur-den than a benefit, more a curse than something coveted.[1]

Anyone who teaches in an American university will certainly recognize Wu's situation. Here is someone who has realized that she has to be a successful consumer of higher education and not, as she had hoped, a young scholar indulging in the romance of learning. Of course, we are persuaded by her argument only to the extent that we accept that she has been forced to this position by the cost of her experience. No matter what the circumstances, once one has entered a university, might not a liberal education be self-fashioned from existing courses, with strong assistance from faculty advisors? The answer, of course, is yes. But that presupposes not only strong advis-ing but shared assumptions about what a liberal education is and whether a university emphasizes its value at all costs. In Wu's case, as in the case of so many others, the credential, very understandably, is the thing.

No one knows exactly how many students see things this way or how many have reacted to tuition costs as this young woman and her friends have done. Statistics do not help much here and Wu's argu-ment for the need for text cribs is not entirely convincing either. Student interest in taking what they perceive to be easy courses in order to maintain a high GPA or to cut a degree program short is nothing new. Students have always read Cliff or Monarch Notes and pursued at least a few so-called fluff courses. There is no reason to believe that, in general, student habits will change if there is more time to read or more money to spend on books. Besides, who is to say, in this age of sophisticated cultural studies—in which NYU faculty are very adept—that courses about Elvis or UFOs are neces-sarily insubstantial?

Furthermore, in the late 1990s, Wu's course of study remained the exception rather than the rule. Only 59 percent of eighteen-year-old students in American public and private universities graduated in four years in 1997, the rest often taking much longer.[2] In 2000, the graduation figure dropped to 53 percent.[3] Gifted students, furthermore, have always earned accelerated degrees. Indeed, in the past decade there has been warm administrative encouragement for a three-year bachelor degree, at least since the president of Oberlin College, S. Frederick Starr, first spoke in favor of this option in 1991, pointing out that it could cut costs for students by as much as 50 percent. Colleges that have no trouble enrolling talented students are looking with some approval on a shortened duration for undergraduate study, so that, as more than one admissions dean has said, the turnstiles can keep turning at a fair clip. Meanwhile, it is only a matter of time before the accelerated degree becomes commonplace in less selective schools, as they seek to find a special niche in the marketplace with compressed diplomas and to promote the connection between a frequently devalued and shortened baccalaureate degree and the more valuable master's degree.

Yet Wu's statement—not to deconstruct it too radically—is not simply about time spent at college or just about the high cost of tuition. It is broadly indicative of several conditions in higher education today that I want to summarize here:

Entrepreneurism. Higher education in the age of late capitalism is looking more and more opportunistic as it readily assumes an entrepreneurial function of its own. "The Halls of Ivy" as a *Wall Street Journal* headline put it in 1997, "imitate Halls of Commerce."[4] And the *Economist* in the same year ran a long, well-researched account of how the modern university is nothing like the old. "Instead of protecting their other-worldliness," the author wrote, "universities nowadays celebrate their achievements as producers of useful knowledge." Thus faculty become "knowledge workers," students become "human capital," and investment in knowledge is investment in growth, for knowledge is "not so much a moral or cultural force, more an incubator of new industries in a technology-dominated economy." In sum, the postmodern university is "the engine room of the knowledge economy."[5]

It is no surprise in an entrepreneurial culture that there is a well-established and growing equation of quality with high cost, which encourages the need to look for bargains and circumvent high cost. One has only to read the definitive College Board web-site to see how we try to put the best face on things and provide encouragement to prospective students in spite of the fact that a high-quality education plainly is prohibitively priced for many. And this has clear social and academic fallout, from limited student access to an affordable education to a lack of incentive to raise standards to a concern to spend money on high tuition only if there is a good chance of a strong investment in future income. A widely read report published in January 2002 claims, for example, that "almost all private colleges and the majority of public institutions are either too selective or too costly for students to attend without putting themselves or their families at a 'serious financial inconvenience' or making an 'extraordinary financial sacrifice.' . . . The report concludes that fewer than 100 of the nation's 1,500 private colleges are 'generally admissible and affordable' to average-performing, needy students because those institutions tend to be more selective and costly than public institutions."[6]

Diversity: Changing Student Demographics and Motives. For much of the 1990s, the competitive, full-time, traditional eighteen-to twenty-one-year-old group seeking a college education shrank noticeably, not even reaching 1980 levels until 1998. "By 1993," notes Arthur Levine, in research conducted with Jeanette Cureton, "38 percent of all college students were over twenty-five years of age; 61 percent were working; 56 percent were female, and 42 percent were attending part-time."[7] Government figures indicate that by 1995, the number of students twenty-five years or older had risen to 44 percent and the number of part-time students to 50 percent. And in spite of a good recovery in enrollment of eighteen- and nineteen-year-olds since 1998, the most recent figures available at time of writing, those for 1998, indicate that the percentage of students over twenty-five holds steady at around 41–42 percent. National Center for Educational Statistics estimates show, however, that from 1999 to 2010, there will be a rise of 24 percent in enrollments of persons under twenty-five and an increase of only 9 percent in the number twenty-five and over.[8] Between 1990 and 1999, the number of white students increased by 22 percent while the number of African Americans grew 70 percent and the Hispanic population rose a remarkable 162 percent. By 1997, 27 percent of students in American colleges were members of minorities, up from 16 percent in 1976.[9]

In short, as everyone knows, in recent years there has been a broad demographic shift to a more mature and more diversified college clientele, one for whom higher education has come to mean many things. For the older student, obtaining a college education is just one of a number of social responsibilities, joining those of work and family. For many minority students, it comes with a particularly urgent mandate to provide social and economic mobility. And for all students, the best quality education seems harder than ever to find at an affordable price. Thus increasingly students look for a college experience that is user-friendly and supportive and provides both good value for the money and useful credentials. Even when students are not overtly consumerist in their demands, those who might traditionally have assumed that a liberal education is designed primarily to shape the sensibility and fashion the intellect are still thinking of a degree more in terms of a passport to prosperity.

Such consumers are also more psychologically vulnerable than ever. Levine notes that today students "are coming to college overwhelmed and more damaged than in the past."[10] He sums up the pessimism concerning student quality in the late 1990s:

Traditional undergraduates are changing in ways that will affect faculty who teach them. They are not as well prepared to enter college as their predecessors. As a result, there is a growing need for remediation. According to a national survey of student-affairs officers that I conducted in 1997, within the last decade nearly three-fourths (73 percent) of all colleges and universities experienced an increase in the proportion of students requiring remedial or developmental education at two-year (91 percent) and four-year (64 percent) colleges. Today, nearly one-third (32 percent) of all undergraduates report having taken a basic skills or remedial course in reading, writing, or math. In 1995, more than three-fourths of all colleges and universities offered remedial reading, writing, or math courses. Between 1990 and 1995, 39 percent of institutions reported that enrollments in these areas had increased while only 14 percent reported a decrease.

According to a survey by the Higher Education Research Institute, only one-quarter (25 percent) of faculty believe their students are "well-prepared academically," while less than four in ten (39 percent) gave them even a "satisfactory" or "very satisfactory" rating in terms of quality. The result is that faculty are being forced to teach more and more basic-skills courses, dumb down the level of their classes, and reduce the number of advanced courses they offer, therefore enjoying their teaching and their students less than in the past. The 1997 student-affairs survey showed that 45 percent of faculty feel less comfortable with students today than in the past. The feeling is more pronounced at four-year schools (53 percent) than at two-year colleges (37 percent).[11]

Few of us in academe can escape either the consumerism or the psychological vulnerability of the current generation of students. Levine notes that his survey "reported rises in eating disorders (on 58 percent of campuses), classroom disruption (on 44 percent), drug abuse (on 42 percent), alcohol abuse (on 35 percent), gambling (on 25 percent), and suicide attempts (on 23 percent)."[12] And as recently as January 13, 2002, a lengthy article in the *New York Times* aptly entitled "The Therapy Generation" reported a heavy increase in therapeutic interventions by college counseling centers. Many more students are making it to college with psychiatric histories, and according to the article "85 percent of those polled by the National Survey of Counseling Center Directors reported seeing more college students with severe disorders, including learning disabilities, clinical depression and bipolar disorder."[13]

Students' study habits have changed too. As the *Chronicle of Higher Education* (January 16, 1998) comments in reporting the results of an annual freshmen survey conducted by the Higher Education Research Institute of the University of California at Los Angeles, "Just 34 percent of this year's [1998] freshmen said they had spent at least six hours per week studying or doing homework, down from 44 percent a decade ago." Students who spent at least six hours a week studying had dropped to 33 percent in the 2000 survey, published in January of 2001. There is speculation, as the *Chronicle* puts it, that "changes in American family life may be contributing to students' apparently lessened interest in what they're learning. About 26 percent of the [1997] freshmen come from divorced families, three times as many as when the question was first asked in 1972. About 39 percent of the freshmen work at least 16 hours per week, up from 35 percent five years ago." Nonetheless, by 2000, student aspirations (as indicated by the UCLA survey) had not lessened: 47 percent today plan to earn a master's degree compared to 34 percent in 1987, 19 percent a doctorate (compared to 10.4 percent), and 21 percent expect to graduate with honors (compared to 11.9 percent).

Levine's research also led him to conclude that plagiarism and cheating, legal threats by students, and student aid costs have risen considerably: "The campus is becoming less and less of a community for faculty and their students," he claims. And "more than 61 percent [of colleges] report expanded use of psychological counseling services."[14] Ted Marchese, editor of *Change: The Magazine of*

Higher Learning, writing in early 1998, backs up these generalizations: "By far the most disturbing stories I've picked up on campus
these past two years have been ones of student disengagement. These
aren't the complaints we've heard for years about student under-
preparation (though that's still real). They're stories about a 1990s
generation described to me as consumerist, uncivil, demanding,
preoccupied with work, and as caring more for GPAs and degrees
than the life of the mind." A few months later he added in another
article, "The typical time budgets of full-time students include 15–
20 hours a week of TV viewing, 20 hours in leisure pursuits, 15–
30 hours a week in paid employment, but just eight to 10 hours a
week in out-of-class study time."[15] Plainly when many speak of the
dumbing down of the curriculum, the reference is to a complex
social reality.

Other salient, often-quoted statistics from the UCLA freshmen
survey flesh out the challenge of educating today's undergraduates.
About a third of entering freshmen in 1996 had an A grade average in
high school, and 85 percent of all students had a B- or better GPA. In
2000, A grades had risen to 43 percent and over 93 percent of entering students had a B- or above. Consistently throughout the 1990s,
over 70 percent of students surveyed gave as the most important
reason for attending college "to be able to get a better job."

The evidence shows, then, that student culture has been changing in character in the past three decades or so to become more like
the market itself: somewhat overvalued and driven by the need for
economic aggrandizement. A college education is widely considered
an entitlement and an entrée to social and economic mobility, and
this presents challenges to the ways we conceive of a liberal education, how we "pitch" the curriculum at large, and how we socialize
students through the organization of student life bureaucracies.

Ironically, even as we bemoan the failing skills of college entrants, the case of Amy Wu, again, is quite common, especially among talented middle-class and low-income students who must work to support themselves and cannot afford to linger in the halls of academe. Statistics in a report of 2002 entitled "The Burden of Borrowing," compiled by the State Public Interest Research Groups, show that student debt doubled between 1992 and 2000, rising from an average of just over $9,000 to nearly $17,000.[16] It is with this group, especially, that the commodification of higher education will most likely only grow more and more anachronistic. On the other hand, it is also likely that college entrants—especially if high schools continue not to prepare their average students any better—will tend to two extremes: those who need remedial assistance and those with high native wit who will seek to finish as fast as possible to avoid the high costs of the credential. The more we help reinforce, through high pricing structures, the notion that a degree can be a commodity credential that comes in various sizes and quality formats, the more we are likely to encourage students with advanced placement credit to shorten their study time. And in 2000, over 43 percent of high school students had taken Advanced Placement exams.

Curricular Change and the Value of the Credential. The content of the undergraduate liberal arts curriculum has been in a state of transition for about two decades, which is one of the major reasons for the culture wars. Increased awareness of the politics of gender, race, class, and ethnicity has driven many academics to revise the general-education course of study. It is difficult to assert the enduring values of white, Western culture, for example, when one faces a multicultural class whose histories serve to remind one of the role of their people as victims in the historical process.

Equally important, perhaps, are the changes resulting from the faculty discovery—widely discussed in educational journals and books—that students learn best when they are placed in active,

problem-solving situations such as internships, independent research projects, and study groups, and not when they are asked
to passively absorb data or abstract knowledge.[17] They respond to
structured, well-connected sources of information and not so well to
broad abstractions. Thus case-centered learning has become important. While the individual disciplines in the academy are at their
strongest point in terms of accumulated historical knowledge, faculty often have to learn how to share and redefine knowledge for a
less centered postmodern world and to effectively show that knowledge, like everyday life, is deeply and inherently interdisciplinary.

Beyond the curriculum lies the controversy over the degree credential itself. As Donald Langenberg, chancellor of the University of
Maryland system, has said, degrees and diplomas are themselves
becoming obsolescent in our digital age, even as they maintain a
credentialist position in the marketplace: "Many academics and em-
ployers complain frequently that colleges' graduation requirements,
based primarily on passing sets of courses, fail to insure that the
graduate has the personal qualities and skills needed to succeed in
graduate or professional training or in the workplace." Langenberg
suggests that

> we must abandon the notion that age and exposure to some
> particular quantity of formal instruction are relevant indicators
> of an individual's educational progress or ability to function in
> the classroom or on the job. . . .
>   It is time to revive the vigorous debates of a century ago
> [about the purposes and layers of our educational system from
> K through 16] and to reconsider the whole structure of the
> system from bottom to top. . . . If we succeed in making the right
> changes, education will become fully accessible to any appropri-
> ately prepared student at any age. We will adapt the delivery of
> instruction to the student's circumstances, rather than force
> the student to accommodate to the educational institution's
> convenience.
>   It will become abnormal to require a student to be in the

same room with a professor precisely 45 times during a semester. Learning will occur wherever students can connect to the World-Wide Web. Students will be able to move easily among educational institutions, perhaps simultaneously enrolling at several real and/or virtual universities, or studying one subject at the high school level and other subjects with college professors.

A universal "college-credit banking system" will have to evolve. Students will demonstrate their mastery of certain skills at different points in their lives and will receive certificates of achievement. . . .

Such an educational system would make more sense in terms of how humans learn. Cognitive scientists tell us what we teachers have long suspected—and long ignored: Different people learn in different ways and at very different rates. Fortunately emerging technology promises to help provide just the customization and "connectivity" that a new educational system would require. We will soon have the opportunity—and the obligation—to adapt courses to the specific cognitive profile of each student. . . .

We mustn't allow milestones to become millstones. We mustn't continue to see diplomas as emblems of the end of an education, or degrees as either necessary or sufficient keys to continued learning. We must rethink the methods by which we encourage, evaluate, and mark the progress of learners of any age. One indication of our success may well be the displacement of degrees and diplomas by more informative—if less hallowed —means of certifying learning. Whatever form a student's performance profile may take in the future, it must convey more useful information and have greater predictive value than the pieces of paper we now bestow at graduation ceremonies.[18]

Given these broad changes in the organization, ends, and audience for higher education—not to mention all the interest in the new "knowledge-based economy"—does it help to return to the romantic argument for a liberal education that Wu outlines? Is there much point in reminding ourselves that the college years are a time for careful intellectual and social growth, for the understanding of what constitutes personal freedom and responsible behavior, for the discovery of options for adult happiness, and even a time for romance? Will things be any different, or any better, if Langenberg's dream is realized?

The romantic critique would hold that Amy Wu may very well have a point and that college should be a time when students with ambitions to expand their knowledge and their interests look forward to a sense of academic accomplishment that is something more than just a piece of decorated paper. But that message seems rather jaded and sentimental to many college students today, who have grown up fast in a world of market pressures and creative, financial problem solving. Competing views of knowledge drawn from the humanities and from the knowledge economy do not make this as easy to decide as many a traditional humanist might think. And consumerism—whether occasioned by genuine financial concern or simply by high sensitivity to value added options—quite understandably drives much thinking in academe today, whether or not it is enhanced by digital means. Given its assumptions, if anything has to be compromised, it is the education process, not the product—as if the two can be separated.

But who can blame students for being such self-conscious consumers? Academe does not consistently preserve the valuable mystique of liberal learning, and students who are bored in high school and are not self-starters—as well as the Wus of this world—will expect little improvement of their lot in college. If the cost of education has become too much to bear, students must find some way to shortcut the process and shrink tuition costs while trying to keep the integrity of the purchased product intact. So if a diploma is simply a credential that can be bought in three years instead of four, and universities encourage such credentialism by thinning down liberal arts curricula at the undergraduate level, why pay the tens of thousands of dollars extra some universities charge?

The Tuition Spiral

Tuition costs remain the biggest issue. For students, parents, and the general public, the clearest symptom of the corporate mentality of the contemporary university is its concern with exacting a cost that the market can bear, a value for the educational experience that also allows for the definition of added value and profit margins in this nonprofit enterprise. Thus one of the first things that comes to mind on hearing Amy Wu's story is that here is a fairly obvious twist on the now-familiar public issue of how escalating college costs increasingly threaten to keep both the poor and the broad bulk of the middle class from attending expensive colleges and rarely allow for added value experiences in the process.

The cost issue is the most public of all crises that face contemporary American higher education. It has been raised and documented many times, nowhere more forcefully perhaps than in a strongly worded but well-argued report from the Council for Aid to Education entitled "Breaking the Social Contract: The Fiscal Crisis in Higher Education" (1997). This report, prepared by a commission of public and private college administrators and corporate executives, asked a simple question: Will "the current revenue base and funding sources be sufficient for meeting higher education's future needs"? The report came to this blunt conclusion: "At a time when the level of education needed for productive employment is increasing, the opportunity to go to college will be denied to millions of Americans unless sweeping changes are made to control costs, halt sharp increases in tuition, and increase other sources of revenue."

The report bases its calculations on the assumption that average tuition rates in higher education will rise between now and 2015 "no faster than inflation." This is optimistic, of course, because such a controlled rise has not been the case either in the past decade or at the start of the new millennium. As the government *Digest of Educational Statistics* explains: "Between 1986–87 and 1996–97, charges at public colleges have risen by 20 percent, and charges at private colleges have increased by 31 percent, after adjustment for inflation."[19] Figures released by the General Accounting Office in 1996 paint an even bleaker picture: "Between academic 1980–81 and 1994–95, tuition increased 234 percent [presumably in unadjusted dollars]. . . . In the same period, incomes rose 82 percent and the cost of consumer goods 74 percent. 'The portion of a household's income needed to pay for college nearly doubled.' "[20] And we can add that from 1996–97 to 2000–01, only five years, tuition has risen a further 18 percent for public schools and 27 percent for private schools. In constant dollars, the increase in public four-year school tuition in the past fifteen years has been 69 percent, and in private four-year schools, 82 percent.[21] True, the stock market boom in the late 1990s helped some people forego the economic strains of paying for an education, but no sensible parent or administrator can rely on market performance to plan for economic stability. And since the collapse of the stock market and the very noticeable decrease in endowment worth in most schools, there are few private colleges and universities in the United States that are not raising tuition 5 percent and more for the 2002–03 year.[22]

Indeed, as the council's report goes on to say, even with a low 2–3 percent growth in tuition each year from 1997 on, "U.S. colleges and universities will fall $38 billion short (in 1995 dollars) of the annual budget they need to educate the student population expected in 2015. If, however, tuition increases at current rates—basically doubling by 2015—the impact on access will be devastating: effectively half of those who want to pursue higher education will be shut out." In 1999 private college tuition rates increased by 4.6 percent, and in 2000 the rise was 5.2 percent; four-year public institution increases were, respectively, 3.4 percent and 4.4 percent. The rate of inflation was only 3.4 percent during this time. In 2002–03, the rise is likely to average out at higher than 5 percent. Signs of financial strain are obvious: 59 percent of all financial aid is now borrowed money, compared with 41 percent in 1980, and "while the average aid per full-time student has increased 74 percent in the past twenty years, tuition and fees, adjusted for inflation, have more than doubled, and family income has risen an average of just 20 percent."[23]

The social, cultural, and economic implications are enormous, and much of our concern over the content of a liberal education will pale beside the problems of tuition costs. It is no hyperbole to say that a high quality liberal education is being priced out of the reach of all but a few, and that relatively cheap, on-line vocational learning or conventional degrees with clearer signs of high returns upon graduation will eventually become the order of the day. Furthermore, all but our richest institutions will implode under the strain of trying to maintain adequate margins between real cost and pricing, seeking revenues to support research, faculty, and student needs, and trying to maintain the expensive physical plants that have sprung up across the country in the past twenty years. And that is nothing compared to the social effects of reduced educational opportunities and extreme financial hardship for a majority of the college population and their families, as we shift the burden of educating the next generation onto that generation itself. How ironic it is that a century after the United States committed itself to mass higher education, and just at the moment when the rest of the world seems to be deciding to follow its example, open access to the best education available is threatened.

As an indication of the financial woes of students today, there has been a dramatic rise in student borrowing, with Family Education Loans, for example, doubling from $12.6 billion in 1990 to over $24 billion in 1999–00. Federal student aid is expected to help families pay for college, but while in 1980 a Pell Grant covered some 38 percent of the average cost of a four-year private college, in 1999–

2000 it covered only 14 percent. And that problem is exacerbated by the fact that Pell Grants comprise only 30 percent of federal student aid, and the maximum grant in 2001 is still barely over $3000.[24] Of the $35 billion spent by the federal government in 1996 on student aid, 70 percent went to loans, a considerably less viable option for poorer families. In 1999–2000, the situation was somewhat better, but still, of the $68 billion available in grant, loan, and work-study funding, according to the College Board, 59 percent was in loans and only 40 percent in grants, a near reversal of the proportions of 1980–81.[25] Meanwhile, because home equity is not counted as a family asset, more upper-income families have been qualifying for loans.

The Department of Education sampled some thirty-five thousand students in 1995–96 and found that half of all baccalaureate students graduate with federal loan debt: "The average amount borrowed by students in 1995–96 was $12,000 at public institutions, compared with $7,400 three years earlier, and $14,300 at private colleges, compared with $10,200 in 1992–93."[26] Another research project by Nellie Mae, the student-loan provider, "found that the average student-loan debt had more than doubled in the preceding six years, from $8,200 in 1991 to $18,800 in 1997."[27] In 2002, according to the "Burden of Borrowing" report cited above, 39 percent of students are graduating with "unmanageable levels of student loan debt." The report estimates that one-third of students graduating owed $20,000 or more in educational loans.[28] Low-income students carry a heavy load of this "unmanageable" debt, as do black (55 percent) and Hispanic students (58 percent). And the U.S. Census data for 2001 "pegged at $32,101 the average income for 18- to 24-year-olds with bachelor's degrees who worked full-time and year-round in 2000."[29] The *Chronicle of Higher Education* in August 1997 summarized yet another report on the debt status of college graduates: "The typical graduate who borrowed to pay for college has total monthly debt payments of $852, which include student loans, car loans, and credit cards. The fastest growing segment of debt includes student loans and credit cards. About 67 percent of college students had a credit card in 1996, compared with 54 percent in 1990."[30] The average card debt for student borrowers who graduated in 2002 was $3,176.[31]

In addition to borrowing more money, students are working many hours while at college—too many hours, in the eyes of the American Council on Education, which has found that 80 percent of students work while completing an undergraduate degree. Indeed, one-third of these students are full-time employees who also attend college. The other two-thirds are traditional undergraduate students who work on average twenty-five hours per week.[32]

There is no question that placing the burden of paying for college on students themselves has raised both moral and practical questions that we seem not to be addressing adequately through federal or state policies. As Terry Hartle of the American Council of Education has said, "The social compact that assumed that the adult generation would pay for the college education of the next generation has been shattered. College students are victims of the popularity of user fees. 'Let the beneficiaries pay' has become a popular refrain at all levels of government. As a result, many financially pressed state legislatures have forced public colleges to increase tuition sharply in recent years, in turn forcing students to borrow more and more."[33] And, of course, increases in tuition and fees in private universities have had an even stronger effect; the freshman attrition rate in private schools rose three percentage points between 1983 and 1996 to nearly 26 percent. (The freshman attrition rate in public colleges meanwhile remained roughly the same at 29 percent.)[34]

This is also a time when schools are finding it very difficult to hold back tuition increases. The real problem is that they cannot discount tuition prices effectively through institutional aid to offset tuition raises, unless, like some Ivy League schools, they have endowment earnings that can be used. Furthermore, in the interests of maintaining or raising the quality of the student body, the use of institutional aid is not uncommonly being deflected away from the economically disadvantaged to students who do not need the money.

But in spite of high tuition—in fact, one might argue, largely because of it—there is a new strain in the telling of the American college story. More students and parents are forced to embrace the inflated economic value of a college degree, based on the often-quoted fact that the earning power of college graduates is much greater than that of high school graduates. There is even a lingering nostalgia for the romance-of-liberal-learning-at-all-costs, now made somewhat elitist by its rarity. But not all Americans would agree that getting a high-quality liberal education should be a grin-and-bear-it experience or like buying a luxury item. Owning an expensive college education may not be a constitutional right, but high tuition costs are jeopardizing the social mobility that we have so long considered a special reason for higher education. And that, ironically, raises another issue—the relation between investing in higher education and an overemphasis on the social mobility such a credential may bring.

The educational sociologist David Labaree has written a fine study of credentialism in higher education that touches on just this point:

> It is time to consider whether the connection between schooling and social mobility is doing more harm than good . . . the process of getting ahead often interferes with getting an education, and . . . the process of getting an education frequently makes it harder to get ahead. . . . Instead of arguing that we need to make education into a more equitable mechanism for getting ahead, I argue that we need to back away from the whole idea that getting ahead should be the central goal of education. . . .
>
> [T]he pursuit of educational advantage has inadvertently threatened to transform the public educational system into a mechanism for personal advancement. In the process, the generous public goals that have been so important in defining the

larger societal interest in education—to produce politically capable and socially productive citizens—have lost significant ground to the narrow pursuit of private advantage at public expense. The result is that the common school has become increasingly uncommon, with growing emphasis on producing selective symbolic distinctions rather than shared substantive accomplishments, and the community interest in education as a public good has increasingly lost ground to the individual interest in education as private property.[35]

It is precisely the importance of a revitalized liberal education as a "shared substantive accomplishment" rather than a "selective symbolic distinction" that is the center of my argument in this book. For it is plain that while barely 9 percent of the population attend schools with an annual tuition of $20,000 and over and 70 percent attend schools priced at $8,000 or less the issue is not simply that of finding a school with the "right tuition," but the availability of any kind of education for those who want it and qualify for it.[36] Given public concerns about tuition costs, the devaluation of the diploma, and student debt, it is evident that the temperature of the academic bathwater has slowly risen in recent years to a point where bathers are starting to scream. And the screams of those who have just noticed that they have been in hot water for some time but cannot figure out how to get out of the bath are often the loudest of all. As the nation enters the new millennium with more muted euphoria over market prospects, we find ourselves raising the big question again of how the social mission and meaning of the undergraduate degree can be somehow insulated from market uncertainties.

The Cost of Doing Business

How did things become so difficult and the culture of academic commerce so contradictory? In part, it is the inevitable result of trusting education to an unregulated market economy. In part, too, as management experts might say, it results from the fact that colleges are only partially corporatized. The crisis in college finances is the result of keeping in place a traditional organization of knowledge in the disciplines while trying to respond to numerous curricular challenges, not to mention operating cost inflation, unpredictable enrollments, strong competition for high-quality students, and government expenditures on higher education that have not kept up with enrollment growth before and after 1990. Historically, too, a serious problem for the market, at least until recently, has been the shrinking pool of traditional students. Between 1960 and 1970, enrollment of first-time freshmen in all public and private four-year schools rose 60 percent—100 percent if one includes community colleges. Between 1970 and 1980, however, first-year freshmen enrollment remained flat in four-year schools and increased 46 percent in two-year colleges. The picture remained the same for public and private universities from 1980 to 1995; the recorded enrollment of first-time freshmen in 1995 is identical to that in 1970; and in 1997 it was almost the same as in 1973.[37]

Perhaps the one consistent problem has been the undercapitalization of higher education and its vulnerability to market changes, especially given the need to discount tuition and provide adequate financial aid. The 1980s and 1990s brought intensifying anxiety over the finances of higher education. As we have noted, tuition rates almost doubled between 1980 and the mid-1990s in public and private four-year schools, and in hindsight it would appear that rate increases went beyond what was needed to meet necessary institutional costs. Although it can be argued that the free-market system inevitably creates wide variations in pricing and value, at the same time there is good reason to think that colleges willingly exploited the market possibilities in a highly aggressive way. On the other hand, defenders of tuition raises point to the rapid growth of curricular offerings at this time to cope with a more diverse student body, along with increased support staff and faculty salaries.

But the 1980s did offer a sound financial basis on which to plan for the future. Revenues per student grew by only about 2 percent a year, an increase nonetheless over the declining revenues of the 1970s. Total revenues, however, more than doubled from 1980 to 1990 (from $60 billion to $135 billion). State funding rose from $20 billion to $40 billion, federal funding doubled (from $10 billion to roughly $20 billion), and there was a considerable growth in sales and services (from $14 billion to $35 billion), providing much-needed investment funds. Bullish markets also brought success for the endowment. In short, the 1980s were a time when colleges and universities could have laid a better foundation for future growth. They started to act decisively in emulation of the corporate style, winning and using large federal "subsidies," building some capital (but not enough), putting stronger public relations units in place, and setting in motion what is now facetiously called the "Chivas Regal effect"—the equation of price with quality. Yet all this did not hold down the numbers of applicants to the best and most expensive schools, any more than they are being held back now, with four-year tuition approaching $140,000. Parents were and are able to use personal resources, credit, financing, and government loans to pursue the golden credential, in spite of the fact that the median family income grew by only 10 percent in the past twenty-five years. Indeed, almost all colleges and universities have felt they can continue even now to raise tuition and fees considerably beyond the rate of inflation, indulging, some commentators say, the greed of our era.

According to *The College Tuition Spiral,* a study commissioned by the American Council of Education and the College Board, the main causes of tuition increases across the nation were a drop in state funding of public universities, competition for a limited number of students, faculty salary raises, and improvements in student facilities.[38] For many schools with poor endowments, increased expenditures were essential to make much-needed improvements in plant and faculty investment in order to remain competitive. But the dramatic tuition increases in general have been challenged by analysts, who emphasize the fact that during this time both state funding and endowment income of public schools did improve. The rich schools got considerably richer, and many did not make marked improvements to their physical plant. In short, many schools continued to raise tuition largely because they thought the market could bear it.

But the real issue, of course, is not just what NYU and Harvard charge. Again, roughly 9 percent of the nation's students go to schools with annual tuition of $20,000 or more. According to the College Board, "Almost half of undergraduate students attending four-year institutions pay less than $4,000 in tuition and fees. . . . And for the 44 percent of undergraduates who attend public two-year colleges, tuition averages less than $2,000."[39] One could argue that it is inappropriate for the best education to necessarily be the most expensive, but then many will also argue that such is not always the case. It has been said that one can get an equally good education at much cheaper market prices. Whether or not that is true—and we have no way of knowing for certain—the concern has to be over the pressure on middle-income student families and those that have no chance at all of meeting high tuition payments. And certainly the value of the credential from a cheaper school is rarely that of our expensive, elite institutions. The gap between rich and poor is widening and making it difficult for many to get any university education of reasonable quality, especially in a country that has devised its market system to cope with mass education. As the same College Board Report comments, "Combined with generally stagnant family income over the past 20 years . . . trends in college tuition present serious problems for low- and moderate-income families. While average inflation-adjusted tuition has more than doubled at both public and private four-year institutions, median family income has risen only 20 percent since 1981. Student aid, meanwhile, has increased in total value, but not enough to keep pace with the rise in tuition, and most of the growth in aid has been in the form of borrowing."

The national median income of a four-person family recorded at the last census—$60,000—limits the ability of most students to earn a college degree, even in public schools. The 70 percent of the student population paying $8,000 or less in tuition a year will have some difficulty with such an income. And the 2000 UCLA Freshman Survey revealed that 46 percent of the student body comes from families earning $60,000 or less. An additional 29 percent of students' families earn between $60,000 and $100,000; and 26 percent earn more than $100,000. Private higher education especially is doubtless not easily available without substantial financial assistance to students from families earning less than $100,000—75 percent of the student body.

All these problems affect poor and minority students in particular, especially at a time when minority populations are growing. Even public school tuition is too high for many, not to mention room and board and other necessary support. Little individual state-funded financial aid is available because most goes as direct subsidies to institutions, not to students. In professional schools above all, where minority students have often relied on aid from affirmative action sources, few are matriculating. The entering class of 1997 at the University of California, Berkeley, Law School, in a state that has banned affirmative action funding, contained no African American students. Ironically, private universities often take in higher percentages of minority students than do public schools, despite their higher tuition rates, because of special institutional subsidies. But graduation rates for such minority students are not high, often because their financial problems make it difficult for them to stay enrolled.

The antidote to rising tuition costs in the market culture of academe is, of course, discounting and subsidies. Some $68 billion of financial aid, mostly federal, was available in 2000, but that includes a 20 percent contribution from the institutions themselves, in the form of grants and loans. This is a doubling in constant-dollar value in the past decade, according to the College Board's *Trends in Student Aid 2000*.

Financial aid expenditures are designed primarily to help students with financial problems and often make attendance at the college of their choice possible. But they are not made simply in the spirit of charity or altruism. Financial aid is also designed to leverage student matriculation in ways that allow schools freedom to shape their preferred student body in terms of numbers, quality, and diversity. And this, in turn, has fast become a euphemism for leveraging the most from tuition resources by returning some of it to good students, regardless of need. Indeed, institutional financial aid is quite a problematic practice because it cuts into revenues and promotes the tuition spiral. A survey conducted by the National Association of College and University Business Officers in 1997 sums up the problem this way: "The average tuition of 212 private colleges that have been involved in the survey from the beginning grew from $5,359 to $15,399 from 1990 to 1997. The colleges' revenue per student, however, grew by only $2,450 to $9,846 over the same period. [Therefore] for every dollar colleges have tacked on to tuition since 1990, they have kept just 46 cents. Over all, colleges are giving 31 percent of their stated prices back to students as financial aid, up from 23 percent in 1990."[40]

Indeed, if one looks at the twenty-year span from 1975–76 to

1994–95 in the Department of Education 1997 statistics—and the 2000 database has a 1995–96 cutoff, which scarcely changes the conclusion—one finds only a modest 32 percent increase in current-fund expenditures per student measured in constant 1994–95 dollars (from $13,351 in 1975–76 to $17,681 in 1994–95). Yet in that time, tuition, room, and board grew on the average more than 400 percent. The portion of the budget allotted to administrative spending (another indirect form of student support) remained roughly constant in both public and private universities (13–15 percent). Research funding saw modest increases, from 19.7 percent to 22.3 percent in public schools, and 7.9 percent to 10.1 percent in private schools. The major area of expenditure growth was in financial aid (scholarships and fellowships) to students, which increased fivefold in public universities and sevenfold in private universities.

Two results of this trend are worth noting. First, many private schools have raised their discount levels dangerously high, even to 40 percent and beyond, to fill a class. Second, many are using their aid to address merit rather than need and are shaping their constituencies by adjusting their prices for *selected* consumers, thereby exacerbating the contradictions created by high tuition in the first place. Most schools have also raised tuition dramatically over this period, as we have seen, relying on bringing in full-paying students who can supplement the less advantaged. They then return a portion of the tuition increase in the form of financial aid to leverage the enrollment of more students, preferably brighter ones, and the circle, then, is closed. Provided that the tuition discount rate does not rise too high, profit margins can remain reasonably good and the financial juggling act can continue. On the other hand, when aid packages, in part subsidized by richer students who may not be so talented, are siphoned off to high-merit students regardless of need, the altruistic motives for financial aid become questionable. They are also often a self-serving, however understandable gesture by schools in the race for high selectivity quotients and a better reputation. But they do little to improve diversity.

There is, therefore, a growing perception that escalating tuition increases in part result from the need for raising student aid—the relation between tuition revenues and aid expenditures is synergistic —and that in some schools an elaborate shell game is in progress, for aid is being used for purposes of balancing a school's budget and raising its competitive worth, rather than building a diverse student body. Indeed, since 1992, when private schools started tuition discounting and loan programs to attract middle-income students,[41] the business of making an expensive education more affordable for the middle class has turned into the buying of rich and middle-class students and increasing a school's reputation through merit-based programs. Even elite schools have moved away from their hitherto need-blind aid policies, which were set on first accepting students on the basis of merit, then allocating aid to those students on the basis of need. Such schools seek to attract the best quality students they can and have announced publicly in the past few years that they have added millions of dollars to institutional financial aid funds. Methods of assessing family need have changed, too, to make it easier for middle-class families—those earning between $60,000 and $100,000 —to obtain aid since it became apparent to elite schools that enrollment yield in the middle-income range was rather lower than those in the high-income range and in the low-income range where students can and do receive very generous financial aid packages. Elaborate formulae were developed so that middle-income parents who have savings will not be penalized for saving instead of spending money on expensive real estate, which would, under older formulae, have qualified parents for aid.

In 1989, two dozen private colleges, including every one of the Ivy League schools (a consortium known as the Overlap Group) "agreed that they would jointly determine the appropriate aid award for each student admitted to one or more of the institutions. The colleges . . . adhered to a financial-aid policy that, many believed, benefited colleges and students alike: Students could choose among the institutions without cost being a significant factor, and colleges could reserve their aid dollars for the neediest students."[42]

Such practices at first had the added value of allowing high-quality students to be spread around a more representative range of schools. Students with merit scholarships to Boston University, for example, have been known to turn down both Harvard and Yale. But the consortium soon caught the attention of the Justice Department, which investigated it. The schools agreed to give up these practices after their activities were deemed a violation of antitrust laws. Supporters of the group's practices believed this brought about the bidding frenzy of the 1990s. Allegations were made that some private schools even ignored home equity in assessing need for students they wanted and included it for less competitive students.[43] And a number of schools still noted the difficulty for middle-income students in affording elite institutions because not all need could be met. But even with the consortium out of action, in the late 1990s increased spending from endowment income has been used by schools like Stanford, Yale, and Princeton to attract middle-income students. But it has also, of course, largely improved the bidding advantage of such schools against those without similar resources.

In 1992, Congress passed an antitrust exemption that permitted private colleges practicing need-blind admissions to "refine the formula for awarding financial aid."[44] Known now as the 568 Group after the section of a law for the improvement of public schools that was invoked by Congress for its new ruling, twenty-eight universities and colleges, all of the highest national rankings (many from the old consortium), from 1999 on aimed to provide additional merit-based aid. They did so by agreeing on elaborate formulae for assessing need, such as considering parental savings for college education as the parents' assets (valued at 5 percent of aid limits) and not the student's (normally considered to be 35 percent of assets for needs analysis). Colleges are now expected to pay much larger amounts toward financial aid, but then not all schools in the new consortium can keep up with the multibillion endowments of schools like Harvard and Yale. And there is growing skepticism that this will stop competition via financial aid to attract students.

Indeed, Peter Carstensen, a professor of law at the University of Wisconsin in Madison, notes,

> The 568 group's 'consensus' strategy invites high-price, brand-name private institutions to eliminate price competition by private collective action. And who would benefit then? The students? Or the colleges themselves, operating much like a cartel? . . . In the world of antitrust, a history of collusive behavior . . . suggest[s] that present activity may be a continuation of past misconduct—especially if an economic rationale for anticompetitive activity still exists. And, of course, in this case, that rationale definitely remains. The plain truth is that private colleges compete for students in the same ways and for the same reasons that producers of other goods and services compete for customers. Selling a college education is a business, and competition for the most coveted students grows keener everyday. . . . The strategy behind colleges' financial aid is no different from rebates and low-cost financing that automobile manufacturers offer to make their products more attractive.

Furthermore, Carstensen notes, "The potential for price-fixing will become greater if more institutions, especially those most directly competitive with the 568 group, adopt the 'consensus approach.' "[45]

There is, of course, a scenario in which elite schools can claim to have democratized the financial aid process more than the earlier, frenzied free-market bidding. Carstensen lists these guidelines as "workable criteria to define need and family resources," "timely and appropriate data," and expert judgment. But these activities simply amount to a growing professionalism and subtlety in the financial aid process, which is undeniable, and really do not speak to the moral question of the broad effects of such a policy, which effectively is a strategy for a group of elite schools to retain its market grip on high quality students. Indeed, Carstensen ends his discussion rather flatly with the comment, "If the standards allow sufficient discretion for aid to be varied, depending on the interest of the institution in making a particular 'sale,' and individual institutions use that discretion, they will not significantly interfere with competition. They may even, through informed discussion and exchange of information, provide a basis to better determine the indeterminate: the need of the student." This is little more than an admission, which Carstensen has already made, that buying a student is like convincing a customer to buy a car. Imagine students shopping among colleges in the same way consumers shop among dealerships for the best deal. In the end, the institution that wins is the one that has best ascertained need and can offer enough money to fill the gap.

This new complex high-stakes financial aid game does not alleviate concern over tuition costs, and it does still favor the wealthy schools, where endowment sizes are at all-time highs and rising fast—more than $90 billion for the top fifty schools in 1997;[46] more than $124 billion for the top twenty-five in 2000.[47] A good deal of money has been freed in these colleges for scholarship aid, but it is unclear exactly how it is being used, whether to address need for the most meritorious or to create a more diverse student body. On the other hand, all these developments are hardly surprising, and it is difficult to blame private schools, especially, which rely heavily on selectivity factors for doing what they do: it is quite legal, and we do live, after all, in a free-market educational setting. Those institutions that do not have endowment resources and who are trying to improve their market reputation have little option but to use financial aid leveraging to improve their lot. Lowering tuition might be a more useful strategy for all schools in the private sector, testing the synergy between quality, wealth, and high cost and aiming for a more democratically representative student body. The alternative is simply a ratcheting up of discounting with all its attendant problems.

For financial aid bidding wars are now well under way, and it is rumored they will become even more common—especially when entrepreneurial students and parents seek to negotiate. It is only a matter of time before the basic strategy of extracting the maximum amount of revenue from all students, regardless of their financial ability to pay, becomes an egregiously obvious public concern. The continuing practice of need-blind admissions is likely to be less prevalent in the not-too-distant future as institutional resources dwindle and federal aid fails to keep up with real costs. And the tactic of tuition discounting to attract wealthy students can be only a stopgap measure in creating strong institutions.[48] As the *Wall Street Journal* put it,

> Most college administrators acknowledge that higher education probably will never again receive the kind of government largesse it once did. Nor do they expect much improvement on the revenue side: Tomorrow's applicant pool, while larger than today's, will be poorer. The general outlook is for cost cutting and fewer services, new strategies such as shrinking the time it takes to earn a degree—and even a shakeout in which some weaker schools go under. But colleges are hard to kill, cautions Christopher Hooker-Haring, dean of admissions at Muhlenberg College in Allentown, Pa. Unbridled discounting may keep some alive, he says, but not without compromising quality. If so, he worries that students and their families may be lulled into buying "a truly inferior educational product simply because someone has thrown a lot of money at them."[49]

Higher education, though, is not very successful in luring and retaining students from middle-income families or below unless schools have private resources and tuition is manageable, simply because the gap between cost and aid is too large—a phenomenon aptly called gapping whereby schools try to draw in students with partial aid and expect them to find the rest. Thus we have a curious situation in which most families—probably three-quarters of those with children attending or seeking to attend college—have to borrow money to send their children to institutions that are in turn struggling to keep their discount levels at 30 percent. It is hard to pick the winner in this scenario.

Nonetheless, financial aid has become the fine art of the college recruiting profession. Calculations and forecasting have become increasingly subtle, if not baroque, with careful massaging of minor differences in offers between student cohorts, based on talent and ability to pay. The trick is to offer the least amount of institutional aid that will tip the balance in favor of one's school, even while maintaining or improving quality and attracting enough students who can afford to pay (sometimes regardless of talent) so that a reasonable margin of gain from tuition revenues can be shown. Financial aid administration, now clearly a branch of statistics and probability theory, is rarely if ever divorced from the overall financial affairs administration and has an important role in determining the nature of an entering class. Any slight deviation from projected income can create troubling budget deficits that have to be met from cuts elsewhere. Indeed, anyone involved in university administration knows that finessing financial aid to produce a reasonably predictable entering class is the key to budget modeling. A sensible projection of student numbers in various cohorts ranging from those with high merit aid to "full pays" lies at the heart of an effective administration.

Along with discounting strategies, colleges are also trying to address the problem of tuition costs by using work-study programs, making special efforts to recruit international students (who are often expected to pay a larger share of tuition than American students) and even offering prepurchase plans that guarantee future tuition. A Manhattan company named Iempower, working through its website, aptly named MyRichUncle.com, matches students with rich investors. Investors pay for the undergraduate education and students pay a fixed percentage of income—starting at 0.2 percent per $1000 of earnings—for a period up to fifteen years.[50] Numerous consulting firms and financial advisors, sometimes even sponsored by institutions, offer advice to parents on planning for the high cost of college with investment and savings plans. The pressure is on because students badly need aid, and schools need student numbers to make budgets and, for the luckier ones who can afford to achieve this, to increase student quality. We are, after all, obsessed with college rankings. Thus, whether students and parents like it or not, they have had to become very savvy consumers. And whether colleges and universities like it or not, they have had to acquire much talent in betting on student futures. Gone are the laid-back, overconfident recruiters for prestigious schools. All but a few schools are having trouble finding well-qualified, full-paying students. (College Board figures in 1998, for example, show that there were a mere 122,383 college students in the United States, with combined SATs of around 1130, from families earning $100,000 or more. This group, which is nearly 90 percent white or Asian, is just over 1 percent of the student body in public and private four-year institutions.)

The tuition and financial crises spawn their own curricular needs—the nurturing of transfer students, for example, even through a growing number of articulation agreements between community colleges and universities. Many students now attend community college for the first two years of their degree work, then transfer to "better-name" schools. Another result is that faculty salaries have rarely risen above 5 percent on the average in the past decade. Meanwhile the number of adjunct faculty, who work for small salaries and no benefits, has risen from one-third of the total faculty in 1987 to 42 percent in 1995.

Yet another effect has been the growth of useful new programing for adults—often taught by adjunct faculty—with strong personal, therapeutic, creative, and work-related emphases that have emerged to cater to this fastest-growing part of the student body. Such continuing education programs, often immensely popular with older students, are the celebrated cash cows of academe (along with professional education) and in some cases have even invaded the territory of traditional programing. Few would question their social usefulness, even while the development of such new courses—a good thing in itself—has done little to stimulate redefinition of the traditional curriculum, in spite of the fact that the adult population is one of the largest growth areas. Finally, and perhaps even more important, as a result of the financial strain of doing the university's business, between 1990 and 1997 enrollment in graduate professional education grew by 9 percent and in graduate education by 10.5 percent, while the undergraduate population has increased by only 4 percent. This has partly been in response to professional openings, but it is also the result of an effort by the university to develop graduate/professional programing with great flexibility.

By and large, institutions of higher education are well aware of the seriousness of their financial problems and have tried to respond to them. In July 1994, the *Chronicle of Higher Education,* using the findings of the American Council of Education's "Campus Trends, 1994," reported that since 1989, "nearly two-thirds of all institutions have reorganized their administration, 80 percent have clamped down on spending, and 71 percent have reviewed the mission of academic programs . . . 45 percent of all institutions have cut their budgets across the board and 58 percent have made reductions in some units. Reorganization and cuts have been made selectively and mostly in public institutions." Predictably, "only 31 percent of the public institutions rated their overall financial condition as 'excellent' or 'very good,' while 45 percent of the private institutions gave themselves such rating."

But to a large extent, as everyone knows, financial anxiety has simply become a daily part of the academic way of life, ameliorated occasionally when the market does well. Such uncertainty often undermines an institution's will to integrate its mission, to take risks with the curriculum. Anxiety over an institution's debt burden, its tuition dependency and revenue diversity, and the amount of net assets available to cover debt service, unforeseen problems, and market fluctuations—all these determine its ethos. And the academic and social implications go beyond even concerns for good accounting and management. The postmodern university, to survive, now has to be a highly diversified corporate entity, serving a vast clientele and most often supplementing its traditional revenue sources from teaching and research with other enterprises. In recent years, the character of the university has changed quite dramatically, from an institution in which learning is a competitive right to one in which it is a purchasable commodity in a consumerist culture.

More Like a Firm

One of the major issues concerning the management of colleges and universities today is why such institutions, in the ironic words of Gordon Winston, a Williams College economist and one of the most lucid experts in the field, "cannot be more like a firm"[51] or, perhaps one should say, even more like a firm. Winston is asking a rhetorical question, but one that is quite serious. Why can't universities be run as efficiently as corporations are said to be run, especially when they plainly want to be corporate in nature? There is a general feeling abroad that fund accounting practices in academe—for example, the use of specific accounts to show the financial conditions of various functions of the university, like plant maintenance, instruction, and so on—are not standardized to any credible extent. They allow for a complex shifting of revenues through various funds and such magical categories as mandatory and non-mandatory transfers. They also allow for off-budget accounting of funds so that actual listings of transactions are incomplete. As Winston points out, "Nowhere is all this put together to tell what the college, *as a whole*, has been up to." Thus, fiscal reports can vary in their bottom lines according to which constituency is being served: the IRS, the public, a board of trustees, faculty, and so on. New rules are in the offing to provide a more realistic revelation of the beginnings and ends of revenue streams, but the fact remains that few university financial statements tell all the subtle mysteries of exact profits and losses, especially when balanced financial statements are prepared.

Of course there are good reasons for this, as Winston points out, and these reasons center on why a college or university is *not* like a corporate for-profit entity. Basing his argument on the work of Henry Hansmann, a Yale Law School professor and economist, Winston summarizes the differences: nonprofit firms can make profits, but they can't distribute those profits to their owners. They function as "trust markets," basically selling services to customers who do not really know what they are buying. While there is little pressure on fund managers to be efficient, these same managers are usually motivated by idealistic goals. Colleges and universities function in this way as a mix of two different kinds of nonprofits: donative, in that they rely on donations for various purposes, and commercial, in that they sell products for a price—like hospital and other auxiliary services. Winston points out that with these two sources of income colleges can subsidize their products. So "in 1991, the average student at the average U.S. college paid $3,100 for an education that cost $10,600 to produce—thus receiving a subsidy of $7,500." (Public school subsidies averaged $7,800 and private school subsidies

$7,200.) What Winston does not deal with is the source of such subsidies, which vary enormously from schools that are heavily endowed and able to subsidize substantially more students than tuition-dependent schools that use tuition revenues to support the education of a smaller number of students. But he does comment on the fact that "in 1991, the 10 percent of U.S. schools with the largest subsidies gave the average student a subsidy worth $21,000 a year; those with the smallest subsidies gave $1,500."

The point, though, is that a university degree, while widely recognized as a product, cannot be sold with a certain degree of precision, as, say, a car that has a specific color, engine size, design, mileage, and so on. Carstensen's analogy with the automobile industry certainly makes sense when it comes to financing the product—be it a car or a degree. But students can never be sure what they are going to get when they take courses, and what they get depends a good deal on their participation in the business of learning. Colleges rely on their customers to be a part of the educational process, to be involved responsibly in what they are doing. Even in the most informal ways, students help educate other students. "Good fellow-students, other things being equal, will lead to a better education than poor fellow-students," as Winston says. For this reason the recruitment transaction between the institution and the student is very important. Good universities care about the students they are selling to, and students, in turn, try to be as well informed as possible about the services they want to buy. But a university education is sought out by people who "don't really know what they're buying. And they can't find out until long after the fact. The idea that higher education represents 'an investment in human capital' is more significant than is often realized, since investment decisions . . . are inherently freighted with uncertainty. . . . Buying a college education," Winston goes on, "is more like buying a cancer cure than a car or a house. There's a strong tendency to avoid regret and play it safe and buy what everyone considers 'the best,' if you can afford it—reputation and animal hunches loom large in the final decision."

Winston also notes the importance (as this chapter has documented) of a university's ability to subsidize costs through endowment income, given that the "difference in schools' ability to pay subsidies to their students is the most fundamental element in the economics of higher education." Obviously, large subsidies translate into better bargains for students and greater selectivity for the institution. The financial aid game played at its best is good for both. If the student body size is controlled, then demand is increased, and as demand rises, so too can subsidies. But in making the decision to be bought, students take reputation into account. As Winston puts it, "It ends with a highly differentiated set of colleges whose initially different wealth has turned into student quality. This may indeed be the *main* way that differences in dollar resources translate into differences in college quality." Schools with wealth and high quality students perpetuate both wealth and quality.

The conclusion is quite clear. The higher education market, like all markets, is not intrinsically egalitarian. Its ways of doing business are in a clearly tensional, even contradictory relation with the kind of social and academic mission I discussed in the first chapter and will again in the last two chapters of this book. But this is not going to change, at least not in the foreseeable future, even though we can begin to understand more clearly how the organization of wealth and power in the college system does influence what we do in the classroom. For the college market, as Winston notes, is hierarchical, and the blue chip players, as we all know, are those with significant donative wealth. Indeed, he admits, "the rich get richer, and the rich have been getting richer for a long time." And the rich schools are somewhat but not totally impervious to sudden changes—such as Winston's warning that "if it comes to pass that 3 million more students enter U.S. colleges and universities [as estimated for the next decade], they will bring with them (based on 1991 numbers) an additional $9.3 billion in net tuition revenues, but also an additional $32 billion in costs—if quality is to be maintained at 1991 levels. That will require $22.7 billion of additional non-tuition resources. From somewhere."

The picture is rather bleak, but the seriousness of it all may escape those who assume that colleges must simply become more efficient, more like well-run businesses. They must be that, of course, but not without a sense of the irony of their position and the tenuousness of their well-being. As Winston points out, and I read his words as in part a critique of academic practices and not just a defense:

> For a firm, increased size often brings economies of scale—fixed costs are spread over more and more output. But for a college that's dependent on endowments and the existing physical plant to support its student subsidies—as most private schools are—increased size spreads those fixed *resources* over more and more students, reducing the average subsidy each one can get [unless, of course, schools are willing to increase their discount rate]. Public schools, in contrast, have usually been supported by "capitation"—appropriations tied to enrollments—to encourage expansion and thereby, citizen access to higher education. They escape the gloomy arithmetic of a larger denominator that rules the private sector. But that's changing; capitation is being replaced by fixed block grants to public colleges, as in the California system. And as public institutions accumulate more endowment wealth, they increasingly will have the same incentives to restrict access as the private schools have had—that is, more students will come to mean more costs but not much more income. So if the trend toward block grants continues, it can be anticipated that public institutions will behave increasingly like private ones, with access restricted by size and selectivity both.[52]

In short, the only hope for maintaining the current market system of higher education, let alone create a democratic agenda for it, is an infusion of substantial capital, in the region of $25–30 billion or so over the next decade, the experts say—money that should be paid directly to students to offset tuition. And, of course, federal and state governments realize this to some extent and have increased their subsidies, though mostly in the form of loans. The money has to be equitably spread, though, especially to students wishing to attend schools with little endowment. And it must be applied where it can best be used: to maintain access and improve the quality of education. But so long as we insist on promoting higher education as a relatively unregulated market system, modeled on the corporate marketplace, the rich will get richer and the poor poorer, a number of schools will die off or reduce their quality, and there will be fewer places for the growing number of students. Another result is likely to be further pressure to curtail faculty tenure and freedoms in the interests of improved productivity and efficiency.

The curriculum, too, will inevitably be held hostage to market fluctuation if we do not introduce more persistent theories of what should be learned to provide a well-rounded undergraduate education, to provide clear value for an expensive degree. That is, we need to radically improve the quality and value of the product. Otherwise we will simply fall into the trap of assuming that knowledge can be delivered to students in different amounts and at different prices depending on their ability to pay. If our system is hierarchical and undemocratic now, it will be considerably worse in the next decade. For market freedom in higher education currently serves to harden social inequality and plays directly to consumer desires. It offers endorsement of the private rather than the public good. So the key question Americans must return to is this: Is an unregulated free-market enterprise the best way to handle something as important as higher education? And if it is, then how best do we adjust the current system to serve the public more equitably?

These questions are difficult to answer because there is a deep tension between the way in which the United States organizes higher education and the results Americans hope to achieve. Unless the academy focuses more on the outcomes of higher education in some coherent, pointedly democratic and integrated way, with tuition-cutting measures and adequate subsidies for students, and unless the academy develops a set of benchmark standards for doing all this, there will be little interest in a liberal education in the eyes of the public except as another branch of top 50 meritocracy training—or its mimicry of the same in other schools' striving for excellence. In a time of scarce resources, many of our most intelligent students will simply study what they want, seek to shortcut the process, or opt for a vocational education as the best use of scarce resources.

At the same time, the sense of public outrage over the cost and value of higher education will increase. This is inevitable so long as the academy continues to refuse to engage the core contradictions of its pricing strategies, which are so intimately linked to the curriculum and the perceived value of a degree. For if one of the great goals of the university is to mediate the contradictions of our market culture, it must seek first to mediate the contradictions of its own in which capitalism and democracy are necessarily yoked: by capitalizing higher education more richly, empowering community colleges to fulfill a larger role and not simply become feeder schools, raising standards and competitiveness in universities themselves, integrating research, inquiry, and learning more fully at all levels, providing a richer and more integrative general education experience, and adhering more closely to the terms of its long-established social mandate to provide a democratic education. In short, it is this set of challenges that liberal education especially must, in its own way, contend with.

CHAPTER 3

A Corporate Ethos

As early as the first decade of the twentieth century, when he wrote *Higher Learning in America,* that astute sociologist of higher education Thorstein Veblen sensed that the modern university was moving with strong purpose to new efficiencies in developing knowledge. He wrote,

> Men dilate on the high necessity of a businesslike organization and control of the university, its equipment, personnel and routine. What is had in mind in this insistence of an efficient system is that these corporations of learning shall set their affairs in order after the pattern of a well-conducted business concern. In this view the university is conceived as a business house dealing in merchantable knowledge, placed under the governing hand of a captain of erudition, whose office it is to turn the means in hand to account in the largest feasible output. . . .
>
> The university is to make good both as a corporation of learning and as a business concern dealing in standardized erudition, and the executive head necessarily assumes the responsibility of making it count wholly and unreservedly in each of these divergent, if not incompatible lines."[1]

Of course, there is some conscious irony propelling Veblen's words, but when we remember that he had little or no time for undergraduate education and saw the primary mission of the university as that of research, we sense that his opposition to "standardized erudition" came from within an academic culture that viewed itself as above the business of merely selling knowledge. Such a concern over an increasingly corporate nature of the university runs deep to this day among faculty in the arts and sciences. But what Veblen saw as a new alliance between erudition and business nearly one hundred years ago has, of course, become the business of higher education. All who work in a college or university know what this is. The process of corporatization takes shape as a combination of the following styles and controls that are used to manage the everyday life of the university:

- *Management and productivity development systems:* Quality management and achievement criteria; academic assessment of learning outcomes; the growth of professional human resources and legal departments to manage an ever more complex and litigious work environment; the use of complex software to organize data, generate reports, keep track of students, alumni, and employees, and to locate and contact prospective students; the use of video communications systems to relate to campuses around the globe; the development of academic divisional structures within schools and colleges to cluster and focus areas of knowledge development; the development of college/university consortia (nationally and internationally) to streamline curricular offerings and nurture knowledge.
- *Budget controls:* Responsibility center budgeting with decentralized budget authority allowing for gainshare options for profit-making departments; cash bonuses and incentives for faculty with merit; contribution margin reports to analyze the productivity and cost effectiveness of programs; complex overhead and flowback systems for research funding.
- *Marketing strategies:* Growing use of media advertising with the targeting of key audiences; the development of public relations offices entrusted with producing favorable and focused press releases, the use of promotional rhetoric and corporate-styled logos, the development of public identity themes, the hiring of state and federal lobbyists; the growth of a new rhetoric of corporate eduspeak that focuses on the language of excellence.
- *The redistribution of labor:* The outsourcing of tasks, the use of outside experts to teach specialized courses, a fondness for consultants, the huge rise in adjunct faculty in recent years to fill positions or to

cope with expansion; buy-out or tenure relinquishment plans to reward faculty who might choose to retire early; the increasing use of computer-generated courses to streamline the presentation of information.

• *The development of research and ancillary enterprises:* Close corporate liaisons for the production and sale of knowledge; focused research programs directly linked to corporate and government needs; the development of patents; the growth of an intellectual property rights bureaucracy; global outreach in seeking "knowledge development partners."

• *Customer service orientation:* In dealing with students and parents, with expanded student-life operations and improved services for students, including mentoring and advising; streamlined digital enrollment systems; therapeutic and career counseling and internship placement services; the growth of corporate connections to enhance the job prospects of graduates.

The development of these so-called corporate styles of management—and more besides, as new services are added almost weekly—has brought improvements to the daily life of students and faculty. Never known for their efficiency in the early to middle years of the twentieth century, universities now have well-developed budget processes and accounting controls. A utilitarian rationality has come slowly but surely to dominate the culture. Students, especially, are served with a heightened concern for their individual well-being. Data are assembled more quickly and efficiently and can often be cross-referenced with ease. Improved incentives are built in to departmental and faculty productivity assessment. The identity of universities is more immediately available to the public through appealing graphic and media presentations.

Of course, universities often still have that slightly worn look that generates a kind of traditional academic warmth and friendliness. Faculty offices are not necessarily any tidier, but then neither are student residence halls. New campus architecture can rather obviously blend the classical, Romanesque, Gothic, and academic functional styles with the most readily available brick, stone, or metal in the area. But some of the more interesting examples of postmodern architecture are to be found on college campuses, which more and more have a kind of corporate office park look— and corporate office parks are now frequently called campuses. Real (and sometimes splendid) efforts have been made to improve facilities for students and faculty, especially during the philanthropic boom of the eighties and nineties. Overall, there is an increased professionalism to campus life, a more efficient, slightly hard-edged but welcoming environment, a kind of postmodern, pastiched functionalism that somehow tries to make sense of the enormous bureaucratic complexity of the academic business.

The problem, however, lies not in efficiency. It lies in the complicated effects of corporate management strategies for handling knowledge, labor, style, and resources in the university. There are clearly perceived threats to faculty autonomy and liberal education from the relentlessness of the market logic. But in some ways, colleges are not like corporations at all, no matter how much we try to demonize corporatism and the growth of the capitalist culture of universities when disciplines fail or faculty find themselves losing the power of self-governance. No successful corporation seeking greater profits or even stability could possibly survive with an administrative power structure like that of the university, or with workers who actually own the means of production and have lifetime job security as well. But that is not to suggest that we should be going all the way with corporate management in the traditional university, though plainly that is the style of the increasing number of for-profit institutions. There has been pressure as well to achieve further efficiencies in recent years with the growth in numbers of activist trustees, often working closely with presidents and chancellors drawn from the political, bureaucratic, and corporate worlds. The creation of specialized university management teams and staff has pushed in this direction too. Subtle and often none-too-subtle ways have been found to circumvent faculty control by adding ancillary programs staffed by nonfaculty, building the adjunct ranks, and developing student life programs as a rival to academic programs.

But the power relations affecting university life are in reality highly complex. They help shape the contradictory culture of academe as much as the complex relations between education and capitalism that I outlined in chapter 2. At least six agencies compete for influence:

1. *Executive boards and college administrations* are institutional caretakers and have broad responsibility for overseeing all the workings of the university as a corporate entity. Theirs is the final responsibility for allocating financial, personnel, and physical resources in order to make an institution work, and to present to the public its best image. They function as guardians of the integrity of an institution—financial and academic—and as overseers of society's best interests. Trustees, that is, play a complex symbolic role, and their power resides in the fact that they represent, above all, social—including commercial—interests in academe.

2. *The faculty*, often represented politically by faculty senates within institutions as well as national organizations, are involved in the pursuit of knowledge and the encouragement of learning. This takes them beyond purely institutional interests to a shared community of learning that is national and international in its professional scope. At the same time, they must operate within the boundaries of their institutions and their specific missions— though these boundaries are being redefined by the Internet—in engaging students in the business of learning. They have a complex allegiance: to their institutions, to their students, and to their disciplines. In faculty hands is the power to set and maintain academic standards based on the essentials of disciplinary learning and the fundamental literacies. The faculty is the primary agency for generating knowledge and giving the university credibility as a credentialing agency.

3. *Students and alumni* have become important players as the market for higher education has matured. Students play the role of consumers and clients who seek to be empowered through the

learning process. This constituency finds the college credential less and less predictable as a preparation for the good life, as we saw in the last chapter, so its anxieties rise, and it becomes more concerned than ever to negotiate the conditions of university life, from tuition payments to grades to the quality of campus living and the curriculum. A stronger sense of entitlement is present among today's student consumers and their parents. The primary aim of the consumer of a university education is to seek empowerment rather than disinterested learning. Alumni, on the other hand, are newly empowered to wield influence on boards through the financial and other booster support of their alma mater. They offer a useful assessment of the quality of the education they received. No institution can afford to ignore alumni, who have long been among the strongest constituencies in the university.

4. *The national and even international market of institutions of higher education* contextualizes the activities of each institution, helping to determine its reputation by comparison and contrast with other institutions, providing accrediting agencies, furthering the growth of knowledge through cooperative efforts, helping to shape general curricula and the disciplines through knowledge trends, and continually defining and redefining in broad terms what it means to be an educated American. While the influence of peer institutions may seem quite abstract, universities are basically known by the company they keep. National media rankings of institutions, based on peer opinion, play an ever greater role in determining a university's reputation.

5. *Federal and state legislatures and educational authorities* attempt to oversee the broad allocation of public tax funds as subsidies for education and research. In the congressional and state legislatures, power is wielded through fund allocations—which are often sorely threatened—and the use of assorted political bully pulpits. Politicians may even attempt to shape the content of the curriculum.

6. *Corporations and corporate interests,* sometimes in alliance with political concerns, wield considerable power in the shaping of universities both through strategic alliances with campuses and as disseminators of commodity knowledge. They also wield power through representation of their culture, as I have outlined

above, along with specific company interests in being represented on boards of trustees. They are noted for their philanthropy, investment in research, special consulting alliances with institutions, and, above all, the encouragement of a corporate management style that has been the strongest influence in the past fifty years on how colleges and universities organize themselves and present themselves to the public. Because colleges and universities recognize that their survival depends on their managerial efficiency, a natural connection has grown up between academic and corporate culture.

This list of the players and their functions in the power games of higher education scarcely does justice to the changing alliances among them, to the shifting role playing of each to maintain their influence, and to the ideological wind changes that affect the curriculum and the economy of higher education in a multitude of ways. To assume that one or more of these sources of power can be pinned down to a fixed position is to oversimplify the fact that the uneasy relations and utopian desires of any of these six players can emerge at any moment and ruffle the texture of everyday academic life. Faculty can call on their traditional rights of self-governance to stall program development or they can be strongly supportive of administrative needs. Students can make their voices heard loudly with great effect. Administrations and trustees can find themselves siding as easily with the student consumer as with external interests. Budgetary formulae can produce growth in some academic areas and not in others and change the whole balance of power in a university when high-income-producing units, usually professional schools, receive a large gainshare of the profits. Overall, though, power settles with those who control the university as a corporation of learning. It may seem split, administratively, with trustees and managers on the one hand and the worker-faculty on the other, those who own the curriculum and the means of work. And both may court students, at least in undergraduate education, as the clientele they are there to serve, at times even competing to show who cares most. But the culture, as seen in the rhetoric we use, is corporate rather than academic.

Excellence

Faculty and administrations do not share, in general, a common language for describing what they do. Faculty have an underdeveloped public discourse for describing their teaching and research mission because they often feel they are not in the business of public relations except in their classrooms and their professional arenas. Faculty in general are also not very good at explaining what they do simply and clearly to the general public. Quite easily in the past few decades, then, a discourse of corporate-styled eduspeak, a rhetoric of service to society such as one might find in a commercial corporation, has been developed by administrations to explain the university's mission and goals. Power has its own shaping discourse in the university through the rhetoric of entrepreneurism and excellence. Increasingly the way we explain ourselves to ourselves in universities —in administrative edicts and annual reports, for example—uses a vocabulary that emphasizes our corporate culture, and the way in which ambiguity arises from this exercise is indicative of how deeply runs the division of labor in academe.

Here is an English professor from Georgetown University, James Slevin, offering his interpretation of such rhetoric in a recent publication from the Modern Language Association:

> We are all familiar with the pervasiveness within the university nowadays of a discourse, derived from finance and accounting, of objectives, accountability, assessment, resources, selling (of credits to customers) and delivery (of instruction to the purchasers of credits and ultimately of the instructed to appropriate work positions). . . . The trick is the way this language is strewn with discourse of another sort, deploying terms like "engage-

ment," "collaboration," "working together," and "collective responsibility" and asking that the faculty look to the "common good" toward which they are to "contribute." This language combines a discourse of commerce and a discourse of community, underwriting it all by using an observation about the calendar ("As we move into the next century") to invoke—without having to explain—a destiny to which we must accommodate ourselves. In this amalgamation, a vehicle of civic responsibility is yoked (like a metaphysical conceit) to a tenor of commodification in the hope that the latter will somehow be understood as the former. This discourse of "collaboration," "collective responsibility," "engagement," "teamwork," and "giving to the whole" at best distracts attention from and at worst intentionally mystifies the far more powerful process of commodification. At the same time it replaces intellectual questioning with civic duty as the obligation of the professoriat.[2]

Reading between the lines of administrative memos is, of course, the oldest academic pastime, and English professors are well trained to do this, perhaps too well trained. Depending on the critical persuasion of the reader, one could be looking for Freudian slips, metaphysical conceits, deconstructive turns, or any other kind of verbal slippage that suggests something secret is happening that could be quite sinister. There is a certain enjoyment afforded these professional readers who are able to prove that all is not well from rhetoric alone. Slevin is writing for an audience of English professors who know that a metaphysical conceit is one of the more challenging of poetic metaphors: a witty but usually surprising connection between things that would not normally be connected. The implication in Slevin's argument, of course, is that there is something deeply wrong and not merely witty about academic administrative discourse: the language of commerce can never be the language of learning; intellectual responsibilities and civic duties are not the same. Indeed, civic duty appears to have actually replaced intellectual questioning as the discourse of choice.

For anyone who has spent much time in universities, Slevin's comments seem very much to the point. Universities have become so entrepreneurial and civic-minded that a dominant organizational discourse, be it from education theory or business, is inevitable. We commodify knowledge and work for the sake of efficiency, and we commodify the language we use to talk about it in a discourse that comes from the real power matrix: the corporate world. Few administrators actually believe that civic duty replaces intellectual activity, but having it all ways at once is precisely what mission statements and administrative reports and memos mean to do. It is the ambivalence of the university's relation to society, itself a mixed metaphor, which indicates the cultural contradictions in academic culture.

The university's mission too has been a mixed metaphor for a very long time, especially in its efforts to link service to society and the economy with intellectual activity. But we should get over the surprise at this (for it has been going on for years) and seek an explanation that tries to come to grips with why the social mandate is as important as it is, why it should be integrated with learning and the inevitably capitalist practices of the university, and why we cannot simply claim that the function of the university is to pursue knowledge on its own terms. That I will explore in the last two chapters, especially in relation to liberal education. The challenge, that is, is to explain our metaphysical as well as pragmatic fate. The implications for liberal learning of merging standardized knowledge with the university's social and economic goals is the major issue, and Slevin's argument does not really deal with our larger needs. But it bears saying here, in agreement with Slevin, that however we interpret the rhetoric of administrative needs, the growth of a discourse of the commerce of learning linked to service to the community at least reveals how much of a metaphysical conceit our daily lives are in higher education.

Administrations are not entirely to blame, though. It is easy for academics to ignore that the move to business-styled bureaucracies for managing university life has been quite relentless since the early years of the past century and has grown as much from the market-styled proliferation of disciplines and departments as it has from the university's participation in global commercial markets. This may not make it right or even more palatable, but it can help explain why liberal education has found it very difficult indeed to mediate the connections between democracy, knowledge, and capitalism.

Similarly, it is all very well complaining, as many humanists do, that universities are not what they used be and that, as Bill Readings has put it, the University of Culture has given way to the University of Excellence.[3] But the University of Culture has never existed in the United States, and the University of Excellence has been devising its format for many years now. The cultural mandate for higher education is certainly included in the university's mission, but it does not dominate. It is very much an imported ideal from the golden age of European (especially German) education theory from the Enlightenment down through the nineteenth century. Even British universities, which preserved the cultural ideal of a university education longer than any others, now have a public mission in a mass education market that is remarkably similar to that of American universities, along with a set of government-controlled, corporate-styled assessment criteria that few American universities would care to live with.

It is commonplace, also, to say that there has been a steady proletarianization of faculty to sustain the corporatization of learning, that teaching has been reduced to knowledge work, and that educational management, public relations, and budgeting strategies ensure that faculty at large remain a proletariat, except in universities where their value is reckoned as a primary resource. All this is more often true than not, but the fact remains that the enemy, if there is one, is within as well as without. The organization of knowledge in academe remains a faculty responsibility, but it has quite literally been driven by a professional marketplace of disciplinary learning since the growth of the first modern universities. The more professionalized departments and disciplines have become, they more they have appeared to be like joint stock companies, entities that are greater than the sum of their parts, founded for the purposes of conducting research, disseminating knowledge, and promoting their own learning within specialized areas of knowledge whose criteria for quality are set by national organizations dedicated to the furtherance of the discipline. Faculty are shareholders in their disciplinary companies with voting rights, self-governance, and ownership of the curriculum. Academically strong departments, that is, have a self-serving and powerful status within universities quite separate from the rights of individual faculty. Furthermore, even though intellectual capital is plainly more tenuous than physical or even social capital, there is no question that "derivatives" from conceptual capital in departmental offshoots or in programs within departments do have a life of their own that faculty are happy to invest in.

In short, the amalgamation of scholars into professionalized disciplines and faculties, beginning in the later years of the nineteenth century and developing more recently with entrepreneurial units in the sciences and professional schools, grows from the fact that faculty have long been willing to move to more professional ways of organizing knowledge in order to subsidize their status and reputation. The development has occurred inevitably alongside an even broader corporatization of learning in the past fifty years or so as universities promote their physical, social, and athletic capital as highly as their conceptual capital in order to enhance their status within a highly competitive market. What I am arguing, then, is that the purity of professionalized disciplinary learning also has more than a faint odor of *lucrum* about it, even if the profit is assessed primarily in terms of the gain or loss of academic reputation.

There has been, though, an overreaching concern with excellence—a term used by all universities to explain what they strive for. Even faculty join in the discourse. The need for a rhetoric of transcendent academic quality is, of course, closely related to the rhetoric of public relations, advertising, and corporate outreach. Most of us in and out of the university know what it means, and we take it for granted and assume it means well. Usually it does in the sense that excellence is hardly a term with pejorative connotations. But *excellence* is not simply a corporate commercial term. It is a corporate academic term, too, a word of substantial grip for those in quality management in all places in the university. As Readings rightly points out,

> Today, all departments of the University can be urged to strive for excellence, since the general applicability of the notion is in direct relation to its emptiness . . . the assumption is that the invocation of excellence overcomes the problem of the question of value across disciplines, since excellence is the common denominator of good research in all fields. Even if this were so, it would mean that excellence could not be invoked as a "criterion," because excellence is not a fixed standard of judgment but a qualifier whose meaning is fixed in relation to something else. An excellent boat is not excellent by the same *criteria* as an excellent plane. So to say that excellence is a criterion is to say absolutely nothing.[4]

Excellence may be damned, then, by its own logic, but neither the term nor what it connotes is going to go away. Besides, alternative terms are hard to find these days, largely because we do not have a common critical and substantive vocabulary based on the disciplines to express our proof of academic quality to the public at large. To speak of the need for high intelligence and high standards is to brand the university as elitist in an egalitarian society. Specific markers of excellence in the individual disciplines are simply too professionalized for the market-driven world of higher education. That is, we have created a split between the content of the curriculum and the public value of learning, something John Dewey warned us not to do, but certainly in our eagerness to be all things to all people, it has happened. And we try to bridge that gap by appealing to the public with terms like *excellence*.

American universities, after all, have never been universities that stand only for the importance of curricular content or for ideologies based on intellectual or cultural beliefs. Theories of social justice have never been ingrained in public philosophy much beyond constitutional rights; Americans have handled race matters with little recourse to academic theory or ideological critique. None of this is surprising or necessarily wrong, but it means that the complex social mission of the American university eyes ideological positions that might provide quality markers other than excellence with a great deal of suspicion, beyond the broad values of free-market democracy. Any contemporary university or college mission statement will promote with little sense of irony a supposedly self-evident alliance between being good, being wise, being just, being socially responsible, and being financially comfortable.

In short, we fall back on *excellence* because we do not have pungent enough discourse of the symbolic intellectual value of knowledge. There has been a deliberate choice not to promote a unifying conceptual ideal for higher education: something akin to Immanuel Kant's allegiance to philosophy, say, or Alexander von Humboldt's insistence on cultural training at the University of Berlin in 1809, or John Henry Newman's mid-nineteenth-century theory of education based on aesthetic culture—though I am not suggesting we should retreat to any one of these. Our particular need in the field of liberal education is for an ideal that unifies intellectual and social capital.

But the meeting and mingling of so many allegories of social virtue in our public philosophy has emphasized social capital above all in a simplified and even sentimentally patriotic and commercial way. The only way universities seem to differ from numerous other social institutions designed to promote the common good is through training the mind. Yet the broad rhetoric of civic sentiment and individual socialization has become the umbrella beneath which most activities of learning can be sheltered. And how does one argue with that?

A recent trend in educational theory and practice serves to emphasize my point about the dominance of socialization as an educational goal and the way in which we market its excellent qualities. Alexander Astin's theory of "talent development" has had enormous cachet in higher education and insists that the major responsibility of universities today is to develop the learning abilities of individual students. This is, of course, a worthy aim. The university's task is to enhance all students' chances of learning and public success and not just to sustain a meritocracy of the gifted. Such a task is itself wedded to ideals of excellence, though, criteria that stray from a traditional interest in normative hierarchies of academic quality based on student test scores, testing, and achievements in acquiring new knowledge. "A talent development approach to excellence," says Astin, "creates a very different scenario. From this perspective, our excellence depends less on who we admit and more on what we do for the students once they are admitted. Thus our excellence is measured in terms of how effectively we _develop_ the educational talents of our students rather than in terms of the mere level of developed talent they exhibit when they enter."[5]

So here is another instance of excellence, this time, however, supposedly measurable—although exactly what is being measured seems rather vague. How clever a student is and how well he or she performs is dependent on progress in charting an individual learning curve, an activity that calls for bureaucracies dedicated to measuring the accumulation of information; this can distract from a concern for the importance of what is being learned. It calls too for intense dealings with statistics, which give a falsely scientific status to achieved learning. And it still does not commit to any clear definition of what excellence is or what the strengths of the curriculum should be because excellence remains purely relative. But at least it does assert the intrinsic importance of each student judged in terms of personal growth, which few would deny is important in a mass education market.

Ironically, it is precisely the scope and complexity of the university's mission and its pursuit of excellence that put an enormous strain on any singularly intellectual motive for higher education. Universities that are not primarily known for research and learning, for example, fall back on social engineering all too readily, on indicators of credential value, on talent development instead of high standards for general achievement, on leadership skills instead of histories of power and political science, on assessment criteria and statistical indicators of excellence instead of honest grading, aiming to grab a market position and to fulfill social aspirations that are far greater than resources can sustain. This is perhaps not fair to say because such criteria do at least give credibility to the curriculum in certain schools that would not have it otherwise, and the response from the public seems to justify these kinds of activities. But it still does not help us find that central idea of the university, for excellence itself and even talent development are simply too vague and rhetorical, too subjectivist and corporate in their connotations to be satisfying.

Again, that is not the fault of the market or of university administrations alone. For more than a century, scholars have been reminding other scholars, as Kant did quite emphatically, that the function of the university is not simply to develop knowledge—

whether it has social applications or not—but to critique it, too, to be reflective of every move we make, even to develop a theory and practice of how academe can and must be self-assessed and self-correcting. But assessment no longer means cultural critique in the university, although responsibility for arguing that it should ought to rest squarely with faculty, especially in the humanities and the social sciences. The sciences have done a rather better job of explaining their protocols, which enjoy high esteem in the eyes of the public as examples of hard research producing useful knowledge. But they too are decidedly uncritical of their own culture. The arts and humanities, meanwhile, are broadly perceived as having lapsed into justifications of professional sensitivity or leftist politics. We may not like speech in praise of excellence and the championing of quality management, identity themes, strategic initiatives, decentralized management strategies, and the university's fascination with a do-it-yourself ethos—but the humanities, especially, have yet to offer a powerful alternative discourse. We are faced with the fact that in the modern university vastly subtle and provocative intellectual agendas are either problematized to the point of no return by scholars or reduced to simple experiences of "learning values" by learning experts and thus remain highly relative, never too threatening.

In short, our current dilemma, as the historian Thomas Bender puts it, is that there is a certain "paradox in the success of academe. Its recognized achievements (disciplinary excellence in the context of dramatic expansion) have not strengthened academic culture as a whole. It has even produced conflicts about its mission, particularly its civic role, and there has been a weakening of the informal compact between the university and society." Bender rightly goes on to say, "The dissolution of a public sphere and the limited role of academic intellect in whatever survives of that sphere is worrisome. . . . Restoring a place for academic knowledge in the public culture and a role for public discussion in academic culture ought to be a high priority of both academic and public leaders."[6] But how can academic knowledge gain a foothold in a culture that is so relentlessly commercial and consumer-oriented even when it does not have a firm grip on the rhetoric by which the university explains itself?

Cultural Hegemony?

No matter how complex the reality of power relations in the university, the play of power in the university has predictable outcomes that do not include restoring academic discourse to a central role. Clyde W. Barrow has argued that the university has been the scene of a continuing class struggle for the past hundred years, since "the corporate ideal as applied to the university [by commercial, philanthropic, and political interests] was actually a class-political program designed to conquer ideological power [that is, the ideological power of academic disciplines]."[7] This explanation has always been an alluring one for faculty, largely because it places the blame squarely on administrations and validates the feeling many faculty have that they are second-class citizens. Barrow points out that between 1860 and 1930, ownership of American colleges and universities passed into the hands of boards controlled by businesspeople, bankers, and lawyers. Fully 74 percent of all board members in 1930 came from the corporate and professional world, compared with only 48 percent in 1860–61, and that high percentage of corporate management of academe has held true since.

The growth of financial power interests in higher education throughout the twentieth century is unquestionable. In America as in no other country in the world, corporate liberalism has gone to great lengths to ensure that the social mission of the university is one that has assimilated capitalist idealism. Barrow even argues that by

1929, the corporate world had mounted a thoroughgoing effort at cultural hegemony for the "national ideological state apparatus." This Althusserian notion that dominant ideologies are institutionalized through various state apparatuses—such as churches, the legal system, schools, corporations, and so on—is somewhat reductionist in both its definitions of the state and its ideology.[8] No one who has worked in an American university or college can deny that corporate leaders to this day are not at all reluctant to make their individual and even collective feelings known to faculty and college administrators. In the mix of social, cultural, academic, and economic influences that drive the higher education enterprise, such terms from corporate life as "excellence of quality," "efficiencies of scale," and "high productivity" have been assimilated into the vocabulary of building institutional prestige. Even more important, programing and the selection of administrators has often even been controlled by a few at the top. But the notion that a corporate class (as opposed to individual members of it) diabolically set about the task of subjugating intellectuals and their discourse is hard to prove, even if it is quite evident that individual cases of subjugation, and even subjugation by certain boards around the country, are not without documentation.

Barrow's assertion also seems to be an oversimplification of the deeply pervasive influence on educational values of an emergent, mass, late-capitalist commercial culture. This rarely clings to a single ideology of class dominance, and its power is determined by the marketplace, by product desirability, and by its communications systems. And purchasing power is widely distributed in today's society. The corporate ethos is one in which egalitarianism, multiculturalism, and "service to society" are indeed strong market values. This is a potent discourse, one that sweeps up important social terminology wherever it finds it. The discourse of the academy and public philosophy are easily accommodated in such rhetoric, as we saw in the last section. It is often difficult to tell these days where corporate jargon ends and academic jargon begins. The language of mission statements, for example, is often the language of corporate humanism.

Barrow's argument, though, does a disservice to the philanthropy of corporations and corporate executives, which has helped to sustain academic institutions for well over a century, sometimes without any real interest in changing faculty values. Furthermore, the culture of corporatism, as powerful as it is, has long been in a conflictual relation with academic principles for organizing knowledge, along with old traditions of faculty collegiality and self-governance. The dynamics of academic power are definable, that is, by highly contradictory relations between academic and bureaucratic bodies. But they are also definable by the discourse of excellence, which, for all its ambiguities, tries to show that both sides are not so far apart, are really trying to say the same thing. And there is a real willingness on the part of faculty to indulge the ambiguities of such a culture, happily following the money trail wherever it leads and working with corporate power interests as a natural extension of the long-held American belief that higher education is an entrepreneurial business and always in service to the economy.

American universities, after all, came into power literally as part of the growth of democracy and a capitalist economy in the late nineteenth century. Barrow himself adduces much convincing evidence that the rise of the American university was paralleled and supported by the transformation of the American economy, beginning with the industrial revolution set in motion by the building of the transnational railway system (1861–1907). During these years, there was extensive migration of labor and capital into factories, mines, and railroad centers, a growing "national network of economic exchange," a sharp increase in manufacturing industries, and the rise of powerful financiers and financial groups like Morgan-First National, Rockefeller, and Mellon that had large stock holdings in various sectors of commerce and a growing interest in the importance of academe. By the end of World War I, American commerce had become a corporate culture, with rationalized production processes and internal organizations, a flow of authority down from centralized power structures, and the pursuit of mergers to protect the capital interests of an important group of financiers. "The net result," as Barrow puts it, "was that by 1929, the 200 largest non-financial corporations [almost all of which had some significant ties to the nation's largest financial institutions] owned 48 percent of the assets of all non-financial businesses in the United States."[9] Along with this came a dramatic concentration of wealth in the hands of a relative few: "By 1893, a U.S. Census Bureau statistician reported that only 9 percent of American families owned 71 percent of all wealth in the country."[10] And with the growth in wealth came the growth not only of commercial power centers that needed better-educated researchers and managers but also of schools of professional development and a strong culture of philanthropic investment in higher education.

The modernization of American universities owes a lot to this pattern of corporate development. Academic institutions in the private sector, especially, were and still are deeply reliant on the generosity of corporate philanthropy for their founding and sustenance. Denominational colleges, powerful driving forces behind the development of American higher education, have long had a comparatively easy if not always deeply rewarding alliance with capitalism. And the example of corporate management and of the strategies and efficiencies needed to succeed in a market economy have had the major influence on American universities and their labor processes since the late nineteenth century. What the academy has learned is the importance of strategic planning and market research, careful product development, a concentration on the means of production (of knowledge), centralization coupled with decentralization in bureaucracies of administrative control, cooperation in developing national academic markets, and what Barrow calls "the rationalization of market relations between competing institutions." To this we must add that the professionalization of the academic worker brought with it concerns for establishing even the most symbolic of humanistic studies as sciences in their own right, along with a concern for measures of achievement in both program and learning outcomes.

Because they exist in a market culture, almost all private and public universities are acutely aware of the fact that their survival depends on adequate capitalization: on trying (often unsuccessfully) to maintain endowments that are at least twice the size of the institution's annual budget. They also espouse strategies of image building, attractive "packaging," clear product definition, and product diversity. They define and target their public, then aim to give it what it wants—in undergraduate education, usually a range of useful, job-enhancing degrees and a basic general education that introduces all students to academe. They know the importance of raising the desire of the public to buy their product, pricing it competitively, seeking good price–cost ratios, and maintaining good public relations. They join the corporate world in assimilating selective aspects of aesthetic culture as part of the language of economic and political achievement. They promote responsible fund and budget management, efficient uses of staff and faculty, and the analysis of margin ratios that allow decentralized budgets to permit profit sharing by units, depending on the extent of their productivity. Many schools may have a long way to go in proving that they understand the importance of responsible management in the eyes of trustees, politicians, and public intellectuals. But many are remarkably well managed corporations of learning.

A number of scholars have offered additional economic explanations for the evolution of the modern university as a business venture: the rise of middle-class professional occupations that needed the efficient development of university degrees as working credentials; a growing interest in education, by the turn of the century, in providing social mobility; and a growing "culture of aspiration," as David O. Levine puts it, created by the Progressive Movement after World War I. As enrollments rose by the end of World War I, university administrations had to become more efficient to handle the boom, and there was a growth in concepts of institutional prestige as colleges competed for students. These are all strong social interests that have supplemented the corporate ideal of enhancing the power of academe to effectively socialize the population and furnish a well-trained workforce.

In short, both inside and outside the gates of academe in America, liberal capitalism has a very strong ideological presence, albeit one that consistently has to deal with an autonomous faculty culture. In the long run, it is hardly surprising that liberal capitalism and corporate interests have gained the upper hand, in spite of shifting power relations within the university. So it is not unusual to find that many public intellectuals and administrators are impatient with the fact that not all faculty see academe as the business it plainly is. Why not simply let the curriculum tell the great cultural history of the growth and hegemony of capitalist values, the story of how we got to this winning moment when history actually ended? Thus it is also not surprising to find a strong allegiance between the old, classical curriculum and more conservative corporate supporters, for the canon can easily be seen as the ultimate scholarly bureaucracy: efficient, memorable, highly focused on matters of power, a kind of *Masterpiece Theater* of the market, properly heroic and quite predictable in its dedication to corporate values. The canon, as John Guillory has pointed out, is above all a form of cultural capital.[11] So too is knowledge itself.

Knowledge and Capital

It is precisely in the nature of knowledge as capital that the cultural contradictions of academe emerge. While corporate practices have the upper hand in running the university, the culture wars that exist in every institution remain a struggle between two major epistemes of academic power: *commodity knowledge,* that is, knowledge that has a use for the world of work, professional and preprofessional training, policy development, inventions, and patents; and *symbolic knowledge,* knowledge that deals with value judgments, ethical, cultural, aesthetic, and philosophical argument, and speculative science. It is foolish to suggest, as some have, that the university is dedicated simply to one or the other kind of knowledge. It must accommodate both. But the tension between the rival knowledges is very real, and the modern episteme of academic and symbolic knowledge, particularly that represented by the liberal arts and humanities, has a much harder time proving its worth as market-driven universities scramble to establish the importance of knowledge that has value in the marketplace.

If the university thrives on its intellectual capital, which it must, then our academic culture wars are fought over the differing valuations of knowledge offered by administrations and faculty. Students and their parents, often not immediately aware of the intricacy of these politics, choose the school that creates for them the right atmosphere of pragmatic or romantic or liberal or simply useful learning. Yet how individual campuses value knowledge and publicly argue for its importance is significant as it sets the tone of their culture, both for faculty and students. Knowledge—who possesses it and why—defines faculty identity and status; curricula and research are guarded jealously; students may be nurtured as colleagues in the search for knowledge; "intellectual property rights" are something academics understand only too well, long before this became a legal term; administrations are courted by faculty with strong opinions about which are important programs and which are not. There is a tacit understanding among faculty, in short, that what matters on campus are the rights of ownership of knowledge as power, and there are clear disputes on every campus as to what are the most powerful forms of knowledge.

Most important for faculty, the politics of academic subjectivity —that complex set of gender, race, ethnic, and class-based epistemologies, along with definitions of professional accomplishment and self-respect—is also defined by the possession of knowledge and how that knowledge is valued on and off campus. But when the corporate practices of the modern university obliterate the nuances of subjectivity in faculty culture, when consumerism and quality control criteria produce new sets of academic cultural values based primarily on participation in what are perceived as the peripherally civic or commercial enterprises of the university, or when they insist on measurable evidence of learning, then faculty self-respect among those working in more symbolic areas of developing knowledge is difficult to maintain. When not feeling peripheral to the academic enterprise or retiring to the privacy of their own academic boudoirs, a kind of lush sentimentality and a tendency to overaestheticize situations and challenges easily takes over in the humanities, for example, as does a strong sense of personal entitlement and lost opportunity. Faculty understandably take seriously that teaching and learning are forms of empowerment, for students and faculty alike. It is not uncommon to find in the arts, humanities, and social sciences the despairing feeling that the academy tends to value intellectual capital only in terms of its measurable power.

But academic knowledge is not simply owned or attached to researchers and scholars and teachers; it also assumes a life of its own. The discourse of knowledge emerges in various sites of academic power: in professional academic organizations, in faculty senates, in commercial contexts, in campus lore and gossip, even in the fitness center. There is a romance of knowledge as a kind of ideal discourse that can bear the disciplines away in flights of discovery and creativity, scarcely pausing to collect rewards. Many faculty, that is, know the pleasures of scholarship and research in their own right, the feeling that knowledge is always stimulated by other knowledge in often ambiguous and challenging relations. Knowledge is interdisciplinary by its very nature. One cannot be an English professor without being a historian of ideas. One cannot be a physicist without being a mathematician and a philosopher. Political scientists are both scientists—seeking the laws of how organizations and states function—and rhetoricians, arguing for a better world.

But academic knowledge as a discourse, no matter how much it is a romantic concept and genuinely exciting for faculty individually, is quite unstable. Any force for social, political, or economic change can affect the reliability of knowledge in the disciplines, and that makes the struggle for the ownership of knowledge more intense and the culture even more contradictory. Sometimes exchange and symbolic values become curiously intertwined. For example, interdisciplinary learning, one of the most exciting of all academic experiences as varying perspectives come to play on single problems or issues, has a problematic status in the modern university. It is now promoted by administrations, only in part because it allows important social themes to emerge for undergraduate or graduate study. It can also break down the rigid barriers of departmental politics and turn faculty into generalists who need representation by fewer numbers. And faculty know this, of course, and are wary of losing a departmental home. Also, administrations widely see the development of interdisciplinarity as a way of handling an alleged surplus of knowledge in the university, especially in the liberal arts. Ironically, though, unless departments are reconfigured, interdisciplinary coursework will actually be more expensive to run, given all the new combinations of knowledge that need to be fashioned. Once institutionalized, the interdisciplinary classroom can be valued not simply for its symbolic knowledge—new and exciting foci on important topics—but for its exchange value too.

The discourse of knowledge in the university, then, its value as intellectual capital and its usefulness as part of the academic economy, has a highly complex career, and we should be very careful about making too many generalizations about the university as merely a corporate center for useful learning. Without question, in the effort to emphasize lucrative programing, the corporate/bureaucratic controls of the university clash frequently with the academic. Increasingly, academics are losing control of the power of generating symbolic knowledge. But in part, my argument runs, that is the fault of "we scholars" too. For it has always been the case that knowledge, if it is to have any lasting value at all, must have value outside the academy. It must also play where we live, currently in a media-infused society that is seduced more by consumer desires, or by the wonder of breakthroughs, discovery, and the thirst for new experiences than by anything else. Academics need to be very astute about their responsibilities for forming public knowledge. As an increasingly digital commodity, even the most complex scientific knowledge or speculation is more malleable in a world of symbolic communication than ever before. Knowledge is in such a state of fluid negotiation and reinvention through digital perspectivism that it is never merely a matter of exchange but is always symbolic in its own right during its few minutes of fame. It is always open to analysis and deconstruction, but it is also open to excellence and a powerpoint presentation.

Thus academic knowledge needs to breed a stronger public understanding of the variety and power of its various discourses, with how knowledge works, how its organization and delivery affect its status, for the corporatization of the university has not led to a clean battle between exchange and symbolic knowledge. The corporate message is that free markets stand for freedom. In our democracy, knowledge (except in the most secret research) is subsidized mainly by free markets, and free markets tend to value knowledge by its public use. The implication of the medium being the message remains as profound as it was when Marshall McLuhan suggested it. As a number of recent cigarette advertisements imply, we only have to admit we are wrong about cigarette companies being all bad to discover that we are right about our love of freedom—to smoke. The paradox of even the healthiest value judgments is that they can limit freedoms; the paradox of freedom is that it cannot survive in a world of political correctness without compromising value judgments. (The cigarette argument is somewhat specious, of course, but only because smoking can harm the unwilling and unsuspecting in proximity of the smokers, not smokers themselves, who surely have the freedom to do what they will.)

What I am getting at is this: People only have to get over their distaste for corporate-styled, "knowledge factory" education to discover that they are right about their inclination to acquire knowledge as an exchange value, to make money and to be entrepreneurial. Isn't that what we all want? That is the power of the corporate argument. Thus corporate values for knowledge—that it be above all useful and thus valuable—have subtly but strongly contended in the university with the more abstract, ethical, and aesthetic values of a liberal education. And they have enormous appeal. The corporate university has claimed often enough by word and deed that it wants to play a major role in allowing knowledge to flow as it will and to be personally empowering, and that, after all, is a celebration of freedom itself.

Markets beget democracy and democracy capitalism. If liberal education cannot keep up with the contradictions this generates, cannot adopt its message to deal with the power of free-market thinking and the new technologies, then, the implication is, it is in deep trouble.

Indeed, the academy has been forced of late into the business of providing an even more symbolic general education than ever before, one in which not only computer technology but social and vocational skills supplement the disciplines and symbolize shortcuts to what knowledge and wisdom really are. All this takes place in a world, as John B. Thompson has pointed out, that is "increasingly traversed by institutionalized networks of communication, and in which the experience of individuals is increasingly mediated by technical systems of symbolic production and transmission."[12] The digital medium has itself become the message of freedom. Even the most practical of knowledges can be made symbolic. The question then is this: How does a liberal education adapt and become powerful in its own right? That I explore in the last three chapters of this book.

I note here, though, that liberal learning resists being turned into mere information, even though mere information often acquires inflated symbolic value. Symbolic knowledge is never finite but a process. It becomes easily professionalized in the disciplines, but then it can also bite its own professional tail, and often does. It is wary of the seductive ease of information transferal, even if most faculty would willingly trade a year's salary to appear on a talk show to discuss their latest book. In general, academic knowledge in the traditional disciplines is conservative, more so than professional knowledge. It assumes that new needs are rather like the old ones because humans have not changed very much and "mankind," as the poet said, still "cannot stand very much reality." It insists on argument and careful value judgments and not simply plying skills for success or measurable progress. It is happy when it makes important connections and can synthesize; it wants to know why it is important and why not. It reflects on its own nature.

Hence there actually is a divide between the merchants of merely skill-based knowledge and the abstract thinkers, and the culture wars that grow out of this run deep. And they run even deeper inside the new communications networks because the media no longer allow knowledge to be merely arcane and mysterious, because faculty can less and less claim to be the shamans of cultural rituals, because knowledge has power, no matter how brilliantly abstract, only to the extent that people need it, want to use it, and find it useful. Yet old academic habits die hard, even if their resilience is not respected by the market, which respects nothing; it merely gets the information out there. Faculty are caught in an ambiguous enterprise. On the one hand, they rightly see themselves in the business— which they think is not a business—of creating knowledge as a way of improving understanding of the world around us. On the other hand, they realize, like all good entrepreneurs, that the commodification of such knowledge brings certain financial rewards and an enhanced reputation. So what is it to be: Babbit or Mr. Chips? Today even the most esoteric theories strain for common currency.

To add to the complexities of the status of knowledge in academe, it is plain that universities are still in transition from the era of Keynesian economics, which has dominated how we organize knowledge and run the curriculum in higher education. We are caught between still powerful Fordist corporatist strategies (of which discipline-based departments are a good example), which have long since gone by the wayside in the larger corporate economy, and new responsibility center theories of management. In an age of flexible, team-centered, pluralistic market thinking, we in academe often continue to sustain a strictly compartmentalized, lockstep model for the production and dissemination of knowledge. We keep in place in our institutions of higher learning a modicum of welfare statism, smoothing over a range of inequalities of student preparation, innate talent, and ability to pay, inequalities, too, of perceived departmental usefulness and productivity. To keep assembly-line academics in action, universities usually organize their academic budgets so that they can allocate some of the assets deriving from more lucrative programing to programs they believe are essential to an undergraduate education, even if not to high income production.

But even such altruism is threatened in the shift to flexible forms of responsibility center budgeting. New management strategies insist that academic units be funded (or not) out of their own success (or failure) in creating resources, which effectively cuts into the initiatives of many liberal arts departments and reduces them to service status. So some branches of knowledge become less important than others. New budgeting strategies are supposed to stimulate faculty to be actively responsible for managing their own "knowledge industries" and to encourage entrepreneurism at all costs, but not always to the advantage of knowledge development. And as I will point out in the next chapter on faculty in the corporate university, they also create a sharp division of labor.

The point, above all, is that these experiments in deregulating and decentralizing budget authority effectively deregulate and decentralize knowledge production. However wise and stimulating they may be as budget management strategies, they are academically very damaging for they pay little attention to how knowledge can aggregate to best effect for its own symbolic reasons. Ironically, they make interdisciplinary studies harder to achieve, as departments are too busy making sure that their units are seen as profit centers and often do not want to share the wealth with other departments. Knowledge development largely becomes a survival of the fiscal fittest with the consumer always in mind.

It is not surprising, then, that those more at home with the efficiencies of corporate economics—where information, above all, needs to have a negotiable price and where downsizing readily occurs to maintain shareholder profitability—are frustrated with the large cost of a college education in apparently less-than-efficient bureaucracies. Knowledge is capital that needs to be reinvested wisely in institutional growth. It is but a short step from that to the realization that tenure is part of the problem. The sense of entitlement in academic work—that faculty should be employed for life simply because they have been productive in the first seven years of the job—obviously leaves institutions with little flexibility to stimulate their growth.

Thus we often hear of the need to reconsider the status of faculty as a protected species because it is felt that they are recalcitrant about updating knowledge capital and too insistent on clinging to departmental homes. Job security, the argument runs, should be a right that is continually earned, as it is in all the other professions. There is, then, a ringing challenge to the long-held faculty belief that when it comes to producing knowledge, faculty are the end, not simply the means of the process. Many administrators with good reason see it the opposite way: faculty are the means to the end, which is student learning. So adjuncts will often do to fill in; professionals from the world of work can replace academics since they have mastered knowledge as exchange; on-line programing may be the most efficient way to develop courses. The market for disciplinary knowledge is too specialized and protected to really be a free market at all, and that must change.

There is even a not unreasonable perception that we have overaccumulated knowledge in the postmodern university through our disciplinary structures. While it may be argued that there can be no such thing as too much knowledge, it is clear that higher education requires us to organize knowledge so that it is useful for something: as part of the mission of liberal learning or of service to society and to the economy. Yet the overaccumulation comes back to haunt us again and again when we do not evaluate our production of knowledge against our mission. And the irony is that this is a direct result of the market culture of academe, which is based not on an intellectual principle for the university but on the flexible accumulation of knowledge depending on market demands.

Academe, in short, is in a problematic phase of late capitalism all of its own when it comes to knowledge production. Symbolic knowledge that is not also useful does not represent the formation of clear social values and is always hard to justify. Given that faculty research is a highly individualized activity, disciplines have a tendency to over accumulate knowledge without careful critique and often do not find the right words to make their symbolic knowledge publicly valuable. In short, ironically, knowledge has become power in the university in much the same way that money is power: not just as a commodity that has value intrinsically but in quantity and in exchange. Yet knowledge is not by nature powerful in the way money is; having lots of it does not necessarily establish its intrinsic worth.

Knowledge, like its corporate paradigm, capital, is caught, then, in a dual role. It has acquired magical powers in our so-called information society, regardless of its worth—as the Internet makes very clear with its extraordinary accretion of information, much of which is quite uncontrolled and of dubious value. Yet as money has value both as the worth of labor and as a symbol of exchange, with the split between the two intimately tied to a division of labor, so knowledge has value as the worth of academic labor and as a symbol of exchange in the business of learning. And the split between these two values is intimately tied to the division of faculty labor in the university. The whole situation is made even more complicated, if not downright anarchic, by the fact that knowledge in our multimediated society has a life of its own, split off from whoever possesses it. It is a commodity in its own right, stripped of ideology and carried by the communications media and the rhetoric of excellence. In a powerful way, the ambiguous status of knowledge and corporate controls of the university have come to symbolize to faculty in the liberal arts and humanities especially their alienation from their own work.

CHAPTER 4

Faculty and the Division of Labor

If the discourse of excellence and the complex relation between knowledge and capital hide a host of ideological tensions in the university, the often tensional power relations among faculty, administrators, and trustees are more clearly in sight. Indeed, for those who love the smell of napalm in the morning, the last twenty years or so have been quite heady political times in academe. Except for a brief spell in the late seventies and early eighties, which Benjamin DeMott appropriately described at the time as a "deeply boring academic peace," there have been widely publicized battles between faculty and others wishing to preserve the traditional humanities canon and those promoting a more multicultural agenda. At the same time, tensions have risen between faculty and activist trustees who, along with a number of university administrators and public intellectuals, complain about faculty productivity and tenure in the light of rising costs of programing. Add to this growing faculty concerns about academic freedom and the ownership of intellectual property, and the academic cultural brew, simmering most of the time at controlled heat, can quickly reach a flash point.

We often forget that U.S. colleges and universities have never been, from their inception, independent scholarly guilds under the control of faculty. The power to run higher education has always been shared by a mix of faculty, administrators, students, alumni, local and federal governments, accrediting agencies, and public representatives on governing boards. And governing boards have always had the last word because, since the Dartmouth College ruling of 1819, colleges and universities have been established as independent corporate entities under the jurisdiction of boards of regents and trustees. Such boards do not often interfere in curricular matters since faculty have long been supported as keepers of the curricular gates. The content of the curriculum, along with its administration and staffing, may be up for some public discussion, but faculty believe that it is not up for negotiation with anyone other than themselves. Nonetheless, it is this assumption of faculty freedom to control the curriculum that is now being more openly challenged. We are perhaps in a new stage of the power struggle between management and workers in the last remaining American industry in which the workers are deemed to have significant control over the means and ends of production.

The tension between managers and teachers/researchers today is widely viewed as a serious one by both sides. There are enough strong feelings to suggest it will be fought to the end, in the next decade or so—especially over the question of academic freedom. As Louis Menand, the editor of a recent important collection of essays on the subject, succinctly puts it,

> At the heart of the political and economic battles over the future of the university is the concept of academic freedom. Academic freedom is not simply a kind of bonus enjoyed by workers within the system, a philosophical luxury universities could function just as effectively, and much more efficiently, without. It is the key legitimating concept of the entire enterprise. Virtually every practice of academic life that we take for granted . . . derives from it. Any internal account of what goes on in the academic world must at the same time be a convincing rationale for maintaining the space defined by academic freedom. The alternative is a political free-for-all, in which the decisions about curricula, funding, employment, classroom practice, and schol-

arly merit are arrived at through a process of negotiation among competing interests. The power in such negotiations will not be wielded by the professors.[1]

There are faculty who would say that the power is already lost because universities are run as corporations of learning, the status of knowledge is changing rapidly to emphasize exchange value, strategies of management are closely linked to corporate-styled organization systems, the public adopts a largely consumerist posture, and administrations have cleverly worked on altering the academic product (favoring professional education) and have thereby undercut the authority of more traditional academics. They have also achieved a reorganization of faculty work through decentered budgeting strategies, which have affected curricular priorities and faculty status.

Civility alone is not going to solve the problem. The comment apocryphally attributed to Woodrow Wilson that the struggles in academe are so vicious because the stakes are so low is simply not true anymore. The stakes may seem low in comparison to the hyperactivity of our merger-preoccupied corporate culture in the larger market. But they are very high for faculty, for students, and for the development of knowledge because they are about whether faculty should retain the freedom of intellectual enterprise.

The issue, too, is not about which side to take, supporting either public-minded trustees seeking management efficiencies or faculty aiming to maintain academic freedom. The positions are more complex, with many shaded agendas and diverse players on each side. Traditional representations of power for the faculty, for example, are rapidly deconstructing as knowledge becomes more and more manipulated by new rhetorics of excellence, decentralized budgeting systems, digital communications networks, and intellectual property partnerships. The more universities become corporations of learning, the more it becomes clear that even innovative academic

CEOs will have little power to build a strong liberal mission for the university against consumerist demands from students, the public need for research, and the increasing presence of for-profit institutions. In the end, even communications software companies will be big winners since they can claim, by making the management of learning the end product, to transmit more cheaply and efficiently the "same" information we do now in a college or university setting.

Indeed, the politics of learning can be quite intense. Consider the following three quotations:

> Since the end of World War II, there has been enormous change. People moved from cities to suburbs, the interstate highways revolutionized transportation, telecommunications have gone through the roof, and there's been a major revolution in health care. Now there's going to be a revolution in higher education. Whether you like it or not, it's going to be broken apart and put back together differently. It won't be the same. Why should it be? Why should everything change except for higher education? —James F. Carlin, insurance executive, chairman, Massachusetts Board of Higher Education,[2] speaking at a Greater Boston Chamber of Commerce luncheon.

> Whether demonizing the campus or promising its redemption, today's conservative activist trustees give in to the temptation to let the balloon of rhetoric float above the messy fields of accuracy and nuanced interpretation. . . . As a faculty member who has worked in both private and public institutions, as a university administrator, and as a college trustee, I have often been dismayed by faculty members who dither about the curriculum, who put their own interests or those of their department before the institution's well-being, or who refuse to think through the fiscal consequences of curricular decisions. However, the reasons why faculty members should determine the curriculum are so compelling that I set aside my occasional grumpiness about their behavior. I urge activist trustees to do the same.—Catherine R. Stimpson, dean of the Graduate School of Arts and Sciences at New York University.[3]

Critics of trustee activism charge partisan (conservative) politics, excessive budget cutting that subordinates educational goals, and hostility to the values of shared governance and academic culture. Defenders of trustee activism claim that higher education administrators have failed to confront serious deficiencies: budget deficits, escalating costs, faculty entitlements and productivity, and political correctness. Both sides are right. Enmity to academic culture is rising as the fiscal bottom line takes precedence. Academic administrators have been slow to get their fiscal houses in order, to challenge campus interest groups, and to hold faculty accountable.—Marvin Lazerson, Carruth Family Professor at the Graduate School of Education, University of Pennsylvania.[4]

In the face of activist trustee rhetoric, Catherine Stimpson's riposte is ameliorative and thoughtful, while showing an appropriate degree of moral outrage. Yet, sadly, it does not deal head-on with the underlying cultural contradictions that have created the attacks on faculty in the first place. Let's start, though, with Stimpson's analysis of the rhetorical strategies of those who would dismantle traditional academic power structures.

Stimpson observes in an article, from which the quotation above is drawn, that "self-described 'activist trustees' . . . have been appointed by conservative governors to the boards of public universities" and "have become a muscular presence on the governing boards of systems of higher education in such key states as California, Massachusetts, Michigan, New York, and Virginia." She goes on,

Activist trustees seem to be adopting the well-worn battle plan that conservatives have long pursued in fighting the equally well-worn "culture wars."

First, tap into the fears of Americans about the cost of higher education by demonizing colleges and universities as radical, slack, and wasteful. Treat faculty members and administrators as adversaries who have earned the suspicion and contempt of right-thinking people. Declare that you cannot trust established sources of information—such as the staff members of a state system or a president. Set up your own research unit on the institution—no matter what the cost—as the board of the City University of New York did. Lament that current trustees have been too negligent, passive, or frightened even to admit to the stink from the Augean stables that higher education has become.

Second, move into curricular issues by offering yourself as a disinterested, diligent party of redemptive virtue who will "take back" the American campus—by restoring academic excellence, freedom of inquiry, and a liberal-arts curriculum that focuses on the great books, great ideas, and achievements of the West. Claim that you will raise Shakespeare from the grave into which the contemporary faculty has stuffed him. And note that, in the process, the purified campus will also have been cleansed of faculty sloth, fiscal bloat, and racial preferences. . . .

Third, enlist high-profile spokesmen and spokeswomen for this struggle . . . establish a national infrastructure that will sustain and train a movement of like-minded critics of higher education . . . [such as] the well-established National Association of Scholars . . . and . . . the national Alumni Forum's ATHENA Project—an acronym for Alumni and Trustees for Higher Education Accountability. . . .

Fourth, once in control, and despite promises to restore a lost freedom of inquiry, be skeptical of independent voices. Silence those who do not obey. Dismiss presidents or directors of state systems if they do not agree with you, no matter how respected they might be. Question faculty tenure, or, at the most extreme, call for its abolition, ignoring the links between tenure and academic freedom.

The rhetoric of conservative intent that Stimpson objects to comes as well from a host of public intellectuals who have written sharp attacks on academe in the past decade. Stimpson notes that the activists are split in how they view the curriculum. Some "evoke an industrial model, in which the curriculum is comparable to a product, and the students to customers, to be served on the lowest possible cost-per-unit basis." Thus, "faculty members are comparable to contract employees who deliver the product, trustees to the corporate board, and the president or chancellor to a crisp but responsive chief executive officer." Other trustees "praise the highly selective liberal-arts college devoted to a canonical curriculum." The real problem, however, is that "activist trustees apparently have no qualms about substituting their judgements—no matter how rash, limited, or rooted in mere opinion—for those of an institution and its faculty." And these opinions tend not to reflect "the pluralism that increasingly characterizes the best American institutions." The solution to the problem, Stimpson suggests, is for college boards to "set a tone of dignity, collegiality, civility, and devotion to educational principles . . . [asking] the hard questions without indulging in the petty pleasures of being hard-nosed . . . [interesting] itself in the curriculum and curricular developments while granting the faculty authority in that domain."

Catherine Stimpson's views are a good example of how many faculty, university administrators, and board members have chosen to draw the battle lines in opposition to activism. The loudest call is for civility; the strongest emotion is dismay that trustees could be so arrogant. But while few could argue with civility as an enduring principle of mature behavior, civility alone has not solved our problems in academe. The apathy and moral lethargy it can induce often leave our cultural contradictions strongly in place. More important, while teaching the differences is always a worthwhile exercise, as Gerald Graff has suggested, we need to move more cogently to an analysis of what shapes the culture of the postmodern university and what fuels attacks on academic freedom. We need to teach the methods of cultural critique, in short, which in this case is more a matter of understanding the politics and economics of how we organize knowledge, rather than indulging yet again the outworn dualities of Left and Right in defining reading lists.

One senses that there are many in and out of academe who might not mind being called activist but who find the language of a

James Carlin too crude for their taste. They still perceive deep problems in higher education related to bureaucratic inefficiencies, an unfocused mission, even perhaps a rather unsubstantiated view of academic freedom based on disciplinary integrity. The above quotation from Marvin Lazerson points in this direction. We scholars have our institutionalized forms of support that bear as much analysis as defense. One could argue even that if academe were not so good at parodying itself, less swashbuckling critiques from activist trustees might have more bite. But we need to remember that the calls for change in higher education are not merely the jeremiads of conservative outsiders. There are many public statements by highly supportive patrons of academe who do not want a bloodletting but speak with increasing lack of patience about what they perceive to be faculty intransigence to any kind of change at all. In short, one can also be tired of the academy's own "balloon of rhetoric float[ing] above the messy fields of accuracy and nuanced interpretation"—for we, too, have left more than a few bubbles unpricked.

Thus, answering, as Stimpson does, that the curriculum is off-limits to the public is not enough, for we know only too well that the curriculum is designed for public consumption. It is also the primary symbol of the power of academic culture, a culture that exists in large part to serve social interests through the development of knowledge. To put it simply, what we teach will survive only so long as it has social significance, only so long as the symbolic and exchange values of knowledge are kept within recognizable distance of each other. It is, after all, through relentless public demand for modernization and intellectual capital that universities have become corporations of learning, and faculty have by and large gone along with the move. This is something the public has learned to expect, even while some academics wonder if they have struck a Faustian deal.

But faculty have historically accepted that social, economic, and academic needs can, in theory, all occupy the same intellectual space. Such a view has long driven the comprehensive mission of the modern university. It is sad, therefore, that institutions of higher education have had only mixed success in integrating social and economic ideals with those of nurturing the intellect. It is difficult to imagine how the academy can be more useful to society and fulfill its social mission without bringing to bear the full interdisciplinary weight of disciplinary analysis of social and cultural issues. The disciplines, that is, may very well be the source of academic freedom, the definable homes of learning, even the power centers of intellectual activity—but they reach full power only in their social significance, to the extent to which they can effectively address the questions of self and society, nature and culture, that define our complex human condition. Thus it seems inevitable that if faculty freedom is to be properly defined for the future it must be in terms of a professionalism that is interdisciplinary and cooperative, even while it continues to safeguard tenure and freedom of research.

One of the strongest challenges facing faculty today, then, is an epistemological one: What is the most effective way of organizing knowledge in the university or college? We seem at times to have a limited awareness of how knowledge has been shaped in the academy in this century through its various relations to the power structures of the university. We have few if any studies, either, of the extent to which higher education has changed and needs to change further in the light of the effects of our information systems on the nature of truth, knowledge, and ethics. In short, we need to understand more clearly the role the academy can and must play in a society whose diversity, market systems, mediazation, and highly flexible economic and political structures are fast making it more and more difficult to talk about knowledge as something that can be pursued for its own sake or mainly from disciplinary perspectives.

Of course, our problems will not disappear if the philosophic mind can put the corporate stars to flight, or if tenure remains in place for ever or disappears, or if we resolve the conflicts between research and teaching to the politicians' liking, or raise standards, or train students better in high school, or even if we can decide once and for all who an American really is. The future of higher education is secure only if we reconceptualize our organization of knowledge to serve a more powerful sense of what liberal education can be and, as I shall argue, return it to its focus on the central issues of a democratic education.

The Division of Labor

No reorganization of knowledge in the university and no response to corporate-styled activism in the university is going to make much sense unless we are willing to explore further how faculty subjectivity and work are defined by the university workplace. Marx first showed how capitalist economies thrive on contradiction, how they are propelled by their crisis-prone cultures. It is appropriate to see how clearly he located the deeply subjective nature of such contradictions, succinctly summed up here by David Harvey in his study *The Condition of Postmodernity:*

> The conditions of labour and life, the sense of joy, anger, or frustration that lie behind the production of commodities, the states of mind of the producers, are all hidden to us as we exchange one object (money) for another (the commodity). We can take our daily breakfast without a thought for the myriad people who engaged in its production. . . . We cannot tell from contemplation of any object in the supermarket what conditions of labour lay behind its production. The [Marxist] concept of fetishism explains how it is that under conditions of capitalist modernization we can be so objectively dependent on "others" whose lives and aspirations remain so totally opaque to us. Marx's meta-theory seeks to tear away that fetishistic mask, and to understand the social relations that lie behind it. He would surely accuse those postmodernists who proclaim the "impene-

trability of the other" as their creed, of overt complicity with the fact of fetishism and of indifference towards underlying social meanings. . . .

Capitalism therefore "produces sophistication of needs and of their means on the one hand, and a bestial barbarization, a complete, unrefined, and abstract simplicity of need, on the other. . . ." Advertising and commercialization destroy all traces of production in their imagery, reinforcing the fetishism that arises automatically in the course of market exchange.

Furthermore, money, as the supreme representation of social power in capitalist society, itself becomes the object of lust, greed, and desire. Yet here, too, we encounter double meanings. . . . Money, in fact, fuses the political and the economic into a genuine political economy of overwhelming power relations. . . . The common material languages of money and commodities provide a universal basis within market capitalism for linking everyone into an identical system of market valuation and so procuring the reproduction of social life through an objectively grounded system of social bonding. Yet within these broad constraints we are "free," as it were, to develop our own personalities and relationships in our way, our own "otherness." . . . Money is a "great leveller and cynic. . ." and a great "democratizer. . . ." Money unifies precisely *through* its capacity to accommodate individualism, otherness, and extraordinary social fragmentation.[5]

The business of developing knowledge as an exchange commodity, as I argued in chapter 3, is not dissimilar to the process of production that Harvey describes. The academy maintains a functioning intellectual economy by hiring faculty, specializing and diversifying its programs, taking care to promote itself, and insisting that teaching is the art of personalizing knowledge for both students and faculty, allowing both to become symbolically attached to what they learn. University administrations, however, do not always have a good reputation for carefully understanding the subjectivism of faculty, "the states of mind of the producers." And faculty and administrations often converse deeply and closely about their differences only when it is too late. Degree programs symbolically unify learning through numerous requirements; departments even try to fetishize knowledge by promoting their importance. That unity is under severe strain in the corporate university, though the mystique of the credential lingers with the general public. So long as faculty participate in the market exchange of knowledge, they become more and more aware of the gap between the subjective meaning of the process for them and the deeply fragmented value of knowledge in the marketplace for the student and for the public. And it is awareness of this violation of what faculty have long seen as their organic relation to their own learning that troubles them most.

I offered some thoughts in the last chapter on the classic division of labor in the modern university between administration experts and knowledge experts, corporate leaders and faculty workers, along with commentary on the relation between knowledge and capital. The situation is indeed serious for faculty in a corporate culture that has little time to value the powerful role of knowledge as symbolic in the development of a public and private philosophy. Faculty, in turn, need to see that the symbolic value of knowledge is not defined by its mere accumulation but must be supplemented by its value in a market system of higher education that insists we explain the social importance of intellectual capital.

There is another aspect to the division of labor that Marx taught us: the demoralization of the worker when his or her work is devalued through repetition or mere service, and when the worker is removed from direct relation to the market and ownership of the work. This is perhaps nowhere more powerfully felt today in the world of knowledge production than in the liberal arts and humanities. There these disciplines are frequently reduced to service status, and faculty lines are often replaced by adjunct or contract workers. Thus even though faculty can speak in the most seductive terms of the cultural value of humanistic learning, the university must also promote the broad social and professional value of such learning. In all but our elite institutions and liberal arts colleges, the humanities are sorely pressed to make their moral and cultural value clear. It is precisely this uncertain and fluctuating market value of humanistic knowledge that has helped devalue a liberal education in the academy. In the meantime the university's ability to trade off both the symbolic and exchange value of the arts and sciences, in fact, fuels the "possessive individualism" of the disciplines of the modern university.

The radical division of faculty labor at large dates back to the earliest American colleges, but the landmark date, again, is the Dartmouth College case of 1819, which established ownership of colleges and universities by their boards of trustees and ensured they would become independent corporate entities. The notion of human capital as an educational product emerged from this corporate ethos, and it is precisely the division of faculty labor that is sometimes misunderstood by a trustee or administrator who complains bitterly about faculty productivity. On the other hand, the situation is not made better by the fact that many faculty do not recognize their predicament and retreat to their disciplinary homes rather than trying to increase the public worth of their knowledge. The non-academic ownership of higher education, however, is what has led to a fundamental contradiction in the way we do business in colleges and universities. Our educational corporations are run by people who generally own the material means of production (buildings, grounds, and so on) but do not own the mental means of production: namely, the faculty. The point about human capital, as Lester Thurow has pointed out, is that it cannot be owned, unless of course we decide to return to the days of slavery. So long as knowledge production is a matter not just of disseminating information but of teaching and learning, then this paradox will stay in place—and one hopes that so long as universities remain corporate, it will always be in place because it is one fundamental contradiction of higher education that keeps academic freedom alive even as it always seems to threaten it. To lose the contradiction in favor of standardized knowledge and mere efficiencies will simply turn all universities into credentialing mills. If anything, we need to maintain the division of labor between those who are academic—who think, teach, and do research for a living—and those who work in or for universities to make sure that such activities produce adequate financial returns.

But it would be much better still to find a way around the division of labor and learn to develop more vital synergies between the major aspects of work in the university: management and learning. Thus one can say, liberally paraphrasing Harvey's comments about money, that in today's society, knowledge could

> fuse the political and the economic into a genuine political economy of overwhelming power relations.... The common material languages of *knowledge* provide a universal basis within market capitalism for linking everyone into an identical system of market valuation and so procure the reproduction of social life through an objectively grounded system of social bonding. Yet within these broad constraints we are "free," as it were, to develop our own personalities and relationships in our way, our own "otherness", *our own disciplinary interests . . . for knowledge* is a "great leveller and cynic"... and a great "democratizer." ... *knowledge* unifies precisely *through* its capacity to accommodate individualism, otherness, and extraordinary social fragmentation.

Right now, though, it is the fragmentation, not the linking together, that is felt most clearly through the organization of knowledge into disciplines. And one senses that the profession itself is not prospering from the way we do business. An editorial in the *New York Times* (29 June 1997) noted the following:

> Tenured professors are held in such contempt that just about everyone feels free to demonize them. But while the country fixates on the cloistered academic with the cushy job for life, tenure is actually withering of its own accord. Data from the United States Department of Education and the American Asso-

ciation of University Professors show that only about 25 percent of America's 1.2 million college teachers are tenured—a proportion that is surprisingly small and decreasing. In addition, of current full-time faculty who do not have tenure, only about 40 percent are eligible to apply, down from about 60 percent two decades ago. Most college teachers can look forward to part-time work at best. Almost half of four-year faculty and 65 percent of two-year faculty are part timers.

Most are the campus equivalent of migrant workers, with no stake at all in the schools for which they work. They earn about $1,500 a course, with no benefits or pension. With such miserly pay, many of them hold several jobs at once, and spend the week rushing from one campus to the next. This leaves little time for faculty meetings, thoughtful readings of assignments or the one-on-one student contact that even middling colleges once took for granted. *The Chronicle of Higher Education* recently referred to adjuncts as "invisible faculty" who stand at the margins of campus life and disappear when the bell rings. Not many industries could flourish with such an atomized work force. Judging from recent articles and complaints, colleges dominated by adjunct labor are colleges to avoid.

But so long as the future of academe is conceived purely in conventional corporate-styled market terms, without an understanding of the deep importance of the division of labor in the university, boards will continue to feel frustrated that they are in the business of producing intellectual capital but do not own the means of production. Faculty, on the other hand, will continue to feel frustrated that they work in legally constituted corporations in which they are central to a labor-intensive production process and yet often receive little respect and remuneration. They are in the position of ensuring product quality control, determining whether students will or will not receive their sought-after credentials. Yet they have little power to determine their own fate within the budgetary contexts of that process or the corporate future of the institutions of which they constitute the major asset. Thus they cling, not surprisingly, to the legalities of tenure and would be deeply foolish to give that up. Better to live with the split consciousness of a knowledge worker with some rights than none at all.

Besides, if the issue must boil down to cost, then the cost of faculty is, in fact, a bargain for the public and a scandal for the profession. No other highly trained professional in today's economy dispenses services that have such social impact and require such intensive training and expertise at such a low average national rate of remuneration. Nonetheless, we often hear that faculty salaries are the major strain on educational budgets, amounting on the average to about 30 percent of university expenditures. In the 1980s, college expenses rose dramatically with the call for more general education, for interdisciplinary and multicultural programs, and for small classes, all amid growing skepticism over the use of teaching assistants. Many schools could not afford to meet these challenges without adding faculty lines. Some did redeploy faculty, carrying out curricular reform to meet actual student needs, and that is an ongoing process now in most universities. But given the current educational philosophy that requires students to major in a specific subject, the only way faculty can be truly redeployed is by moving responsibilities from disciplinary teaching to teaching in general education, and even that will not guarantee a reduction in numbers.

Curricular changes have had their economic impact in other ways. More and more colleges have realized the importance of faculty development programs as fewer lines open up and the talents of existing faculty have to be rechanneled. It is not uncommon to offer released time and additional money to faculty to encourage curricular innovation, which in the end can only benefit the student. This, however, is costly for colleges and not made more palatable by the fact that aging faculty cannot easily be replaced by new, fresh talent. The compulsory faculty retirement age of seventy has been revoked by federal law, and tenure remains a sacred right recognized even by the courts, except in conditions of extreme financial exigency. So faculty are staying longer in the classroom and the laboratory.

It is not surprising, therefore, that largely for economic and political reasons, many governing boards and presidents have considered tenure the primary problem in the academic community. Their thinking often runs like this: If each college could keep only productive faculty—for which read good teachers or researchers with reputations—then curricular configurations could be developed that make best use of each school's resources. These fine faculty, no less, could be paid more and would feel better about themselves. Productivity could be maintained by regular reviews with the explicit threat of removal if performance is not adequate. The profession would be enhanced and would become more competitive.

If it were possible to keep only the most productive faculty in terms of teaching and research, and we were able to measure this productivity sensibly, then there is a chance that universities would have higher standards and greater reputations. But cost effectiveness would not necessarily follow, and there are concerns about how one would determine which are the best faculty. Teaching is a notoriously impressionistic exercise to judge (even by students), and the value of research likewise is very difficult to settle. Who is to say that modern literary theory, for example, should be privileged over medieval studies in an English department? or work in biology over work in physics? or who can say that some seemingly minor contribution in chemistry research will not prove important at a later date?

The point is that universities, for hundreds of years, have made contributions to society only because professors have had freedom to configure themselves into groupings that best aid their pursuit of knowledge and best serve their teaching. So if at some point it becomes apparent to foreign languages faculty, for example, that they have more in common with English faculty—and vice versa—then maybe lively disciplinary connections can be made and efficiencies realized. But the overall principle of departmental and disciplinary structure, along with faculty rights to hire within those departments, and tenured faculty rights to pursue the research they want to pursue, are all quite understandably viewed by faculty as sacred obligations. This is not to say that faculty should not be held accountable to combine their talents and relate to each other more productively than at present, as I have been arguing, especially for the purposes of improving knowledge development and learning opportunities for students. Nor is it to say that faculty should not be nudged strongly to find more synergistic relations between the disciplines. Faculty culture is badly in need of reorganization and invigoration in many schools for precisely that reason. But the basic principle of tenure in departments maintains both the freedom of thought and expression and the definition and preservation of a knowledge base. The attack on tenure is not an attack on faculty alone, it is interpreted by faculty as an attack on knowledge itself as a disciplinary construct. Any reason to change that requires a good deal of explanation, I have been arguing, has nothing to do with the market and everything to do with how we value knowledge.

Corporatism and Faculty Life in the Modern University

The historian Michael B. Katz has explained our current situation in higher education in terms that are close to those I have used in my argument:

> The conflict between . . . the forces of the marketplace and community in higher education echoes an old struggle. For centuries, faculty argued that universities should be self-governing communities of scholars and tried to resist the pull of church or state, which sought the inculcation of orthodoxy and the training of

loyal servants. However the ascendancy of liberal economics in the nineteenth century reshaped the ancient tensions within higher education. For liberal economics substituted the demands of an impersonal marketplace for the intrusive authority of church or crown. Under the mantle of service to the whole community and relevance to contemporary life, some university reformers attempted to apply the principles of supply and demand to the evaluation of economic institutions.[6]

The rise of liberal capitalism and its patronage of institutions of higher education by the turn of this century brought a social mission to higher education that forced the American academy to deal with the challenge of explaining the seductiveness of Capital as a Common Good and Knowledge as a Symbolic Good. Philosophically, it has come up somewhat short, I have been arguing, largely through a confusion of the two versions of the good. It would have been even more bereft of theory were it not for the development of Deweyan pragmatism, which I will explore in chapter 6.

Higher education, though, has always been conscious of higher powers—from God to Mammon—and the dominant twentieth-century model for academic institutions is unmistakably that of an independent corporation (even within state systems). "Corporate voluntarism" takes over by the turn of the century with little protest, simply because the state did not take responsibility for higher education. Katz points out that "the conduct of single institutions" is defined by their status as "individual corporations operated by self-perpetuating boards of trustees and financed either wholly through endowment or through a combination of endowment and tuition (sometimes with help from the state)."[7] That is what the Dartmouth decision required. The meshing of the growing market mentality and the social mission of higher education followed soon after. By adopting a divisional administrative structure for clustering departments that anticipated many a large corporate organization today, universities, Katz points out, became "federations whose components were coupled by bureaucracy, which was grafted onto their earlier corporate voluntarist structure." It is the bureaucratization of modern universities by universities—mainly to handle the enormous spread of knowledge building—that left such institutions open to the strong corporate influence we see today. Katz quotes the educational historian Laurence Veysey's perceptive arguments that "bureaucratic administration was the structural device which made possible the new epoch of institutional empire-building without recourse to specific values. Thus while unity of purpose disintegrated, a uniformity of standardized practices was coming into being.... Losing a clear sense of purpose, spokesmen for the American university around the turn of the century ran the danger of casually, even unconsciously, accepting the dominant codes of action of their more numerous and influential peers, the leaders of business and industry."[8]

At this historical point, as corporate managerial strategies came to the fore and the university's mission began to pull in several directions at once, trustees assumed the dominance they have today. Policies of unequal pay to faculty were instituted. Faculty became employees, and in some famous instances were summarily fired for their views. The labor of faculty, as Katz notes, was "transformed into a commodity whose price was determined by value in a novel arena: the academic marketplace." Higher education and capitalism came to work hand in hand, and it was the university, ironically, that took the initiative:

> The transformation of the leading universities signaled a new era in the history of capital. In a dramatic and novel way, knowledge—advanced technical and managerial knowledge—had become a resource essential to the progress of the vast new corporations and bureaucracies that dominated economic and social life. Science and technology, production and administration, coordination and marketing: all required experts and expert knowledge. Until the late nineteenth century, most experts and

expert knowledge had been produced outside universities. By capturing the process through which they were produced and transferring the actual production of much new knowledge from outside their walls to within them, universities staged one of the great coups in the history of capitalism. They met only minimal resistance, however, because the imperial interests of universities and the self-protective interests of professionals reinforced each other nicely. Together, they made credentials dispensed by universities the hallmark of professional expertise. Universities thereby became the gatekeepers of the advanced technical-managerial society.[9]

This explanation by Katz of why the corporatization of the university was so swift and relatively unchallenged hangs perhaps on a too neat focus on the emerging importance of technoscience. True, this did exert an enormous power, but the new market economy, the fresh emphasis on a social and democratic mission, and the increasing perception that a liberal education was more a luxury than a necessity also played a strong role. The importance of professional education made it inevitable that liberal education alone would not have a firm grip on higher learning, even though much deference was and still is paid to its importance. Furthermore, while it is true that faculty have won, from 1915 on, through the American Association of University Professors, rights of tenure and academic freedom, these are the last line of defense against the complete corporatization of the university, as I have been arguing. More important is the fact that knowledge has such a powerful connection to capital, and the division of labor continues to leave faculty in such a contradictory condition.

Indeed, faculty mobilization of its forces at various times in this century—in the promotion of tenure rights, in the culture wars, and in defense of recent attacks by politicians and boards of regents—has at best produced a stalemate. Sadly, the most effective faculty defense seems to be to keep that stalemate alive. Faculty may retain academic rights, but their work is patently standardized. Even noble efforts to insist on the humanistic roots of general education—from Columbia University's Contemporary Civilization Course of 1915 to Ernest Boyer's pleas for a revitalized core education in the 1980s—have resulted in no persistent theory of general education that has a clear set of core values that empower knowledge beyond its social mission. The student revolts of the sixties may have redefined relevance, but the market has redefined it back to its economic roots. "Faculty," as Katz says, "realize that universities grow only in response to the 'needs' of the economy, society, technology, or some other great force. A reified imperative drives the history of higher learning and narrowly constricts the availability of alternatives at any point in time. The character of universities becomes inevitable, and their legitimacy rests on their service to the great forces over which they have no control."[10]

For all this, however, we must not forget that the culture of academe is contradictory at heart largely because faculty and intellectuals have not only an unstable alliance with the growing corporate power of the university, but also an uneasy alliance with the knowledge they produce. The political scientist Clyde Barrow may have mistaken the power of capitalism to override the free-thinking motives of intellectuals—or he may yet be proven right if faculty lose the rights of tenure and academic freedom. But one can easily admit the aptness of Barrow's analysis of the strong link between capitalism and academe that shaped faculty as a class of knowledge workers, which substantiates the findings of other historians, like Veysey and Katz. As Barrow puts it,

> The educational processes and conflicts set in motion during the age of reform [1894–1928] remain important because this period established the basic institutional contours that shape the practical class consciousness of contemporary American intellectuals. . . . The institutionalized self-image through which

American intellectuals now understand themselves was itself a historically contingent political accommodation of this period that has been carried forward into contemporary social theory as a form of intellectual false consciousness. . . . The unstable accommodation between intellectuals, capitalism, and the state has, after all, long been referred to as "the problem of the intellectuals." Thus, the current educational crisis is partly a question of whether or not the intelligentsia can live up to its own historical mission. . . . Attempts to reject the corporate ideal through an alliance with the working class have failed to materialize except in scattered instances. Most intellectuals have chosen to negotiate an opportunistic historical accommodation with business interests and the state by accepting the new organizational structure of university life in exchange for limited procedural guarantees of personal security, which has not included academic freedom.[11]

That "opportunistic historical accommodation with business interests and the state" by faculty, ironically, is what has kept universities alive, or at least has kept faculty alive. But it is also what compromises the pursuit of symbolic knowledge. Furthermore, we have seen recently the cozying up of intellectuals, adjunct instructors, and graduate teaching assistants to union leadership in just an attempt to "reject the corporate ideal through an alliance with the working class." The problem is that nontenure-track instructors in America have no option to do otherwise and survive in the marketplace.

Alienation and Ideology

Generalization about the extent of faculty alienation needs to be tempered, at least outside the arts, humanities, and social sciences. For one thing, many faculty do enjoy their new status as the corporate stars of academe and also reap good rewards as consultants. Many are happy teaching and ask for little more than the stimulation of intelligent and responsive students. But more important is the fact that the shared culture of the classroom, the mass circulation of corporate-managed symbolic forms—media, entertainment, goods, travel, and globalization—have come to dominate the values, experiences, and modes of interaction of faculty, students, and the public at large.

As John Thompson has pointed out, "Contemporary theorists who employ the concept of ideology have failed to deal adequately with the nature and development of mass communication, and with its role as a medium of ideology in modern societies. In some cases this is because the concept of ideology is part of a grand theoretical narrative concerning the cultural transformations associated with the rise of modern industrial societies."[12] The need for a grand narrative, for a utopian system, is deeply suspicious these days, not because humans are intrinsically imperfect, but because, as Isaiah Berlin has pointed out in the wake of Kant, there is no straightening the crooked timber of humanity.

Yet implicitly the grand narrative sustaining both Katz's and Barrow's critique of the rise of the corporate state is that ideas do matter above all and can change the world, and somehow that sustains hope in liberal learning. Yet we have to question this, and question too whether capitalist ideology stands still long enough to be a clear target, and whether its power structures are always repressive. The rise of the modern university, for example, was driven by the same science-and-technology-inspired, modernist, utopian, post-Enlightenment faith in reason that has sustained the rise of capitalism in this century. But today the modernist myth of democratic capitalism has deconstructed itself into media culture, a subtle massaging of consumer desire, the radical impulses of mass electronic communications, and even some fruitful disciplinary interconnections in the world of academe. Many years of the development of the ultrarationalist discipline of economics, for example, and many Nobel prizes to the University of Chicago ironically symbolize both our success and failure in attempting to understand market forces. Contemporary culture has only one grand narrative to sustain, and that is that there is no single narrative at all but the endless changing of communications modes, market trends, and the values they convey.

The university tends to function in this world like other cultural institutions, by doing the best it can to strengthen its own power and by changing itself when it can to meet social needs. Thus faculty culture has changed and will probably continue to do so, as it has been swept along by the communications systems of late capitalism. The corporate impulse to work for profit, even by our most euphemistic of non-profit social institutions, is especially strong, as is the culture of consumerist desire and its competitive ethos. But again, this is a world, as Thompson points out, that is sustained less by distinct class ideologies than by the contradictory symbolism of desire and gratification generated by our mass communication systems. The meaning of knowledge in the contemporary university is mediated and shaped as much, I have argued, by the symbolic systems of everyday market culture as it has by the discourses of academic learning and disciplinary knowledge. In the public eye, the university is about information itself, not about its disciplines, and increasingly students are coming to university not with a strong desire for a particular major, but for a general education. The need to produce knowledge for profit and social well-being and to package it in highly attractive ways has also brought the university closer to the high-tech arrangement of symbolic forms in the world of corporate mass culture. The challenge, therefore, is to understand how the symbolic knowledge of the disciplines is related to the kinds of meaning we want students to be able to *make* in this multimediated world, and not merely in the university. In short, knowledge can be power in the contemporary university only to the extent that it assimilates and becomes the proving ground for the social power of knowledge. Yet at the same time, that social power must be defined as something more than merely the acquisition of a strong credential.

For we have to emphasize, contra Barrow, that corporatism is not merely the activity of a commercial class. Through its mediazation it is now a process that has deeply and inevitably infiltrated all aspects of everyday living, including academic life as well, following our mission of serving society. Of course the academic disciplines remain deeply, professionally interested in their own forms of organization. Ironically, such professionalism also dominates the academic urge to decentralize, not just an institution's finances but its organization of knowledge, too. Departments often retreat intact to create small schools-within-a-college, ostensibly to cooperate more closely with each other, but also to form alliances that afford a kind of protection against other disciplines. More and more, however, the importance of undergraduate education—which demands close forms of cooperation among the disciplines—is challenging this. It sets up an option for knowledge that takes us back, ironically, to that time in the university's history when disciplines were not so professionalized, when knowledge was a kind of *bricolage*. The excitement of learning in a digital age is once again the gathering of information from any and all sources, a process that belies the singularity of disciplinary approaches.

Cultural Contradictions and "Liberal Anxiety"

What I have been implying is that the cultural contradictions of the university are really symptoms of the cultural contradictions of liberal capitalist democracy itself. My argument is that instead of mediating the problem effectively, the university has become part of the problem. The discontents of contemporary higher education result, ironically, from the fact that the university has always been split between all aspects of its complex mission: research, liberal education, service to society, and service to the economy. The deep division of labor and the complex nature of knowledge as power have only contributed to this.

On the other hand, if one buys into Daniel Bell's analysis of the cultural contradictions of capitalism, the university might be deemed a success at mediation. For Bell, the question is how "one can discern the structural sources of tension in . . . society: between a social structure (primarily techno-economic) which is bureaucratic and hierarchical, and a polity which believes, formally, in equality and participation; between a social structure that is organized fundamentally in terms of roles and specialization, and a culture which is concerned with the enhancement and fulfillment of the self and the 'whole' person. In these contradictions, one perceives many of the latent social conflicts that have been expressed ideologically as alienation, depersonalization, the attack on authority and the like."[13] Elsewhere, Bell uses the term "cultural contradictions" to explain "the tension between asceticism and acquisitiveness," "the tension between bourgeois society and modernism," and "the separation of law from morality."[14]

The contemporary capitalist American university generates more potent causes of alienation than Bell specifies. But if one sees the contradictions of capitalism, as Bell does, as a series of tensions that actually propel capitalism forward rather than holding it up, then the university has had success in alleviating the problems of modernism for the public. Apart from the obvious, such as educating a professional class and providing much of the new knowledge needed to develop the economy, it has been in favor of propagating modernism as technological innovation. It has supported the social science of liberal democracy, focusing on ways of accommodating or eradicating problematic behavior, rather than arguing for its cause through any social conditions. It has developed the utopian cultural values of modernism so that they become more bourgeois and forged a link between specialization and the whole person in numerous student life programs. It has even assumed it can teach ethical behavior. Few can have any doubt that part of the enormous influence of the modern American university system at home and overseas has been the obvious evidence of this success. The American university literally makes liberal capitalism possible by providing the knowledge it needs, by educating for such a society, and by neatly smoothing over deep fissures in the system. And it has done so without extreme or ideologically based criticism, indeed, some would say, without standing for enough critique. It has also made a special effort to reestablish the link between morality and the law and business practices, and it has been outspoken about the multicultural nature of American society.

But this has come at a price: the downgrading of education as a critical reflection on modernity as well as on the disciplines of learning that constitute modernity in the university, especially those in the arts and humanities. The university, that is, has not always nurtured a strong role in developing public philosophy. It is not as dedicated as it might be to developing a thick description for knowledge in undergraduate education, as Clifford Geertz might say, to nurturing the life of the mind because the mind is a terrible thing to oversimplify. Instead, development has been largely in the areas of research and professional education, with the latter even occupying a remarkably large place in undergraduate learning. In 1994–95 there were 234,323 bachelor's degrees in business awarded in the United States and 13,775 in foreign languages and literatures, a ratio that changed little in 1997–98—which raises a question about how we are educating people for the much vaunted global economy built on intercultural understanding.[15]

Perhaps the strongest source of anxiety, however, is that the contradictions of higher education are not easily resolved through social agendas for higher education that are embedded in liberal philosophy. As Alan Ryan, warden of New College, Oxford, put it recently in examining "liberal anxieties and liberal education" in America,

> Liberals are . . . more inclined than most to see differences of language and geography as something to be overcome rather than to be taken as setting the boundaries of comprehension and enjoyment. This is true, even of those liberals who are most eloquent in insisting on the importance of the "small platoons" to which we feel most intimately attached. Most liberals believe—even if they only admit it somewhat blushingly—that the processes of economic and scientific modernization will bring all or almost all societies to a liberal, egalitarian, secular view of politics and culture and therefore of education, and that given a clear field a local version of a liberal society will secure the loyalties and affections of its inhabitants. Needless to say, anyone who believes this, in the teeth of the horrors of the twentieth century, the resurgence of religious fundamentalism in the West as well as elsewhere, and the vitality of a conservative tradition that regards a faith in progress as foolishness, must temper hope with anxiety—but they ought also to temper anxiety with hope.[16]

We have to do better than hope or anxiety. We must devolve a critique for examining not simply how the university shapes the politics of citizenship but how the contradictions of academe can also shape an unstable identity for both knowledge and knowledge workers. These are, after all, public moral dilemmas that need to be resolved not by partisan politics, but by a persuasive analysis of how higher education tries to unify society at large through the strength of its public philosophy. This is an issue, in short, that has to be addressed by the academy itself with the careful understanding and cooperation of its administrations. Simply letting things go on as they are in the spirit of liberal mindedness, or tweaking the agendas here and there with the same motives, is not going to stave off the inevitable: the demoralization of undergraduate and graduate education and the denigration of critical knowledge.

Such a critical analysis is unavoidably political. But it is a process that needs to be deeply embedded in the business of liberal education itself, without the attendant liberal euphoria that Ryan so rightly criticizes. Democracy's discontents are inevitable, simply because democracy tolerates differences and a market culture. But one of the issues to engage is the deep contradiction of the ideal of individual independence restrained by constitutional limits. As Michael Sandel has pointed out, our reigning public philosophy is liberal not in the sense that people today value participating in government, but because they expect government to be neutral and "not to affirm in law any version of the good life."[17] The only kind of liberal philosophy we like is one that is completely laissez-faire, and that has certainly been the politics of liberal learning.

We should have a more complex relation with "liberal learning" in higher education, one that will not easily tolerate neutrality or assertions that it is only for itself. A reinvigorated role in *cultural mediation* is very much needed as an academic activity, as is a fresh approach to an interdisciplinary and democratic education, as I shall argue in the concluding chapters. Critical neutrality is not a position the academy naturally falls into because of the deeply controversial nature of knowledge and the fact that argument is the primary rhetoric of all academic discourse. Yet we try so hard to be neutral and collegial in the American university, in order not to offend our peers and to sustain the market at all costs, and that results only in a blurring of differences. It would be better if the university would seek not to be so accommodating of cultural contradictions and be damned for standing for too much rather than too little.

CHAPTER 5

The Ideal of a Liberal Education

In these last three chapters I want to examine options for defining a critical and democratic liberal education. The challenge to do this does not come from the marketplace, for the market for higher education and the commercial knowledge economy are largely content with open-ended rationales for excellence and useful knowledge. Markets are neither critical nor democratic. But liberal education remains an issue for almost every university because few are willing to completely give up the idea that something has to stiffen the glue that holds capitalist education together. Markets do not give prizes to the principled, but we can at least search for an idea of the university that can relate to our need for a democratic education that can combine, say, the traditional ideals of cognitive rationality, social responsibility, and cultural values with the realpolitik of liberal capitalism. Yet, at no time in its modern history has the American university ever been widely attached to an ideal that unifies these concerns, even though, as we have seen, the fourfold mission of liberal, vocational, social, and research-based education has loosely held together in an unholy alliance over the past century and has intended to support the economy as much as the development of knowledge.

John Dewey made a very important point when he said that philosophy is always the philosophy of education, deeply existential in its demands, not merely idealist or subjective, but concerned to situate the business of learning and understanding within the context of living. In this chapter, then, I want to explore, through a historical survey, some options for developing a philosophy of general liberal education that works to define the social mission of the university and the cultivation of the intellect. Of course one can ask: Isn't it taking too much for granted to insist that a democratic education is the place to start? My argument is that it is an appropriate starting point given the dominant culture of American higher education: the fact that universities seem to mostly agree on the broad social mission and its egalitarian ideals. It has not been a quirk of history that the university system has grown as a corollary to the rise of the American liberal economy and the persistent belief that democracy is all-important. True, there are deeply cynical moments in American university life when its commercialism emerges the winner, when student aspirations are compromised by costs, and when the division of labor in the university between academic and administrative responsibilities does not support productivity, but leads instead to faculty alienation. Yet the impulse to define some kind of liberal learning that might mediate the split between the academic and the corporate remains essential and intriguing. Bureaucracies can be tampered with endlessly—and in universities they are—but without some persistently persuasive intellectual ideal dominating the mission, the social idealism of the modern university simply becomes social engineering.

Classical Heritage

It is often argued that liberal education began in the fourth century B.C. when, in opposition to the Sophists' moral relativism and oratorical hyperbole, Socrates (ca. 469–399 B.C.) emphasized that stable truths and principles of knowledge are discoverable by the educated mind. The four major philosophic schools of ancient Greece kept this metaphysical option alive for some nine centuries.

Plato's Academy (ca. 428–348 B.C.), the first of these schools, supported an intellectual elite that worked with a curriculum that included metaphysical inquiry, mathematics, and dialectics. The educational mission was to idealize philosophy as a body of knowledge that would guide the individual and the state wisely, even if not through principles that we would consider democratic today. After teaching some twenty years in Plato's Academy, Aristotle (384/3–322 B.C.) founded his Lyceum, the second major school, with a curriculum based on logic, ethics, biology, physics, politics, and rhetoric, probably favoring the natural sciences among educational subjects.

The Aristotelian antirelativist agenda produced what remains to this day the most influential body of philosophic works covering the metaphysical approach to ethics, epistemology, the nature of reality, the relation between logic and language, and the practice of interpretation. For the Aristotelian, truth in higher education remains a logical possibility. True virtue is not simply a matter of doing good things but a unified state of being good that has to be attained through careful study of concepts of goodness. One cannot acquire moral skills through skills training alone. One does good not simply by choosing to do good, but as a result of developing a practiced sensibility, which can be gained only from a sound theoretical education. Happiness is to be valued over wealth and results from the pursuit of reason. Living well is above all a matter of cultivating excellence of mind through practical wisdom. In short, Aristotle's was the earliest and, for many, still the most powerful argument ever offered for a liberal education for its own sake, as John Henry Newman well knew. Higher education was defined by Aristotle as an education that above all could mold character of intrinsic worth and not merely pursue expedient outcomes.

The third major school was no less intent on establishing the moral nature of a liberal education. Stoicism, founded by Zeno (334–262 B.C.), was developed primarily by Chrysippus (ca .280–ca. 206) and was carried through the Roman years by Cicero (106–43 B.C.), Seneca (4 B.C–A.D. 65), Epictetus (ca. A.D. 55–135), and Emperor Marcus Aurelius (A.D. 121–180). It too proposed a nonrelativistic, metaphysically based philosophy of education. Once again, the emphasis was on training reason to attain its highest effectiveness, working from its beginnings in intuition and sense impressions and exercising itself through the disciplines of dialectic, rhetoric, logic, grammar, poetry, and music. But reason for the Stoics, as for Aristotle, aimed to achieve a definable end. The Stoics believed that reason can reach conclusions and discover the inherent design of the world, which reflects a divine presence, or *logos*. At its highest point, human reason identifies, through rigorous study, with logos itself. While in practice Stoicism offered a fatalistic view of a complex, fluxual universe that predetermines human activity, it nonetheless emphasized the enormously influential ideal (especially for the Renaissance and the growth of modern science) that a rigorous training of the intellect, stripped of the passions, could achieve a purely rationalistic and not merely opinionated view of the world.

The fourth major philosophical school of education in the Hellenist world was more tolerant of relativity and perhaps closest to our current mainstream thinking in the liberal arts and sciences, consumed as we are with theories of relativity, uncertainty, and the quantum nature of reality. Epicurus (341–271 B.C.), whose philosophy was later immortalized in the Roman world in the *De Rerum Natura* of Lucretius (99 or 94–55 B.C.), established a school that admitted both men and women for enlightened discussion in a garden setting. The Epicurean theory of knowledge was unashamedly sensationalist and mystical rather than dependent on logical first principles. Space is pure void and relies on no immanent divinity; the world is in perpetual motion and is atomic in structure; divinity is simply a human idealization—and so too is hell. Contradictory explanations of the way the world works are not only possible but inevitable because they are all based on the evidence of the senses and their differing perspectives. And when it comes to ethics, personal pleasure—the goal of every individual—is the measure of what is right or wrong. The greatest good and the purest pleasure, though, are closely linked and are achieved not through stimulation of the bodily senses alone but through a mind refined in contemplation, exercising its free will. Yet Epicureanism was no mere hedonism, and the end of education was no mere justification for any or all actions. The body should be trained to enjoy the simple life, the soul nurtured through the study of physics and not the contemplation of divine subjects, and the mind honed through careful argument.

This brief description of the main ideological issues driving higher learning from the Hellenist period down through the beginnings of Rome's preeminence in the Mediterranean is, of course, quite oversimplified. But my point is a simple one, too: Remarkably, almost all the classic options for valuing learning—from the emphasis on reason to a political education to an aesthetic education— were experimented with in this astonishingly fertile period of educational idealism. We recognize many of our educational issues now. The tension between the symbolic and the exchange (rhetorical) value of knowledge that preoccupies us is as old as the Greeks. Our culture wars are ancient indeed when we exam the battles between truth telling and deconstruction, first principles and relativism, canonic culture and contingent cultures. They grow inevitably out of the contemplation of the nature of knowledge. For those more concerned with language as the philosophical medium and an end in itself, common sense tells us that all philosophy, as Ludwig Wittgenstein would have it, can be described as a problem of language. But that does not disarm the standoff in the history of educational ideas between the essentialists and the pluralists—or the traditionalists and the reformers—because most of us would like to believe that our experience is not simply limited to the words we use to describe it.

Yet when we consider the ideological subtlety with which the definition of knowledge was addressed two thousand years ago, as if the mind always needed to start from scratch and be walked through a critical history of itself, then perhaps we are missing something today in the erosion of philosophy at the heart of the undergraduate curriculum. Perhaps we should still be dealing, even at an elementary level, with the burning questions of how we know anything at all and whether it makes sense to pursue something called truth. The ancient art of educating the free mind naturally turned to such matters, yet even though we emphasize critical thinking, we most often do not assume that higher education is about learning to understand how the mind knows what it thinks it knows.

But that is not surprising, for the Greeks, too, had their practical and political interests in educational philosophy and did not want to leave it all in the hands of epistemology. Metaphysics soon developed into rhetorical strategizing; questions of being became allied with matters of persuasion. The burden of providing curricular instruction was taken on by numerous schools of oratorical rhetoric and not by the established academies. It is somewhat chastening to realize that when offered the choice of learning metaphysics or rhetorical cleverness, the majority of the ancient world came to opt for the latter. Rhetoric as oratorical skill rather than philosophical finesse is the primary legacy from the Greeks to the Roman world. The liberal arts went into business formally with the Roman *artes liberales*, subjects of study that were befitting an argumentatively free and not servile person. These subjects, though, as we shall see, were emphasized not so much to nurture curiosity and imaginative thinking as to promote enlightened service to the state. Roman education is the beginning of a liberal education that is fused with professional and nationalistic aims as well as with educating a dominant political class. No matter how much lip service we pay to Aristotle and the importance of educating the philosophic mind, we are very much the inheritors of the Roman tradition of education for power.

Indeed, there is little that is new in the politics of the contemporary academy in terms of the educational status of knowledge. Beyond that Aristotelian moment that Newman tried to revive, the outcomes of learning have long been linked to motives other than its own intrinsic pleasures. Rarely has knowledge ever been promoted purely for its own sake in education systems, and, ironically, it was not till Newman's idea of the university that we find a "purist" definition of disinterested learning. That was relatively short-lived, anyway, being quickly absorbed into an interest in aesthetics and a literary education in British universities. With the growth of professional academic disciplines by the end of the nineteenth century, such theorizing had little chance of widespread survival and became buried in liberal arts colleges and, particularly, in English departments, where literary culture became the ideological heart of liberal education. In short, for centuries the knowledge derived from liberal learning has always seemed to embody a tension between utilitarian outcomes and learning for its own sake.

Of the Liberal Persuasion

Bruce Kimball has dramatized this development in another way as an ongoing battle throughout the classical period between skills of persuasion and skills of critical thinking. He has described the growth of ideas about liberal education as a "long and confusing debate," dating from the fifth century B.C., in which two opposing "semantic branches of the Greek term _logos_ . . . [were] thought to define the nature of civilization and of a civilized being." He continues,

On one branch were orators and rhetors, who emphasized the newly invented arts of grammar and rhetoric and the skills of composing, delivering, and analyzing a speech. These skills were paramount in a democratic city-state or a republic where persuasion determined the outcome of every question arising in the political and judicial assemblies. On the other branch were those who regarded rhetoric as an imprecise and practical tool that constituted but a shadow of the true essence of logos. These others, including Plato (427–347 B.C.) and Aristotle (384–322 B.C.), searched for a precise, rational method of pursuing knowledge, and regarded the new arts of mathematics and syllogistic logic as conveying the essential nature of logos.[1]

Again, we would find it difficult today to claim that the tension between cognitive reason in the name of science and rhetorical strategies of argument common to the humanities has disappeared. Some might say that the philosophers have lost out to the orators, who are now politicians, public relations experts, spin doctors, advertising copywriters, talking heads, and promoters of the habits of our "most effective people." The Romans, on the other hand, at least made oratory central to the rhetorical cause and emphasized a respect for history and literature. "The Romans, being builders, lawyers, and administrators of an emerging empire," says Kimball, "felt most sympathetic toward a theory of education emphasizing public expression, political and legal discourse, and general and ethical training in the literary tradition that described the noble virtues and orderly society of the past."[2]

Literature, that is, was seen to have more than a humanistic influence. It was considered descriptive, grammatical, and rhetorical. It existed for social and political purposes at once. The function of literature was to deliver a persuasive fusion of aesthetic effects, convincing argument, and morally uplifting historical commentary. Hence the powerful concept of literature as performative, which has been taught through the classics from the Renaissance to the present day. Hence, too, the fact that a liberal education based on the study of literary texts has been associated, even before our time, with social empowerment as well as with an aesthetic education.

A liberal education for the Romans offered training in literature and language, some mathematics, astronomy, logic, dialectics, and, above all, the art of persuasion itself: rhetoric. These were the Roman *artes liberales,* an organization of knowledge later adapted by Christian scholars, who restored the importance of the pagan liberal arts. The seven liberal arts—grammar, logic, rhetoric, arithmetic, geometry, music, and astronomy—came to dominate Christian education in western Europe throughout the medieval period, even though, as Kimball points out, "specialization and advanced study were not encouraged by the Christians and were even criticized as leading to self-indulgence."

In the twelfth and thirteenth centuries, however, scholars like Thomas Aquinas revived Aristotelian logic, momentarily displaced rhetoric and literature from their pedestal, and brought a distinctly rationalist bent to the business of studying religious doctrine, the Bible, and patristic texts. But the Scholastics' interest in linguistic analysis and philosophical argument in turn gave way, during the rise of Renaissance humanism, to the rediscovery of Cicero and other Roman authors. Once again, the classic tension between the philosophers and the poets, between the language of objective reason and the language of persuasive metaphor, provided the deep structure for the mythology of higher education. Christian education was dedicated to an understanding of the power of authoritative texts through the rhetorical nature of language, for the study of the literary qualities of language had always been associated with the study of language for its persuasive effects. Literature was important not simply for its aesthetic form but as a moral *exemplum* dedicated to a social education. "This humanist model of rhetorical and literary learning," says Kimball, "was amplified with Christian ethics and with notions of courtesy derived from the medieval tradition of knighthood. These three normative traditions—the humanist model of learning, the social etiquette of courtesy, and Christian ethics—coalesced to yield the ideal of Christian gentility, which became the archetype of a liberally educated person in sixteenth- and seventeenth-century England."[3] It was this "model of Christian gentility [that] was readily endorsed by the founders of Harvard College in 1636, as well as in the eight other colleges subsequently founded in the American colonies." Thus was developed a curriculum dedicated to "rhetoric and grammar, to reading, memorizing, and interpreting literary and theological texts that defined the virtues of a citizen in God's commonwealth."[4]

While the religious motives of such a mission varied in intensity, the liberal arts curriculum of British colleges from the mid–seventeenth to the mid–nineteenth centuries maintained a humanist interest in Greek and Latin texts as the moral exemplum of a dominant class, one dedicated to political power and public virtue, and not simply the massaging of an aesthetic or religious sensibility. Mathematics, history, logic, theology, natural science, and moral philosophy were important, too, but humanistic ideals dominated liberal education, largely because humanism itself was a comprehensive term of some public authority. Humanism was able to explain that the functions of public and private power had some kind of moral, religious, and aesthetic meaning, even if that power, in the British case, was closely aligned to imperial yearnings.

But humanism contained within its boundaries, from the Renaissance to the nineteenth century, a burgeoning fascination (nowhere seen better than in the drama of the Renaissance) with the tension between worldly power and personal desire, between thinking and acting, language and truth, poetry and rational discourse. The rise of modern science did little to disturb this, in large part because the empiricism of science (and the emerging social sciences) was easily adapted to the pragmatic needs of a growing imperial culture. The Renaissance fashioning of power grew from its discovery that the word is not incarnate, that knowledge is pursuable for its own sake and may be created with secular authority in a wide range of fields. It was in this context that the art of classical rhetoric became again the most important of the public arts, since the use of language molds the moral universe and mediates truth.

Thus develops the modern sensibility and modern education, both of which are understandably still confused about exactly how language can shape the truth. Our curriculum to this day swings between the extremes of open-ended interpretative play and rationalist, social scientific taxonomies of human behavior. The Renaissance, without conclusive leadership from science, was in a position to emphasize a rhetoric-based education in which the pursuit of knowledge and the use of language to a large extent existed as subjects of study in themselves. Language, after the rise of Ramist logic, is transparent and value free and must be judged by the strength of its use in argument. Thus, once again classical concerns arose about whether good rhetoric is necessarily symbolic of good ideas and moral virtue or mere sophistry at work. These issues certainly revitalized philosophy as one of several disciplines, including mathematics and astronomy, which could examine the symbolic value of knowledge.

The real battle over the modern university curriculum surely begins here, with the desacralization of language and the growing belief that language is too unstable for us to be sure that it can carry clear meaning and essential truths. Renaissance humanism, therefore, is important to us not so much because it revived classicism with a nostalgic concern for authoritative texts, but because it paid special attention to the aesthetic, scientific, and argumentative uses of language together: in short, rhetoric. Even though the Scholastic influence did not disappear, the whole point of education lay not just in what should be taught, but in examining the world through the medium of language. The boldest of rhetorics—the Ciceronian fascination with the language of public power—was deeply influential because it blended the philosophic with language at its most socially persuasive. In short, this was a time—as Richard McKeon, one of our best historians of rhetorical practices, has noted—when "rhetoric replaces metaphysics as an architectonic art."[5] This is a time, that is, when rhetoric, politics, and aesthetics had an extraordinarily happy collaboration, as we can see in the plays of Shakespeare and in metaphysical poetry. Humanism quickly learned to promote an alliance between the seductive pleasures of metaphor and an insistent questioning of issues of power, morality, and an increasingly complex psychology of the self.

Of course, this social and political power of a literature-based humanistic education has long been admired in the West. But what was so often passed off as a great Victorian restoration of liberal education in nineteenth-century British schools and colleges, under the influence of Cardinal Newman's *Idea of a University* and Matthew Arnold's *Culture and Anarchy*, became a rather egregious use of literature in the services of something that might be called heroic vitalism, the stirrings of imperial glory, the aestheticization of knowledge in conjunction with power. The play of rhetoric we have just been discussing during and following the Renaissance appeared the most appropriate way to educate men of breeding, especially in the ways of public power. It aimed as much to fashion leaderly sensibilities and heroic skills of expression as to impart a sense of history that might support Britain's own imperial expansion.

This political use of literary-styled rhetoric went unquestioned for years. So it was not surprising that C. P. Snow created a considerable intellectual stir in Britain and elsewhere with his "two cultures" argument in 1959. Ostensibly a promotion of science education, Snow's argument was deeply political. He played off humanistic education against scientific education and said the standoff was all about the British class struggle in that humanism had been the guiding force of the ruling classes and science had been left to languish in the care of those who had relatively little class influence.

But this deep, underlying tension in modern education transcended class, and Snow was aware of that. The real issue came down to whether philosophical reason and science can somehow control the endless reach of language, whether language's inevitable expansion into metaphor can be stopped somewhere along the line, and whether truth will out. In short, the old Platonic argument between the poets and philosophers lies at the heart of Snow's concern, as it does behind any effort to assert the curricular priority of either the humanities or the sciences. The two are equally imperialistic. Once you give the poets a line, they can metaphorize the whole text—and may even turn it into every other text. Once you give the scientific or philosophic method full purchase—at least until quantum theories come into play—the only questions worth asking are those to which answers are empirically possible. And when quantum theory is in play, scientists and philosophers become poets.

Snow's class allegory may seem too limited for the American context. But it embodies the key dilemma of relating language and truth that still drives all our curricular issues. The art of rhetoric, the orator's rhetoric, is the art of fashioning language into a philosophic and aesthetic medium; but it is also the art of politically motivated persuasion and the art of delivering information to strong effect. It is difficult to think of a subject that is more important to study these days than rhetoric, especially the rhetoric of the electronic word, and it does not take a cloying nostalgia for Ramist thought to figure out why.

The genius of the Renaissance, after all, was to brilliantly reveal the poet and the philosopher at work *together* in the great humanistic texts of the period. One is aware of a creative tension between ratiocination and argument, on the one hand, and rhetorical verve and poetic aptness, on the other. There is a connection between power and metaphor in the service of moral complexity, which is indeed what a classical liberal education found so inspiring. Language is a transparency through which one sees the struggle between the public and private self as it comes into consciousness. It is also densely suggestive of what that self is and what it wants to be. It dramatizes the subtlety of the psychology of personality. In short, as the Renaissance seemed to understand so well in all its arts, truth is open to interpretation, and psychological self-fashioning is above all a rhetorical, social act.

What has this to do with liberal education and the curriculum today? After Ramus finally wrenched apart language and truth in the mid–sixteenth century—a historical moment that had been brewing for many years and is still simmering—education was faced with an extraordinary dilemma. Can we put language and truth back together again? or must we teach the arts of reading, speaking, and writing as merely playful, even deconstructive social exercises of the art of persuasion? One part of our educational mission has always emphasized the former, the pulling together of language and truth, and we have tended now to turn those activities over to the sciences and social sciences. We have also wanted to keep the latter option open in the name of a humanistic education. But they are still at odds with each other.

But it is important to note that all the classical theories of the importance of rhetoric to a liberal education elaborated their arguments through an analysis of how language shapes public versions of the truth, be that through logical argument, metaphorical persuasion, or both. At heart, the classical philosophers were interested not only in the best way to explicate a problem philosophically or even how to appreciate the aesthetic delights of poetry and music. They were fascinated by how language can persuade us to action and can

deeply influential with scholars who believe that a liberal education lies at the heart of the university's mission. As I have mentioned, Newman's study has been powerful, too, when coupled with the work of Matthew Arnold in articulating the cultural mission of British universities in the late nineteenth and early twentieth centuries. It has also understandably become a touchstone for humanists in the United States, where there has been a persistent concern that a liberal education has lost its way amid determined vocationalist goals.

For one thing, Newman's grand narrative is thoroughgoing in its belief that sustaining the intellect is the real business of the university. Reason, as Newman puts it, "considers itself from first to last independent and supreme; it requires no external authority; it makes a religion for itself."[6] Start with reason and the intellect, and the rest will surely follow. Here, for example, is how Newman expresses his idealism in a famous passage from *The Idea of a University:*

> Surely it is very intelligible to say, and that is what I say here, that liberal education, viewed in itself, is simply the cultivation of the intellect, as such, and its object is nothing more or less than intellectual excellence. Everything has its own perfection, be it higher or lower in the scale of things; and the perfection of one is not the perfection of another. Things animate, inanimate, visible, invisible, all are good in their kind, and have a *best* of themselves, which is an object of pursuit. Why do you take such pains with your garden or your park? You see to your walks and turf and shrubberies; to your trees and drives; not as if you meant to make an orchard of the one, or corn or pastureland of the other, but because there is a special beauty in all that is goodly in wood, water, plain, and slope, brought all together by art into one shape, and grouped into one whole. Your cities are beautiful, your palaces, your public buildings, your territorial mansions, your churches; and their beauty leads to nothing beyond itself. There is a physical beauty and a moral: there is a beauty of person, there is a beauty of our moral being, which is natural virtue; and in like manner there is a beauty, there is a

perfection, of the intellect. . . . The artist puts before him beauty of feature and form; the poet, beauty of mind; the preacher, the beauty of grace: then intellect, too, I repeat, has its beauty, and it has those who aim at it. To open the mind, to correct it, to refine it, to enable it to know, and to digest, master, rule, and use its knowledge, to give it power over its own faculties, application, flexibility, method, critical exactness, sagacity, resource, address, eloquent expression, is an object as intelligible (for here we are inquiring, not what the object of a liberal education is worth, not what use the Church makes of it, but what it is in itself), I say, an object as intelligible as the cultivation of virtue, while, at the same time, it is absolutely distinct from it.[7]

Apart from the interesting fact that not even Newman is without a passion for excellence, this is clearly a strong statement that liberal education is about "cultivating the intellect" as a faculty of reasoning that opens the mind to powers of engagement. Newman's argument is that this is indeed the starting point for any social, practical, or religious agenda. If reason gets itself right—and presumably logic and rhetoric have something to do with this—it will find virtue on its own. But everything depends on nurturing the life of the mind, a notion both Plato and Aristotle would have agreed with. The question still arises, when we contemplate the social mission for higher education, whether it might be wiser to start from purer, more essentialist motives like Newman's, to begin with mind as the seat of learning and concentrate on the opening and refining functions of its activities. Newman himself is not unaware of the importance of enlightenment as a social virtue, of a university education for the social good. And this he sees as the clear consequence of intellectual activity:

Training of the intellect, which is best for the individual himself, best enables him to discharge his duties to society. The philosopher, indeed, and the man of the world differ in their very motion, but the methods, by which they are respectively formed, are pretty much the same. The philosopher has the same com-

mand of matters of thought, which the true citizen and gentleman has of matters of business and conduct. If then a practical
end must be assigned to a university course, I say it is that of
training good members of society. Its art is the art of social life,
and its end is fitness for the world. It neither confines its views to
particular professions on the one hand, nor creates heroes or
inspires genius on the other. Works indeed of genius fall under
no art; heroic minds come under no rule; a university is not
a birthplace of poets or of immortal authors, of founders of
schools, leaders of colonies, or conquerors of nations. It does not
promise a generation of Aristotles or Newtons, of Napoleons or
Washingtons, of Raphaels or Shakespeares, though such miracles
of nature it has before now contained within its precincts. Nor is
it content on the other hand with forming the critic or the
experimentalist, the economist or the engineer, though such too
it includes within its scope. But a university training is the great
ordinary means to a great but ordinary end; it aims at raising the
intellectual tone of society, at cultivating the public mind, at
purifying the national taste, at supplying true principles to popular enthusiasm and fixed aims to popular aspiration, at giving
enlargement and sobriety to the ideas of the age, at facilitating the
exercise of political power, and refining the intercourse of private
life. It is the education which gives a man a clear conscious view
of his own opinions and judgments, a truth in developing them,
an eloquence in expressing them, and a force in urging them.[8]

Newman, brilliant public philosopher and theologian that he
was, senses that the pragmatic and the politically rhetorical have a
way of complicating and even tainting the purity of reason. Yet he
knows he has to preserve the social mandate for education. On the
one hand, he offers as exhaustive a definition of the Platonic value of
the human intellect as we have in modern educational theory. The
mind has its own standards, its own natural virtues, its own perfect-
ible shape. On the other hand, the result of shaping the mind is to
create the self-confidence and habits of thought that best breed
responsible citizens and leaders in a great but ordinary society. This
is indeed a strong theory, for intelligence, that most differentiating

of measurable factors in the human population, is not itself the issue. Reason incarnate in the rhetorical moment, one might extrapolate, is the issue. One can be tempted even to argue that American education may actually be more elitist in its pragmatic concerns, that its inordinate affection for measuring the mind's capacity through endless testing, aptitude scores, and intelligence quotients, in order to define cleverness and the likelihood of success, is perhaps no less likely to produce an undemocratic society than Newman's passion for aesthetic perfection.

The mind for Newman is a kind of intellectual engine for the soul, delighting not only in the power of the beautiful but in the beauty of its own power. It has a life of its own, for in those communities of learning that value minds for their own sake, nothing is more important than a large, well-decorated brain. And there is no question that lurking in the background of the great but ordinary society are those beautiful minds that can be set free from mundane earthly uses. "Reason," he pointed out, "is the principle of that intrinsic fecundity of knowledge, which, to those who possess it, is its especial value, and which dispenses with the necessity of their looking abroad for any end to rest upon external to itself. Knowledge, indeed, when thus exalted into scientific form, is also power; not only is it excellent in itself, but whatever such excellence may be, it is something more, it has a result beyond itself."[9]

Newman makes a distinction between learning that is liberal and learning that is useful. To do this, he leans heavily on Aristotle's distinction between the purity of form and the impurity of function: " 'Of possessions . . . those rather are useful, which bear fruit; those *liberal, which tend to enjoyment*. By fruitful, I mean, which yield revenue; by enjoyable, where *nothing accrues of consequence beyond the using*' " (*Rhetoric*, i, 5). The other oppositions in Newman's theory thus quickly fall into place: the great and the ordinary, the Shakespeares and the commonfolk, genius and the common mind. One senses that Newman realizes the dualism of this arrangement but is sure it can be overcome through reason itself. His values are aristocratic and aestheticist at heart, yet his intelligence tells him that that is not in itself always good, that whatever must work for higher education must work to produce not only an elite but a more generically high achievement for all who study in universities, again through valuing knowledge for its own sake. The dualism that subtends all his argument is stubborn indeed, though, and the Neoplatonic view that ideas in themselves are somehow pure and transcendent and can be disattached from their extensions in the empirical world, or even from moral values, remains consistent. Ever since Newman's reworking of classical epistemology into a modern theory of liberal versus pragmatic knowledge, liberal learning has been suspicious of teaching ends, not means. At the same time a suspicion of knowledge for its own sake persists because reason left to its own devices cannot be trusted to guarantee its usefulness or its virtue. That is the rock and the hard place of modern liberal education theory: knowledge for its own sake must be as much an end as any utilitarian uses of knowledge, and that end can be aesthetic, rhetorical, or positivist. But that, as many have pointed out, is how the twentieth century got itself into trouble—when reason cannot see the political wood for the theoretical trees (and here one thinks of Martin Heidegger), or when we have been so intent on the exchange value of knowledge that we ignore the cultural contradictions that result.

Newman seems to insist that the pleasure of being in the company of people with splendid minds resides in the aesthetic delight derived from the experience, simply, of thinking something through. Our real admiration of a work of art, and its ability to propose that truth and beauty are somehow closely related, lies in contemplation of the work itself. The aesthetic experience may be moral in linking truth and beauty, but the operations of mind in themselves are primarily aesthetic: "The artist puts before him beauty of feature and form; the poet beauty of mind; the preacher, the beauty of grace: then intellect too, I repeat, has its beauty, and it has those who aim at it."[10] The mind itself, claims Newman, in the intelligence it exhibits, can be contemplated in its self-containedness, its flexibility, its form and expressiveness, and admiration can only grow for "the repose of a mind which lives in itself, while it lives in the world, and which has resources for its happiness at home when it cannot go abroad."[11]

For good reason—and the irrationality of much utopian and neofascist thinking in the twentieth century has served only to support this position—Americans have been less aesthetic and more pragmatic about education as an experience that links the body and mind and does not merely celebrate a powerful intellect. While we retain a necessary affection for the phenomenological pleasures of thinking as an end in itself, and a great admiration lives on among humanists for Newman's calm and happily self-composed intellect, the metaphysical inclinations of his theory of liberal education have been nudged aside by definitions of how the mind explains itself through its working values, the outcomes of its expression, and its calls to action. Understandably, Americans find it difficult to separate things from their use, mind from matter, form from function. With its intensely social mandate, American education espouses a pragmatic humanism. As John Dewey put it, "Only living, not metaphysics any more than psychology, can 'give' an ideal."[12] But perhaps, in the process, we have lost in our theories of liberal education admiration for "the repose of the mind which lies in itself"?

The American Version of Liberal Education

While European concerns about liberal education took the philosophical route by the eighteenth century, the history of higher education in America has always been driven by concerns that cultural, social, and economic practices drive the academic curriculum together. The colonial colleges were founded by ideological communities, not by groups of scholars as in Britain and Europe. They were governed by boards of ministers and businessmen who combined the requirements of piety and the polity. True, these colleges thought of themselves as communities of scholars and, with much rhetorical flourish, extolled the value of learning offered through the classical European curriculum of the time. They held strict entrance requirements, which included an adequate reading knowledge of Latin and Greek. They taught the old *artes liberales* (again, logic, rhetoric, Hebrew, Latin, Greek, natural philosophy or physics, metaphysics, ethics, and mathematics). But they never conceived of themselves as self-governing, independent guilds of faculty, as were the early European schools, and their curricula had clear religious agendas. Rhetoric as argument, in short, never received full curricular play in the early years of higher education in America.

Those Puritan settlers knew what their priorities were: they wanted their own schools to show that their New World experiment had come of age, and they wanted to prepare young men for the work of God and the community. In 1646, the Statutes of Harvard insisted that everyone at the college "shall consider the main End of his life and studies, to know God and Jesus Christ which is Eternal life." For, as Cotton Mather put it some sixty years later, "They foresaw, that without such a provision for a sufficient ministry, the churches of New England must have been less than a business of one age, and soon have come to nothing . . . without a nursery for such men among ourselves darkness must have soon covered the land, and gross darkness the people."[13]

For two centuries after its beginnings, the redemptive ethos of American higher education was dominated by the social values of the idealized Christian gentleman: one who was successful in a patriarchal New World society, had a passing knowledge of classical rhetoric, and was generally comfortable with biblical ethics. Through a respect for classical learning, higher education aimed to encourage such pleasures of mind and spirit as would promote the social values and independent character of the new Republic, even while it provided a sense of belonging to a European-styled educational elite. With the colonial colleges on hand, families would not have to send their sons to the old country. Yet even this relatively unified cultural theory did not stop persistent and well-documented public complaints about everything ranging from the content of the curriculum to student discipline and the behavior of faculty, complaints that were often exacerbated by the colleges' struggles to survive financially. Benjamin Franklin, for one, complained that the colonial colleges were little better than finishing schools.

Then, as small college education waned in popularity by the mid–nineteenth century, the moral and religious ideals of a Protestant liberal education clashed strongly with the emergence of science and freethinking objectivism. Both collided with the expanding power of late-nineteenth-century corporate liberalism, which learned to cleverly hedge its bets by standing for a combination of conservative moral values, a nationalistic entrepreneurism, and a creative affection for feeding its own self-fulfilling prophecies about what the public really wanted based on economic needs.

The religion of education and education through religion were to dominate for many years, at least until the mid–nineteenth century. In spite of support from Jefferson and Washington, a secular national university never assumed the same importance as the socioreligious ideal of a liberal education. The crucial document defining this ideal was the Yale Report of 1828,[14] which asserted the importance of a classical education centered on Greek and Latin. Thus part of higher education at least became officially dedicated to a liberal arts concept that derived from Renaissance humanism and its revival of classical texts, the study of languages and some logic, and a smattering of science. Education was primarily literary in nature, though not in the philosophic and political senses that we understand literary studies now. Textual scholarship, not the interpretation of texts, was uppermost in scholarly minds. Students were exposed to great works and, as if by a process of osmosis, beauty and wisdom flowed through the eyes of the beholder. Those were the days, as nostalgia merchants would have it, when America's mind was freely open and not cluttered by the reflexiveness of doubt.

But the Yale Report reveals little understanding of the subtleties and ironies of training students in classical rhetoric or a literary education. It unashamedly focuses not on an education for open argument but on education for social power, as embodied in the connection between Christian beliefs and the heroics of classical texts. The report had a strong influence until just after the Civil War, when the gap between the elitist content of a Christian liberal education and the commercial desires of a democratic industrial society began to widen. Then the curriculum became increasingly professionalized in the disciplines, and a sense of the centrality of rhetoric to the curriculum receded even further from view.

After the Civil War began the great American age of public education, which we still inhabit, in which education sees itself as feeding society's needs and ameliorating civic tensions. In the 1860s and 1870s, American higher education was both liberalized and professionalized at once; the study of elitist notions of power shifted to the installation of egalitarian opportunities. The collegiate rights of women were established with Vassar College in the early 1860s. Cornell University was founded with a commitment to student diversity in 1869. And President Charles Eliot introduced the first elective curriculum at Harvard in the 1870s, breaking the grip of religious moralism on higher education. This period, too, saw the rise of western and midwestern land grant universities, with their democratic and vocational missions. At the same time came the development of professional research studies, starting with the founding of

Johns Hopkins in 1867, dedicated to the Germanic belief that truth was discoverable through rational, methodical means and that such methods of study could dominate any discipline worthy of the name. In short, service to learning and service to society became clearly established as related ideals, even though the tension between the two increased as the disciplines took on new seriousness through advanced research and doctoral study.

Not surprisingly, the old creative tensions at the heart of ancient rhetoric were again glossed over, this time in the rush to discover truth by a scientific method, regardless of whether the discipline was in the arts or the sciences. Academe took on new self-esteem, but it also became a profession of some strain as it tried to pry deeper into the whereabouts of knowledge, as if it could be excavated from language with the right philological skills and might be rationally verifiable if one asked the right questions. The study of rhetoric itself came under this spell in the last two decades of the nineteenth century in the formation of English studies as a discipline with its own canonical reading list. The classical interest in literature as exhibiting rhetorical power, linguistic subtlety, and philosophical import did not wholly disappear. For centuries, knowledge of Latin or Greek texts had been one of the touchstones of social breeding, even in America, and through the rise of importance of the elite liberal arts colleges and Ivy League schools in the nineteenth and early twentieth centuries, the classical tradition remained strong.

But the problem was that this concern for an aesthetic of power in the study of literature—devoid as it was of any sense of thoroughgoing irony—soon became somewhat languid, introverted, and belletristic in its scholarly emphases. A rigorous, open-ended dialectic between what language said it was doing and what it could be interpreted as doing was simply not promoted. Great texts became cultural icons, carefully assigned to display cases in the museum of literary history. Writing about those texts became a weighty, self-consciously embellished, celebratory gloss on the vocabulary of good taste. In the end, cultural criticism turned inward—rather like those eighteenth-century novels that borrow each other's characters —in order to establish a common high culture.

Thus it was in this period—from the turn of the nineteenth century through the first three decades of the twentieth century— that a powerful concern arose to extol the social power of the literary canon in the name of humanism, to ground the rhetoric of cultural greatness in a view of humanity that had more to do with white European bourgeois virtues than with the lives of the majority of the American population, and certainly not those who were women or people of color. Indeed, for many years, even until the 1930s, the scholarly reading of English literary texts was patterned on the exegetical and philological interests of Christianized classical scholarship. Students were taught to read English literature as if it were Roman or Greek literature—with professors providing a translation, as it were, so as not to mistake the real meaning. The whole exercise in a modest but nonetheless persistent way seemed to be about remythologizing classical values.

This nostalgic, neoclassical tradition of liberal learning remained a strong influence in liberal arts colleges until well into the twentieth century, and its presence is felt even to this day. True, the rise of the modern American university coincided with the ascendancy of Enlightenment philosophy and the new science over the literary tradition of Christian humanism. But if, by the end of the nineteenth century, the scientists appeared to have won that war, they had by no means managed to reshape humanism into a more objective or more philosophically problematic set of ideas. Opposition from liberal arts colleges and religious schools intent on pursuing the ways of the old humanism remained strong. Sectarian colleges and universities, particularly Roman Catholic institutions, clung to the program of classical studies, with an emphasis on literary and rhetorical training that could be traced back through Ignatius Loyola to Cicero and then to Isocrates. Yet it is only recently that we have rediscovered the importance of Isocrates as a theorist of a deeply argumentative and ironic rhetoric.

At the same time, though, many American universities, encouraged by the scientific emphasis on value-free research, abandoned the idea of training the virtuous citizen through a broad course of classical study. They introduced the undergraduate major, a specialized preparation for the pursuit of truth modeled on graduate study in the disciplines of the arts and sciences, especially the sciences, and grounded in a rationalist, objectivist methodology. The English major was left as the site of the old humanist battle—a history well charted by Gerald Graff in *Professing Literature*[15]—and it is largely within English departments that the battle between philosophy and poetry, theory and literature, humanism and science has continued.

The professionalization of study in the arts and sciences, which began in the universities before World War I, may seem rather quiet in comparison with today's fervid theorizing, ideological battles, and cultish self-promotion at conferences, but it was not without considerable confidence. Certainly, American scholarship developed a measure of self-sufficiency during the interwar years, when the research institutions came into their own.[16] After World War II, there was an explosive growth in enrollment and disciplinary emphases, and universities began to acquire an even more complex, rationalist mission, one that sought to promote both research and undergraduate education in state schools and elite private universities. Soon there appeared a conscientious concern for undergraduate education as a systematic curricular focus. The Harvard study (the famous "Red Book"), *General Education in a Free Society* (1945) and the President's Commission for Higher Education Report in 1947, *Higher Education for a Democracy,* had great influence on the conscious shaping of undergraduate education to provide what the commission report called "general education." The Red Book still leaned somewhat on classical humanism, but it at least recognized the ironies of doing this. The commission report, however, was quite distinct about revising the elitist tone of liberal education.

A transformation from liberal education to general education— at least in universities, if not liberal arts colleges—was well under way by the late 1940s. The humanistic cultural mission of higher education that had been strongly implicit from the beginnings of American higher education was now overtly challenged by the scientific culture of cognitive reason. The disciplines were deemed worthy of undergraduate study, and their methodologies became the new touchstones for a sound liberal education. But it was research that had the strongest draw for faculty. Here is how Thomas Bender describes this momentous shift in academic politics:

> Faculty values—research opportunities, better colleagues, better students, greater autonomy—drove university development and established the standards by which universities were judged and ranked, at least those universities that aspired to distinction. . . . So radical was this transformation that Christopher Jencks and David Riesman called it, in the title of their book of 1968, *The Academic Revolution.*
>
> This pattern of change freed faculty for a stronger research orientation, and it enabled a firmer sense of academic autonomy and disciplinary professionalism. Whereas the Red Book had asked philosophers to investigate and teach "the place of human aspirations and ideals in the total scheme of things," the postwar discipline, embracing the inward-looking and donnish analytical movement, eschewed such a civic role. In retrospect it appears that the disciplines were redefined over the course of the half century following the war: from the means to an end they increasingly became an end in themselves, the possession of the

scholars who constituted them. To a greater or lesser degree, academics sought some distance from civics.[17]

In the service of graduate training and nurturing the disciplines in competition with the all-powerful sciences, the liberal arts became highly specialized. At the same time, the rhetorical heart of their enterprise, something that could help them define the practical mission of the university, not to mention its humanist and civic responsibility, was weakened. The professionalization of the disciplines, as much as the growing utilitarian motive for higher education and the huge development of mass education in the second half of the twentieth century, has ironically driven the liberal arts to their current defensive position. Once knowledge gained power primarily for its professional usefulness, then even attempts at public discourse were often replaced by the language of relatively arcane interpretation theories.

This also opened the way for the growth of the public power of the social and natural sciences, for those disciplines understandably stayed closer than the humanities to objectivist research protocols. As knowledge became modernized, more harnessed to economic and nationalist agendas of the United States as the emerging, dominant world power, usefully applied learning grew in importance. And things have changed little since. Efforts in the 1970s and 1980s by the humanities to establish a stronger presence for the "human sciences" (Jacques Derrida's term) have met a whimsical and at times derisive response from the public and the media, largely because of the extraordinary introversion and fastidiousness of their vocabularies. Few academic enterprises have been more perplexing to the public than humanist fascination with deconstruction theory, for example. Even the broad authority of the humanities on matters of social justice and cultural value—after the "student revolt" of 1968 and through the growing diversification of the American university

—has not had a profound effect on American public life. The academic critique of gender, race, and culture politics continues to be deeply embedded within the specialized discourse of the disciplines. Ironically, though, even as poststructuralist interpretation theories seem to lay the basis for broader cross-disciplinary learning through their work on the nature of power—not to mention their understanding of the instability of the human subject—and as pragmatists become experts in contingency, the disciplines of the arts and humanities remain obsessed with their heady professionalism. Interdisciplinary learning has scarcely grown at the pace many hoped it would. As Bender wryly remarks, "It is striking how little the structure of the university has altered since the 1920s. . . . The department remains the basic organizational unit."[18]

What I am arguing, therefore, is that American liberal education has followed the uses of knowledge for social power, first defined in the Renaissance through the currency of classical revivalism and Christian culture. It then found itself shaped by the growing egalitarianism and faith in scientific reason of the new universities born in the latter half of the nineteenth century. And in the interests of research agendas and academic professionalism today, liberal learning not surprisingly embraces a complex and rather arcane politics of interpretation. From a purely professional perspective, the disciplines must go where knowledge takes them. But the steady corporatization of the American university has ironically supported this professionalization of learning rather than demanding a more public role for the humanities. Indeed, the humanities have yet to recover a publicly persuasive rhetorical stance and the distance between even the humanist disciplines remains very real. So too do student needs for a substantive, issue-centered general education that they can take into everyday life.

CHAPTER 6

Knowledge, Modernity, and Pragmatism

In the past fifteen years, liberal education has become the focus of a number of widely read studies arguing for curriculum reform in undergraduate education.[1] Nearly all these studies reasonably assume that undergraduate general education is where we find liberal education most clearly at work today. In response to calls for basic and connected learning in the arts and sciences, many universities have devised special core programing taught mainly at the first-year level, often with additional courses required before graduation. Certain practices have become common in general education courses: a more inclusive definition of American culture, the use of multicultural texts, a growing internationalism, a concern for values and service to society, remedial programs to prepare students in the basic literacies (writing, computers, mathematics), service learning, a growing concern for a democratic education, inquiry-based pedagogies, and assessment of student learning.[2]

One would think that with all this going on there would be little need for concern about the future of liberal education. Is it not the case, as Bruce Kimball has argued, that "pragmatism and liberal education are converging" and that this is a promising development? After all, American education theory has had great affection in the past fifty years or so for the thinking of John Dewey and, as Kimball explains, most of the general education practices listed above "have conceptual and historical roots or find a principled rationale in pragmatism."[3] True, universities are concerned with how social values can define undergraduate education, how we can "teach the conflicts" and use various kinds of interdisciplinary strategies in doing so. But as lively as the activity of liberal education may seem to be, learning is rarely connected, we still cling to rather hopeful notions of humanizing readers by exposure to great texts, and general education remains more traditional than not in its desire to expose students to disciplinary methodologies. We do not operate from a broad idea of the university, a cooperative intellectual culture that focuses on learning interdisciplinarily. We have not budged from the hegemony of the disciplines. And we have yet to devise a strong enough idea of a democratic liberal education that most schools will find irresistible and want to put in place.

There is, of course, frequent dismay at how slowly things are changing in the world of the arts and sciences to accommodate what are euphemistically known as new challenges for learning. There is equal dismay over what the liberal arts, especially, are up against in the university in facing those challenges, the kinds of issues— economic, political, and cultural—that I have been outlining in detail in this book. And a few academics, including Henry Giroux and Stanley Aronowitz, finger corporatism as the culprit. Aronowitz, for example, a sociology professor, has recently written a scathing attack on the "corporate university," proposing that it be "dismantled," that liberal education be reformed, and that four key knowledge areas (history, literature, science, and philosophy) be applied to "specific historical periods," with the aim of examining these periods through the cooperation of the four disciplines.[4]

I think it is quite apparent that the corporate university shows few signs of being dismantled, that it will remain product (degree)-centered in its thinking, intensely bureaucratic in its functions, focused on the professionalism of the disciplines, and beholden to the academic marketplace to set its practices. Corporate culture in the university is not merely in place, it is hegemonic: the main context for any and every curriculum. The nature of knowledge has changed in the past fifty years or so away from symbolic to exchange modes, away from an integrative view of knowledge (the old primacy of moral philosophy) to specialized skills. And indeed, the consumerist public seems to want it this way, as much as some students bemoan the loss of the romance of learning. I have argued too that the mission of the American university is so complex and unprioritized, so lacking in any integrative idea and given over to an entrepreneurial opportunism, that we can barely deal with the contradictions of our own culture, let alone those of the society we serve. The practices of general education are under constant revision to try to cope with the increasing fragmentation of knowledge, but they rarely pursue thoroughgoing cross-disciplinary strategies, and their good intentions are frequently undercut by structural ambiguities in the university and by budgetary constraints. Faculty freedoms are threatened more than ever, and the division of labor can only become an increased source of anxiety.

In short, the intellectual ideals of liberal education that sustained it for so long—its concern for the nature of knowledge, its passion for defining reason and truth, its need to fit together an analytic, ethical, aesthetic, and ideological making of a worldview, its insistence on the importance of rhetoric and argument—cannot be effectively replaced simply by a theory of market responsiveness within the professionalized disciplines. They might be replaced by an agenda that Aronowitz outlines, but that too is not pointed enough to focus activity on a well-theorized democratic education, one that has strong interest in addressing key intellectual topics and social issues that have remained perennially provocative. Interest in reforming liberal education is compromised not simply by the onrush of academic professionalism and research for profit, and by agendas that have veered too easily toward political correctness and tax-onomic learning, but also by the failures of liberal philosophy to rework the primacy of intellectual agendas convincingly.

In a curious way, too, liberal education rarely talks about what constitutes personal happiness. Consider George Washington's re-marks to Congress in 1790, which got to the point of what the knowledge business was all about then, and still is. "Knowledge," he said, "is in every country the surest basis of public happiness. . . . To the security of a free Constitution it contributes in various ways: By convincing those who are entrusted with the public administration, that every valuable end of Government is best answered by the enlightened confidence of the people: and by teaching the people themselves to know and to value their own rights; to discern and provide against invasions of them; to distinguish between oppres-sion and the necessary exercise of lawful authority . . . to discrimi-nate the spirit of Liberty from that of licentiousness."[5] That is, knowledge is a necessity for preserving basic human freedoms and for acquiring the personal confidence necessary for happiness. This is not to say that happiness will necessarily follow from knowledge or that an enlightened populace is necessarily a contented one. Ob-viously knowledge can lead to discontent with one's lot, as faculty know well in the university. But the assumption that happiness is a function of enlightenment, and enlightenment is a theory of what knowledge can do, surely remains a powerful concept. The argu-ment that an enlightened happiness is the happiest of convergences is very persuasive.

Our problem, though, is that enlightenment is not a pressing goal in liberal education today, and the public tends to have a dif-ferent definition of happiness for students, one that declares all too often that knowledge and the ability to be critical and argumentative are not the source of joy; happiness is more likely to be found through a good job. Many of us know that when our politicians, university presidents, and corporate leaders talk about the importance of education as a public good—not the purest of public goods because there are few public subsidies for goodness, but at least a good to the extent that general entitlement is met—they are referring to the effectiveness of higher education in delivering workers for the knowledge-based economy. The more knowledge that is accumulated and made accessible, the more apparently democratic our education is, and the happier we all can be.

As the dean of educational historians, Frederick Rudolph, noted in a memoir written after a fiftieth-year reunion at his college, Williams, there have been three stages of cultural development in American higher education: "Christian, Gentleman's, and Consumer."[6] While I do not quote this with any yearning to return to the first two stages, certainly the proliferation of the knowledge economy as we know it today has resulted above all from a strong consumer demand for credentials in every vocational field. Knowledge has bloomed richly as the legacy of what Europeans label the "massification" of higher education. Europe, too, has recently discovered mass and professional education and, having plunged in, now looks perhaps more fondly toward American universities, maybe this time in an effort to redeem what the French critic Jean Baudrillard has wryly called the Euro-American habit of indulging in "unhappy transferences."

For the knowledge boom in America and Europe is, from an economic standpoint, a very happy one. The academic knowledge business, as we have noted, has entered into an alliance with liberal capitalism. The evolution of modern information systems—their consumer values, corporate and state power bases, the decentralized governance they encourage, their advertising subsidies, and their need to be a part of the new global knowledge economy—has plainly become a driving motive for the development of knowledge in the university itself. Higher education has inevitably grown closer to corporate life because the university is the major social institution dedicated to propagating the modernization of knowledge. Less and less, though, has it been trusted by society to explain itself to itself, to say unpopular things about what modernization actually means.

The Modernization of Knowledge

A contradiction arises when we contrast the intellectual challenge of higher education to "cultivate humanity," as the scholar Martha Nussbaum puts it, with its role in purveying specialized credentials for a society that equates knowledge with economic value and national prestige. The battle has been fought many times before over the centuries, for Veblen's opposition between erudition and applied knowledge is as old as the Greeks. But the battle, I have been saying, is no longer the philosophical one it once was, and it is unclear that simply returning to old ideals of liberal education without revising them will work.

Revisit for a moment the classic definition of what a liberal education can provide in the way of nonspecialized knowledge. Here is Nussbaum's eloquent description:

> Three capacities, above all, are essential for the cultivation of humanity in today's world. First is the capacity for critical examination of oneself and one's traditions—for living what, following Socrates, we may call "the examined life." This means a life that accepts no belief as authoritative simply because it has been handed down by tradition or become familiar through habit, a life that questions all beliefs and accepts only those that survive reason's demand for consistency and for justification. . . . We need Socratic teaching to fulfill the promise of democratic citizenship.
> Citizens who cultivate their humanity need, further, an ability to see themselves not simply as citizens of some local region or group but also, and above all, as human beings bound to all other human beings by ties of recognition and concern. The world around us is inescapably international. . . . Cultivating

our humanity in a complex, interlocking world involves understanding the ways in which common needs and aims are differently realized in different circumstances. . . .

But citizens cannot think well on the basis of factual knowledge alone. The third ability of the citizen, closely related to the
first two, can be called the narrative imagination. This means
the ability to think what it might be like in the shoes of a person
different from oneself, to be an intelligent reader of that person's
story, and to understand the emotions and wishes and desires
that someone so placed might have. . . . The third ability our
students should attain is the ability to decipher such meanings
through the use of imagination.[7]

The modernization of knowledge for Nussbaum and many humanists rightly requires a long memory. Nussbaum is describing the
traditional role of higher education as the transmitter of critical
cultural history and social values. Such an education is a matter of
training conscience, imagination, and logic through close encoun-
ters with many versions of the other—texts and cultural experiences
—in order to create a responsible, enlightened, and self-reflective
citizenry. One might guess that such a citizenry could also be con-
fident of its rights and have good prospects for gaining happiness.
College is the place where we train future generations to think critically and ethically, to develop empathy for others, and to share
important social values that are open to change. While there are
more radically liberal and revisionist theories than Nussbaum's, and
more conservative ones as well, she is plainly encouraging traditional liberal education to nod in the direction of the current calls
for critical thinking and multiculturalism.

On the other hand, another definition of modern knowledge
related to the knowledge economy has emerged in recent years, one
which seems to have a much wider purchase in the commercial
marketplace and even in the corporate university. This other definition does not resonate with Socratic references, but it has a powerful

influence on how we run higher education and on the way education is valued outside the university. It opens up some important issues humanists must address about what it means to be educated in a modern world. Here, then, is one of the leading new "knowledge economists," Dale Neef:

> The basic thesis behind the emergence of a knowledge-based economy is that . . . there has been a unique combination of focused market incentives that have led to immense technical progress in the areas of computing, biotechnology, telecommunications, and transportation (to name only a few) and which have begun to foster dramatic changes in the way in which economies, organizations, and governments will function in the future. Indeed, there is now compelling evidence that the sudden and ever-accelerating burst of growth in high-technology and high-skill services and in the new products and service structure they are creating may bring about some of the most profound and unexpected changes to the way in which we live and work witnessed since the nineteenth-century transition from an agricultural to an industrial society. . . .
>
> As a result, it is becoming obvious that individuals (and organizations) who are best able to leverage their knowledge advantage will increasingly account for a greater portion of total output. They will also become the recipients of a consistently greater portion of relative earnings. In short, for developed economies, knowledge work—activities that involve complex problem identification, problem solution, or high-technology design and that result in innovative new products or services or create new ways of exploiting markets—has quickly become the focus for economic growth and individual and organizational prosperity. This change will have profound effects on our way of life at both organizational and national levels.[8]

Neef, of course, is primarily defining "knowledge work" in terms of the dramatic challenges posed by the growth of technoscience. Necessary changes in public policy, an understanding of the ethical and cultural implications of new scientific discoveries and technological change, the replacement of knowledge as a search for essential meaning by knowledge as unending innovation. But for thinkers like Neef, "knowledge work" can easily be largely a matter of problem solving and design, as if problems have no historical, ideological, or political context—all that a liberal education aims to offer through the arts, humanities, and social sciences. There still is in the university and in the world of public philosophy a more than lingering belief that science above all provides true knowledge, even if, as Neef declares, science is driven by market principles.

Nonetheless, Neef's point is no overstatement: the world *is* a place in which everyday culture changes rapidly not through the work of philosophers but through those who do have skills in identifying and solving technological problems. The challenge goes out to the liberal arts, as it has for over a century, to create a response to this. One might assume, for example, that there is market "exploitation" available even for liberal learning as part of "complex problem identification and solution," simply because the liberal arts are all about the ethical, aesthetic, economic, and political implications of any problem that affects the name and nature of society. But most in the liberal arts would be content for a serious acknowledgment that those disciplines do have a place in the postmodern world and play an essential role in understanding and evaluating social change and the effects of technoscience.

A more classically enlightened, but still provocative definition of knowledge within the postmodern context is offered by the most prominent theoretician of the corporate knowledge economy, Peter Drucker. Note how he has coopted a more humanistic vocabulary for his definition of knowledge, but still says essentially the same thing as Neef:

> The knowledge society *must* have at its core the concept of the educated person. It will have to be a universal concept, precisely because the knowledge society is a society of knowledges and because it is global-in its money, its economics, its careers, its

technology, its central issues, and above all, in its information. Post-capitalist society requires a unifying force. It requires a leadership group, which can focus local, particular, separate traditions onto a common and shared commitment to values, a common concept of excellence, and on mutual respect. . . .

Yet the knowledge society needs a different kind of educated person from the ideal for which the Humanists are fighting. . . . "Liberal education" and *Allgemeine Bildung* are in crisis today because they have become a *Glasperlenspiel* [glass bead game, after the title of Hermann Hesse's novel] which the brightest desert for crass, vulgar, money-grabbing reality. The ablest students appreciate the liberal arts. . . . But all over the world today's students, a few years after they have graduated, complain that "what I have learned so eagerly has no meaning; it has no relevance to anything I am interested in or want to become." They still want a liberal arts curriculum for their own children— Princeton or Carleton; Oxbridge; Tokyo University; the *Lycee;* the *Gymnasium*—though mainly for social status and access to good jobs. But in their own lives they repudiate such values. They repudiate the educated person of the Humanists. . . .

Post-capitalist society is both a knowledge society and a society of organizations, each dependent on the other and yet each very different in its concepts, views, and values. Most, if not all, educated persons will practice their knowledge as members of an organization. The educated person will therefore have to be prepared to live and work simultaneously in two cultures— that of the "intellectual," who focuses on words and ideas, and that of the "manager," who focuses on people and work.[9]

It is in higher education that this struggle to define the educated person takes place between the intellectual and the managerial, between the humanities and professional education. The battle is over outside the academy, for the media managers and political spin doctors have decisively beaten out those who prize complex solutions for complex problems. But in the academy the tension still exists, as Drucker admits, between humanistic knowledge and knowledge that is primarily information or skill. But by "intellectual work," Drucker means the pursuit of specialized and useful information that has some "universal" principles that might be profitably taught. As he says, "The knowledge we now consider knowledge proves itself in action. What we now mean by knowledge is information effective in action, information focused on results."[10] So, he believes that

> the future does not belong to the "polymath," but to the special-ist, and the challenge to higher education is to integrate the knowledges into a "universe of knowledge . . ." what we do need—and what will define the educated person in the knowledge society—is the ability to *understand* the various knowledges. . . . Without such understanding, the knowledges themselves will become sterile . . . intellectually arrogant, and unproductive. For the major new insights in every one of the specialized knowl-edges arise out of another, separate specialty, out of another one of the knowledges.
>
> There is no "Queen of the Knowledges" in the knowledge society. All knowledges are equally valuable; all knowledges . . . lead equally to the truth. But to make them paths to truth, paths to knowledge, has to be the responsibility of the men and women who own these knowledges. Collectively, they hold knowledge in trust.[11]

Drucker is right that there is no Queen of Knowledges in the knowledge society. Competitive jostling for central stage between the academic disciplines continues, but no one discipline has full purchase on knowledge of the workings of the individual, society, or nature. But this is not to say that knowledge cannot be guided by the urge to make connections and to synthesize its components as an end in itself. What happens, after all, when we are selective, as Druc-ker is, about which "specialists" make sense and which do not? What larger knowledge informs that decision? The claim that "all knowl-edges are equally valuable" and "lead equally to the truth" is difficult to believe when Drucker attacks traditional humanists and what he calls "the motley crew of post-Marxists, radical feminists, and other 'antis'" along with "those new nihilists, the 'Deconstructionists.'" Drucker does not think the truth lies in any of these ways, and he is hardly in the minority. The often politicized versions of knowledge offered by the academy in the past decade, even if they rightly engage the inequalities of everyday power, have perhaps left many in the general public quite unsure of the meaning and worth of "radical humanism." But even if it is impossible for knowledge to avoid the political, the academy must accept blame for its failure to develop a strong public philosophy in plain terms, one that does not veer to political or aesthetic extremes. The irony is that in our knowledge society we rarely teach what knowledge is, we only teach knowledges. In the public eye, learning in the humanities has been eclipsed by what appear to be more robust and neutral social and natural science protocols of inquiry. After all, as Drucker none-too-subtly states, those philosophical concerns that have traditionally shaped a liberal education do not pack sufficient punch to sustain the economic motives of higher education. And of late there has been increasing criticism of the academy as not always on board with the patriotic agenda of keeping America strong. It's simply too risky to leave knowledge to the "polymaths." The shared values and trust in knowledge that is celebrated by Drucker and others are plainly those of Western corporate and military power.

One cannot deny that in the world of commerce and international finance, Western power appears to be all the power there is, however vulnerable it is to market fluctuations, however possible it is that it will not last forever. But economic power alone cannot support a vital culture or lend understanding to the complexities of our human fate. Drucker does not seem to have a strong interest in an education that tolerates ambiguity. He seems little concerned with sustaining the conditions of happiness beyond the need for getting and spending. True, Drucker rightly bemoans the fact that "crass, vulgar, money-grabbers" do not understand the value of a liberal education except, as he says, for reasons of promoting social status. But this clever adoption of the opponent's rhetoric should not fool us. Drucker's interest is not so much with liberal learning as with corporate-styled power itself.

But, ironically, that is why Drucker has such an important message to convey. As he implies, learning without a concern for the social uses of power is highly ineffective. The liberal arts need to take heed of that. But we do not need to celebrate the triumph of the West in doing so: "The Western tradition will . . . still have to be at the core. . . . Its material civilization and its knowledges all rest on Western foundations: Western science; tools and technology; production; economics; Western-style finance and banking. None of these can work unless grounded in an understanding and acceptance of Western ideas and of the entire western tradition."[12] The notion that good finances and banking necessarily require "acceptance of Western ideas and of the entire Western tradition" is highly provocative. But such ideology is not unusual, even elsewhere in the American academy. Drucker is simply repeating the reasons some of our business and political leaders have supported the classical curriculum: the grandeur that was Rome reminds them of the late-capitalist American *imperium*.

Liberal learning itself is not about establishing or sustaining power elites, even as intellectual elites in the disciplines come and go. It is about examining why we have them at all, why we have been fascinated by power for as long as people have lived together in societies; why Drucker's view of knowledge is influential in our time. It is about gaining the confidence that derives from being able to argue for how societies and nature work. It is about critically reviewing the history of ideas of what it means to be not just an American but a citizen of a much larger world, engaging the amazing complexity of that experience, most of which has not been developed by people made euphoric by the flush of wealth or power. There is little ambiguity, though, about the nationalism and consumerism happily promoted by those who do not see the importance of liberal educa-tion as history-based cultural critique.

So is there any point in harking back to at least a review of the traditional liberal arts curriculum? The answer is no and yes. No, if the traditional liberal education curriculum simply seeks to pro-mote some nostalgic mystique of the past. Learning in the arts and humanities can easily become merely aestheticized and lose any crit-ical edge, can subsidizes the arts, for example, as a kind of connois-seurship, or spiritualism of the aesthetically inspired. This is not to say that we should lose touch with aesthetics or spiritual issues, for such have their own distinct rewards. But our obsession with the power of a highly aestheticized or fastidiously overnuanced culture —pure or revised—seems a last-ditch reaching out for a truth that leaves most of society far behind.

On the other hand, yes, we should turn back to review the tradi-tional idea of the liberal arts because only a critical historical per-spective can remind us of the irony of believing the importance of our own rhetoric today. We have made little progress understanding how to teach the nature of knowledge itself. Look, for example, as the last chapter documents, at how strongly interested the Greeks and Romans were with a practical, political, rhetorical education. It was not all about metaphysics, aesthetics, and theories of knowl-edge; it was about politics and social power. But without those theo-ries of knowledge, how could they possible know what power was? Look too at how the Renaissance revival of humanism as a politi-cal, philosophical, and rhetorical fact—a conscious shaping of lan-guage for subtly layered effect—often seems more pragmatic and certainly more poetic than most public philosophy today. Look at the enormous power of the University of Reason in nineteenth-century Germany, the world's first country dedicated to a nationalist research agenda at the same time, and compare that to our own deep relationship between capitalism and science today, with little concern to teach at the undergraduate level the complexities of reason itself.

Nussbaum's benign humanism calling for self-examination and empathy for other perspectives is a step in the right direction. That said, though, we have something serious to learn from Drucker as well as from Nussbaum. No matter what he intends as an outcome, Drucker makes an important point when he says we will have a poor future in higher education unless we integrate useful with theoretical knowledge, theory with praxis, if only because the public will have it no other way, and the educational marketplace will only sustain the value of what the public perceives is necessary. Drucker is right when he says that since "the *technes* have become knowledges in the plural, they have to be integrated into knowledge. The *technes* have to become part of what it means to be an educated person." And this is the very issue the liberal arts must focus on: the power of integrative knowledge.

Pragmatism

The modern American university has long known the important connection among knowledge, pragmatism, and learning. In spite of many a nostalgic look back at Newman among apologists for liberal learning in the United States, there is consensus that American higher education favors a process of learning by doing.[13] The distinctively American contribution to the argument over liberal education is perhaps best understood by referring to what I would call Dewey's pragmatic humanism, his definition of the habits of analytic, reflective, and creative thinking that lead to moral action:

> There is all the difference in the world whether the acquisition
> of information is treated as an end in itself, or is made an
> integral portion of the training of thought. The assumption that

information that has been accumulated apart from use in the recognition and solution of a problem may later on be, at will, freely employed by thought is false. The skill at the ready command of intelligence is the skill acquired with the aid of intelligence; the only information which, otherwise than by accident, can be put to logical use is that acquired in the course of thinking. Because their knowledge has been achieved in connection with the needs of specific situations, men of little book-learning are often able to put to effective use every ounce of knowledge they possess; while men of vast erudition are often swamped by the mere bulk of their learning, because memory, rather than thinking, has been operative in obtaining it.[14]

As Dewey explains it, education is anything but abstract or merely aesthetic. It is a process of coming into understanding by engaging issues, learning through active participation in the context of problem solving. Knowledge not learned as part of a pattern of use remains mere theory. The only way to make a person "conscious of his social heritage," says Dewey, "is to enable him to perform those fundamental types of activity that make civilization what it is." Educational progress is measured not simply in "the succession of studies, but in the development of new attitudes towards, and new interests in, experience. . . . Education must be conceived as a continuing reconstruction of experience." Dewey's subject, then, is the modernity of real knowledge, the capacity for experience to refresh itself in reflection and social action. "If we can only secure right habits of action and thought," he says, "with reference to the good, the true, and the beautiful, the emotions will for the most part take care of themselves." Therefore, "education is a regulation of the process of coming to share in the social consciousness."[15]

Like Newman, Dewey sees the definition of intelligence as key to the idea of philosophy as well as education. While Newman's religious faith made it difficult for him to avoid a split between mind and body, Dewey would have nothing of that. Acting, suffering, and knowing are the functions of an integrated consciousness, and it is through the body in action that knowledge results, not simply through contemplation by a beautiful mind. While learning for Newman is theoretically an out-of-body experience, for Dewey it is quite visceral, the body in action discovering problems in situations, hypothesizing and sharing solutions. Pedagogically, that is, Dewey puts in motion the theory, somewhat oversimplified today by the knowledge economists, that it is important to link learning with a process of discovery and experiment.

Embedding learning in this process, however, begs the question of how engagement with the other shapes one's own learning. Dewey's epistemology is not empirical in a clinically materialistic kind of way, nor is it based on a complex phenomenology of consciousness, one that must constantly reflect on its own profession of strain. It is rooted in a concept of human nature that is more organic and unified than Drucker's; even nature itself is a kind of interrelated whole, society is naturally democratic at its best, and community is the source of fundamental human values created by human interactions. In short, there is great optimism in Dewey's humanist position. He believes that there are moments, which he described as aesthetic, when the problematic nature of experience resolves itself through active inquiry and when a "consummation" takes place in a wave of understanding. In his organic philosophy, the modernist's need for an "epiphany" lives on.

Dewey's theory of learning, however, presupposes a naturally inquisitive mind seeking pleasurable and socially advantageous inquiry. Like Newman, Dewey believed in the pleasures of thinking but did not accept any inherent morality to thinking itself. Moral choices arise from situations; morality is a function of thinking through competing values. For Dewey, though, bypassing the duality of secular and religious, liberal and useful through use of the creative intelligence became not simply a reaching out for an elegant hypothesis, but a trust in developing habits of mind that can integrate an understanding of a wide range of human activities.

As he explained in *Human Nature and Conduct,* "Utilitarianism . . . was concerned not with extracting the honey of the passing moment but with breeding improved bees and constructing hives. After all, the object of foresight of consequences is not to predict the future. It is to ascertain the meaning of present activities and to secure, so far as possible, a present activity with a unified meaning. We are not the creators of heaven and earth. . . . Our concern is with the significance of that slight fraction of total activity which starts from ourselves."[16] Such a concern serves Dewey's emphasis on education as the training of minds capable of integrating experience. Romantic about his modernism, Dewey nonetheless sets himself apart from both idealistic and subjectivist theories of knowledge in that immediate sensations are part of a process of constructing knowledge in a context. The phenomenology of consciousness is not of great interest to him; the social drama and intersubjectivity of coming into understanding is. Knowledge is not crudely rationalistic—he is well aware of the emotional intelligence—but it is scientific in that common sense reviews experience and assumes the fundamental value of rational inquiry within a democratic society, one that can tolerate openness and promote reason as a link between self and the world.

So Dewey circumvents questions about the mind-body problem and acts as though reason can be defined by its functions, for it has no intrinsic value on its own. His optimistic faith in education as a means of shaping consciousness to be critical and integrative within a liberal democracy—for Dewey was a spokesperson for the social psychology of the new republic—has become the classic American ideal of modern learning, though an ideal too easily forgotten in the rush these days to standardize knowledge. It speaks to an education that frees the mind to be creative and foster happiness because it is fashioned through experience of its natural and cultural contexts. It is not surprising, then, that in any serious theoretical disquisition about the democratic value of education today, Dewey's argument inevitably drives the agenda.

But enticing as this is as a working theory of teaching and learning, Dewey's emphasis on the mind at work can lead to a focus on the discovery process as an end in itself—as it has in the new knowledge economy. In allowing for intellect to be defined by its application and mind by its use, educational ideals can become merely functionalist, even if Dewey did not intend it that way. It is but a short step from learning as a process useful for obtaining knowledge of self and society to learning whose importance is determined by the process of understanding itself and its measurable outcomes. For then all knowledge becomes quite relative, all knowledges are equal, as they are for Drucker, and taxonomies of learning assume more importance than learning itself. Another corollary of functionalism is that the value of the learning process can only be determined by whether we can quantify assessment instead of turning to more subtle descriptions of how the intelligence has actually performed creatively.

This is not what Dewey would have wanted, I think. Today, we are often distant from Newman's aesthetics of mind in arguing for what is important in undergraduate education. But in spite of the optimism expressed by Kimball and others that pragmatism and liberal education are close to united, it strikes me that we are also often far from Dewey's concern for "a present activity with a unified meaning": the importance of learning as discovery is too often shaped by a sentimental process of accepting the other without argument. We rightly have mandates for diversity in higher education and a deep interest in ethics and community service. But these ideals, when simply taught as values, become mere exercises for shaping a society according to rules of correct behavior and desirable outcomes.

Our fragmented degree requirements, too, leave little time for students to treat learning as a potentially unified experience, which Dewey argued for. Even when we value existential theories of learning above all, we often revert to a kind of materialism of method and an education by distribution requirements. True, too, there is a putative bond these days between disciplinary learning, social responsibility, and practical training for the world of work. But we are often more intent on educating for assimilation into society at all costs than for society's change for the better. We tend to promote the need for a productive citizenry rather than a critical, socially responsive, reflective individualism, and it is this latter concern that drives Dewey's pragmatic humanism and that must drive liberal humanism today. In short, the ideal of a democratic, liberal education that Dewey proposes is not the same as Drucker's theory of knowledge, and it does not conspire easily with the university's efforts to promote the importance of human capital in the marketplace. In a very real way, Dewey and the market are not compatible. For with the latter, knowledge is commodified into *technes*, while for the former it is ever-changing in its fascination with processing and reflecting on experience.

Enlightenment, Modernity, and Truth

Dewey's pragmatism seeks that moment, as he puts it, of "consummation," and that I suspect is another word for "enlightenment," which in turn historically summarizes the culture of reason. But how important is enlightenment in higher education in the new millennium? Few social institutions, after all, carry more responsibility for meeting public needs for a better society than the university. Americans go to college not simply to improve their minds and to develop critical thinking, but to learn what it is to become an American. Too often, though, the university does not promote the impression that being an American is a complex work in progress, a mandate to work on achieving enlightenment, an identity to be argued for, and less a matter of entitlement, of achieving economic independence, and of fitting into some predictable and even patriotic paradigms. And too often the problem lies in the failure of liberal education to provide a grounding in learning as the construction of social values.

How then can American higher education reinvigorate the dialectic between the value of knowledge as a process of growing up in a democratic society and its commodity value in the marketplace? Will Dewey's theory of the creative intelligence do this work? Liberal education in recent years, after all, has failed to arrive at a coherent theory or praxis that can resist the power of market forces, in spite of the enormous theoretical influence of Deweyan pragmatism. We have looked at Dewey's theories selectively—favoring the passages on learning-by-doing—and have missed his syncretistic intent. Experiential learning is admirable, but it does not commit us to value knowledge in the university as somehow connected and pervasively cultural.

Are we perhaps better off focusing less on the social mission and more on a traditional concern with enlightenment in developing the undergraduate curriculum? Does it matter, too, that enlightenment has something to do with understanding our own modernity? The theme of the modernity of knowledge is not incompatible with Deweyan pragmatism as an educational ideal. The project of modernity has occupied us for the past three hundred years or more and is difficult to avoid in any serious pursuit of liberal learning. Inevitably a liberal education, whether pragmatic or not, is about understanding one's own time and one's own place in it.

To explain the relationship of enlightenment to the concept of modernity requires a book in itself. But it has become commonplace to argue for the continuation or termination of the project of modernity as a product of our so-called Age of Enlightenment in the eighteenth century, with its fascination with science and a growing understanding of our increasingly symbiotic relation to nature. Enlightenment thought told a powerful and somewhat optimistic story about the development of culture as well. With its concern to account for the complex work of describing nature, progress, science, social reform, the law, aesthetics, natural rights, the social contract, epistemology, and democratic theories, the Enlightenment focused in effect on defining the terms of modernity through the play of reason. We may find it difficult to reenact this confidence in the wake of our past century and beyond, but only a reactionary would blame the failure of reason for it all. No matter how radically the twentieth century lapsed into such frightening contradictions in the name of rational progress, we are left with having to make reasonable sense of it all or be doomed to repeat it.

As Jürgen Habermas has made clear, modernity itself is an "unfinished project" of the Enlightenment. This is not simply because some think that reason has been discredited in its failure to stop the evil of wars and pogroms, but because modernity is always an ongoing valuation of the complex experience of the present, not only in relation to the past, but as a moment that must be renewed to have meaning at all. The paradox of modernity, of course, is that it never stays still long enough for us to know what is really modern and what is not. And that is especially true for us living in a consumer-driven postmodern world of competitive markets, slippery but alluring cultural representations, chameleonlike values, and knowledge that claims to know too much about itself to be sure enough of what can actually be known.

The challenge to liberal education in the postmodern age is that students at least engage the ever-open question of what it is to be modern: the history of its ideas, its theories of power, what the term modernity has meant historically—for it is the one quality of experience that all ages share. If we are to find some defining set of values for our social mission and if we are to forge a much-needed connection between matters of the mind, the demands of liberal democracy, and service to the economy, then we need to make sure that somewhere, somehow, we address the questions of how far we are enlightened and what constitutes our modernity.

Culture and Truth

To be fascinated by modernity is to be concerned, sooner or later, with the question of culture. The pragmatist epistemology insists we deal with the question of how cultural values are produced and how social experience shapes what we know and believe. We talk a lot in the university about the social construction of reality, how values are defined by the power of social institutions and the language we use. But if we buy into a pragmatic pedagogy, then we have no option but to study the operations of power critically, a topic that needs to make its way into the undergraduate curriculum as a way of trying to understand the connection between culture and society, between how we shape our values and how our values shape us. Without even an elementary understanding of the workings of power in democratic (and any other kind of) society, we have little understanding of the true challenges to social responsibility. The curriculum for a liberal education, after all, is probably the only place where the delights and discontents of democracy can be explored. Options for democratizing the curriculum in a highly symbolic way—such as through a concern for marginalized and postcolonial cultures—have presented themselves continually in recent times and are most important. But so too is a consideration of democracy itself, as I will show in the last chapter, and the culture that democracy tries to shape.

It has become commonplace for academics to valorize many cultural voices at once in the interest of creating a model of a democratic society in the academy and of trying to influence society beyond. But in academe, the difficulty of reconciling a pluralist culture with the need for shared, pragmatic values is acutely felt. Concepts of culture are provocative because they threaten the plurality of societies and propose sameness. Indeed, the word *culture* looms very large on the academic agenda, particularly as the teaching of cultural values is inevitably implied by the social mission of the university and because such values always seem to be at war with each other. What the recent culture wars have dramatized for us, especially, is the highly problematic status of the term *culture* itself, at least in the singular. To a great extent, the questions in and out of the university about liberal and illiberal learning, lie in the concern that we will overtheorize a political definition of an undergraduate education and therefore not only teach the conflicts but simply encourage bitter argument.

A *New York Times* op-ed page in 1998 carried a lead article by John Ellis, a prominent figure in the Association of Literary Scholars and Critics, entitled "Poisoning the Wells of Knowledge."[17] He makes a call to "the entire community that cares about education" to change "the current orthodoxy" in the humanities, for "it is a disgrace that universities can no longer afford to protect." The orthodoxy Ellis refers to is that represented by the "crude reductionism" and the allegedly unoriginal thinking of scholars who work with deconstructive and postmodern cultural theories.

While there is no shortage of philosophical memory in the major texts of contemporary cultural criticism by major figures—Jacques

Derrida, Michel Foucault, Jean-François Lyotard, Hans-Georg Gad-
amer, Habermas, and Fredric Jameson are all philosophers as well as
theorists—one can agree with Ellis that often in academe lesser mor-
tals have not done their homework and loudly claim to have invented the ideological wheel. Invention without memory breeds
hyperbole—which may also have something to do with the tone of
any number of academic critiques. But even if the scholarship of
postmodern academics was uniformly respectable, not everyone
would be convinced of the importance of the study of culture as part
of a general, liberal education. Theories of culture are social epistemologies: how we come to understand and describe what people do
together and how they create social values and customs. The field of
cultural studies, for example—that collection of literary and sociological disciplines—deals with the circulation of power and its
representations in society. This is an important part of the teaching
of culture but is often cited as too political. Critiquing the role of
romance literature in constructing female subjectivity, say, or discussing the manipulative design of shopping malls, or reading into
the pastiched styles of postmodern architecture for corporate motives are fascinating exercises in explicating the hidden meanings of
power. But this still does not always tell us why cultures sustain
society and are not simply manipulative, how they embody enduring values even while they are ambiguous and double-edged. There
never has been a culture without provocative and often dangerous
ambiguities. The current dilemma of cultural studies is that it has
not yet established how postmodern culture—which often appears
to be a matter of throwing everything together seamlessly for effect,
usually with commercial motives—has a predominantly integrative
or moral motive. The assumption is that it doesn't, that there are no
master narratives; in short, there is no sense at all to it all. And we
have not given up on reason or enlightenment in higher education,
so no sense appears to many to be nonsense.

This may very well be the problem of culture rather than academic inquiry, but one suspects it may be the latter, for we too have little interest in defining knowledge in a syncretistic way. In the corporate culture of the university, the curriculum itself is chameleonlike on the tree of market-produced knowledge; when the intellectual foliage changes, it does too. Our own academic world is one of endless curricular representations, some might say simulacra of knowledge. Traditional scholarship and cultural studies are just two options. But even if the market itself seems to be powered by shareholders who deconstruct its value at whim, it remains true that no amount of deconstruction theory seems to have persuaded everyone in and out of academe that the possibility of Truth has gone the way of Nietzsche's God, or that cultural relativism rules absolutely, or that moral objectivity is impossible to define. In American culture, God, deconstruction, and the market make curious bedfellows, but cohabit they do. Along with wanting to know what culture is and not just what it does, there has been a persistent need to not let the concept of truth go down the drain. But we have no way of knowing who is closer to the truth on cultural matters because we make little effort to bring the disciplines into consort. That alone will not do the trick of course, but my argument is about the curriculum, teaching, and learning, not about the proofs for God. What about a special emphasis in general liberal education on Truth itself? Is this the responsibility alone of those clever readers between the cultural lines? The rhetorician's responsibility? The concern primarily of those social scientists and humanists who believe in cultural relativism and nurture over nature? Or is it the purview of those humanists and scientists who have a metaphysical view of the world and see their lives and nature itself guided by some larger principles—or perhaps, as the new old physicists put it, a unified field theory? Or is it, as E. O. Wilson claims, that even morality is genetic?

Of course, one cannot consign all relativists to one camp and all essentialists to another and expect to do any theory justice. But one can teach the options for defining epistemology and ethics in the interests of understanding that in the end education is about knowledge itself. The ancients were not in such a hurry to give up the discussion of knowledge in their academies, even though they had covered all the same theoretical bases we have within a few hundred years. Our culture wars have thrived on the ambiguous relations between idealism and realism, humanism and scientism, as well as the clash of ideologies and beliefs. The modern university has become a carnival of conflicting theories inherent in the different academic disciplines. So it makes sense to teach the reasons for knowledge as carnival as a way of foregrounding the moral importance of intellectual conflict.

What troubles some academics, though, who have pondered life after the major battles of the culture wars, is that the battles go on. We are still fighting value wars. We have not regained much faith in higher education as the business of framing knowledge with a concern for how values are made. Of course, the conflicts will always remain specifically political in many ways. Voices will claim that metaphysics was not fully deconstructed when Derrida did his awesome number on those transcendental signifiers. Others still believe that the philosophical (Marxian) pursuit of totality did not die when the Evil Empire collapsed. On the Left and the Right there are signs that we reach for political abstractions that are really traces of special interest leaving their slimy trail, leading to shells that keep crunching under foot, only to reveal battered but not quite dead bodies within. But how can we get liberal education to remain political—that is, concerned about which values are right or wrong—yet apolitical enough to want to know why different views exist?

Indeed, with some irony, Ellis's article, implying that truth lives on in spite of flabby postmodern thinking, sits in the *Times* op-ed page, right next to another provocative column, which also happens to ponder a serious question of the morality of culture. Here the *Times* columnist, Frank Rich, contemplates the 1998 ambush murder in Arkansas of four classmates and a teacher by two boys aged eleven and thirteen. "Why did they do it?" asks Rich. He quotes the Arkansas governor and the National Rifle Association, who agree, in the words of the NRA, that "this is not a gun issue, it's a society issue." Perhaps, though, they really meant to say it is a cultural issue, if indeed Daniel Bell is right in saying that what is "striking today is the radical disjunction between the social structure (the techno-economic order) and the culture. The former is ruled by economic principles defined in terms of efficiency and functional rationality. The latter is prodigal, promiscuous, dominated by an anti-rational, anti-intellectual temper in which the self is taken as the touchstone of cultural judgments, paradoxically, because of the workings of the capitalist economic system itself."[18]

In trying to understand such tragedies as the one in Arkansas and at Columbine High School in Colorado, not to mention several other incidents of high school shootings since, it is tempting to radically split off culture—that which can be learned and even bought, our values and preferred moral activities, even our "irrational" nature, according to Bell—from society, that supposedly rationalized institution, consigned to the Constitution, the law, and the workings of civil society, not to mention the market. Exactly how the Darwinian economic forces of the market are rational is unclear, but let us assume—I think safely—that this posited split between culture and society is one that has a wide purchase outside Bell's writing and even turns up regularly in the cultural battles of the university.

For those who see culture (especially popular culture) as the antirational and promiscuous and society as the seat of reason and the law, that bit of human activity we have a better chance of controlling, it is natural to confine sin, evil, and even guilt to culture itself, maybe even a culture that is not our own. (Faculty often do this with themselves and administrations, and administrations with faculty, disciplines with disciplines, academic cultures with each other. The division of labor in the university has created, after all, two major academic cultures: knowledge work and administrative work.) Being willing dualists, we can do this so easily. We also become very suspicious of whether culture can provide a reliable value system. We are ambivalent about culture because we know it can do evil as readily as good; it is after all irrational at heart. So the columnist Frank Rich asks his thirteen-year-old son if the Arkansas killers could be "under the influence of the TV cartoon 'South Park.' . . . Couldn't Nintendo be teaching boys your age to kill?" And he is told "dismissively" by his son that the young killers are simply "evil. It's 'Lord of the Flies.' . . . They [society] need to find a solution, because if there isn't a solution, it's anarchy. They can't blame the kids because kids are supposed to be innocent. So they have to blame someone else to make an easy solution for themselves." The problem isn't with nurture, it's with human nature—and some people are bad.

If guilt has to be assigned, then we can pinpoint and blame those who are guilty, but it is an easy step to summon up the presence of evil itself as a prime motive for human behavior, a presence embedded in our culture. Either way, the guilty are left available for various rituals of exorcism in the name of cleansing culture, our own or someone else's. The law can be quickly invoked. Find the boys guilty because of natural, even original sin, and we can justify a punitive response. But we cannot stop there; we have to know why, and the answer is not just that human nature can be evil but that American culture can also be a bad influence or even nurture the evil. That is Rich senior's take, while Rich junior favors a more Darwinian view.

The issue of how sin and guilt are part of culture or not, as we all know, gets more complicated on an international scale, but it still follows the same cultural paths. The U.S. invasion of Afghanistan was (and is) not simply an attack made to destroy the home of a major terrorist group, or to gain revenge, or to catch the devil, though it was and is all those things. In a curious way, it was also to exorcize the culture of Islam, as many thought, of something that was not essentially it. Islam, after all, could not simply be the other. In this age proclaimed by the West to be one of vast global interdependencies, Islam, the argument runs, has to be somehow reconcilable with liberal democratic values. The horror at September 11 in all Islamic countries could be interpreted as support for this. But someone then has to police culture because it cannot police itself. Postmodern international relations—and some would argue the "new Western colonialism" of developing nations—are as thoroughly about cultural anxieties as they are political and economic. So one of the reasons for the exorcism in Afghanistan, beyond all understandable concerns for security, was that it was about world order, the maintenance of the new global political economy.

The invasion might prove by the way it was handled (through support from Islamic and European countries, "surgical" attacks on Al Qaeda, and good intentions to rebuild the country), that both West and East are capable of subtle moral distinctions, unlike those who flew planes into the Twin Towers, who were of course conducting their own holy cultural war. They are especially capable of sharing cultural values, and not just a connected set of economies. But the West was careful to make clear that its invasion was ostensibly not a holy war, for it was not about dealing with a whole "evil" culture—though articles and even learned books soon after questioned the stability and motives of Islam at large—but rather with a small part of that culture (even a "primitive" tribal culture) that could be held accountable. Nonetheless, it still became very difficult for many in Islamic countries to understand this; the symbolism of the invasion left little doubt in the minds of people in the Middle East that it was Islam that was being attacked and not simply Al

Qaeda. Other, equally important kinds of cultural values that have to do with one's own identity and its integrity, quite apart from what is right or wrong, slipped quickly into place.

My point is that any radical cultural critique, military or theoretical, is fraught with danger because it brings out an extraordinary complex of contradictory assumptions about what culture is and how powerful it is. It is not enough to teach cultural differences, not enough even to simply accept the differences, to tolerate the other. Civility goes a long way, but we need to teach, too, how cultures and their values work, something that can be done only in universities with the close cooperation of political scientists, sociologists, anthropologists, philosophers, and semioticians. Our own culture wars in the university have evoked extraordinary anger because people feel that the culture they identify with is somehow being questioned and by implication their own social identity and academic reputation. And, again, those are the rather tedious wars we are going to continue to fight unless we focus more on the umbrella terms like culture itself.

Let's return, though, to the question of popular reaction to the killings of high school students by their peers. As Rich *fils* implies in the *Times* article, one can still retain a curious sympathy for Matthew Arnold's Victorian view of culture as the place where we can make society better and stave off anarchy. Culture itself is not bad, only some people in it. Frank Rich agrees with his son, too, saying, "Though few Americans like to say so out loud, children can be evil— or, to put it antiseptically, sociopaths."[19] Thus culture in general is let off the hook and is the place where bad things can happen and bad people just happen to be. That too is an easy way out, saying that culture itself is not really to blame. One can get gratification at least from the fact that both young and old still derive moral insights from reading literature, for young Rich has done his reading. But the problem of cultural generalizations arises from knowing how to read and write, how those texts (be they books or entire cultures) create cultural meanings. For example, *Lord of the Flies*, which Rich junior has been reading, has become a modern "classic" because it does not deconstruct juvenile guilt and wrongdoing as cultural facts but simply lets stand the theory of the bad seed, the religious view that some people are just plain evil. Henry James's *Turn of the Screw*, though, another modern classic, flirts with the same question of evil in the young, but seems in the end to allow no easy way out. Evil is both in and out of human nature, it is environmental, and it is very ambiguous indeed as a representation of reality; it can at times just be a matter of interpretation and is possibly a figment of the imagination.

There is no doubting the evil of the actions in Arkansas, or Colorado (the Columbine high school killings), or the New York massacre of September 11. But how we make judgments of a cultural nature about such actions—and about evil itself—is quite problematic. Moral judgments, after all, as we see in all the incidents mentioned, easily become tied up with cultural assumptions, and examining how this happens, even in an elementary way, makes for a powerful general education. This is the kind of public issue that can be dramatized for its ethical, philosophical, sociological, and political import. Whether we interpret evil as having a presence or not in the world—in people, cultures, subgroups, and so on—we have to deal with the culture itself. Rich's editorial is an example of how alive the argument still is over whether human nature can be anything at all intrinsically, or whether culture makes us what we are. The whole issue of nature or nurture lies behind our fears and delights in culture: fear that we are inevitably who we are, delight that we are not; fear that we are formed largely by culture, delight that we can change who we are.

Thus young Rich makes his father feel better by suggesting that it's a matter of nature not nurture. But we cannot feel better about this. Naming evil as sociopathic does not relieve culture of guilt because, after all, culture can still help the enterprise of evil—and even the devil can be a part of that, an insight that has made Stephen King the best-selling novelist of our time. Whether we like it or not, culture remains extraordinarily complex. It is a convenient repository for our sense of what is evil. It is also the repository in other circumstances of goodness and happiness. It remains resolutely Manichean, sustaining precisely the kind of oppositional thinking that propelled the culture wars and showing us that we have made little progress over the centuries in solving the dilemma of philosophical objectivity.

Thus Ellis seems to be right about contemporary scholars spinning their wheels, whether one likes his reading of the humanities "disgrace" or not. So long as we simply argue about conflicting values and ignore the nature of value, we will spin our academic wheels. The alleged split between culture as the place where we deposit our values and society as the place where we try to live in a civilized way has long been held as strongly inside academe as beyond it. The university mission ignores culture except as a celebration of the arts. It has a social mission, not a cultural mission, and it should have both. It somehow tolerates disciplines that make culture their subject on the grounds that this is a traditional activity of learning and a way of subsidizing creativity. It is society and science, the potential rationales for good living, that have a more obvious role to play. Of course no good administrator is ever going to admit this, and few faculty will either. But the sad state of teaching "culture" in the humanities results from the fact that few theoreticians put culture and society together.

But that is another discussion. My point is that in the university we traditionally assign aesthetic, moral, and intellectual culture to the arts and humanities—those are the traditional trouble spots, the places where sensitive but radical people roam, where faculty are most likely "political" and discontented. On the other hand, cognitive reason rules in the social and natural sciences, for the social sciences especially discuss how self and society are formed by the state, its rituals, its behavior, its institutions such as the law, welfare, marriage customs, health services, the environment, child development, and the economy. And most faculty are happy to play out these roles. The disciplines, which do not have to cooperate as they once did to offer a running commentary on the nature of knowledge itself, are homes away from the home of knowledge. But such faculty, I think, miss the point when they insist that general education is just about learning what the disciplines have to offer. It is also about how we can discuss with a few well-chosen case studies how we create values, develop democratic social practices, tell right from wrong, value social justice, and make sense of what nature tells us about ourselves.

In short, general liberal education really is the place where we can tackle head on our love and suspicion of culture, our sentimental and even mystifying way of dealing with it. It is the business of a liberal education, surely, to try to close the gap between culture and society not simply by celebrating great creative moments but by showing, pragmatically, how human values are made.

CHAPTER 7

Democratic Education

Culture and society have long glared at each other across an academic no-man's-land strewn with philosophical land mines. Numerous other foundational issues, too, have complicated life in academe: social justice, truth, the nature of creativity, civilization's discontents, and so on. Our problem in establishing a liberal education curriculum in the university is not just a matter of how to respond with adequate zeal to the knowledge economy of the corporate university through the disciplines. We have no trouble putting together an aggressive sampler of general education courses that celebrate the texts and interpretation theories of all the academic departments. And often an individual discipline does get to a big foundational issue, at least from the perspective of how that discipline sees it. The problem we have is that foundational issues beg for interdisciplinary treatment. Even if undergraduates never get to hear all the complicated reasons why, I have been arguing, we need to focus a liberal education in a modest but lively way on the very question of what constitutes knowledge we can live with, argument that works, evidence that persuades. Inevitably, for example, we are going to fight intellectual wars over whether it is wiser to explain human behavior in genetic or in socially constructed terms, or whether meaning is singular or plural, or whether culture has a causal or casual relation to society. Better to have these wars sooner rather than later, dramatized not simply as theory but as they arise from practical, everyday issues: like making sense of the news, understanding the conditions for war, and so on. Foundational issues derive from the contradictory culture of everyday life, and in their filtered and often overtheorized forms, they lie at the heart of the disciplines as well as public philosophy. Unfamiliarity with the fact that knowledge, argument, and justification take different forms to be effective in different ways can lead later to dramatic oversimplifications, wrong-headedness, even cases of terminally bad metaphysics in making judgments and developing opinions.

In short, the earlier in a university career that liberal education deals with complex relations that are not going to go away—like the relation of culture to society, truth to reality, language to meaning, experience to ideas—the easier it is for students to argue in the disciplines later and apply more specialized viewpoints if needed. But how we make sense of experience, since experience is whole, in the end has less to do with an education in one or two disciplines than with general education. We will always bring to experience our own developing worldviews, our empirical profile, as William Gass has called it. And general education is above all about empirical profiling: how we can develop the ways we make sense of the world. It is not just about having ideas; it's about what we do with them when we have them.

That most American educators seem to speak out in favor of the Deweyan epistemological profiling is more than useful in this regard. Perhaps any position—metaphysical or empirical—would do as a starting point, because all we need is just that: a perspective from which to dramatize a problem and set up options for solving it. But the pragmatic approach emphasizes that knowledge, truth, and morality are contingent on how we deal with specific problems. In general education, we are not teaching beliefs, we are teaching ways of seeing and questioning, how to deal with questions about who we are and why we are here, the problem of understanding what it is to be modern (or postmodern), the limits of rationality, the elusive nature of nature, the remarkable complexity of culture. Working on the theory that such an agenda is bigger than all of us, it is perhaps wise to handle an agenda of this seriousness modestly, in pragmatic, inquiry-based, problem-centered, case-book fashion. General education is not the place to just celebrate the disciplines themselves, it is the place to celebrate the issues they all have in common: questions of knowledge and power.

Why is this important? Because the link between education, democracy, and public knowledge is deeply embedded in concepts of American culture. It is no surprise, as Elizabeth Kelly puts it, that much of the struggle for democracy has taken place within the university. As she says,

> That is where much of the collective historical memory of a particular culture is generated, collected, analyzed, and preserved. As institutions, universities are distinguished from other public and private arenas because of venerable traditions of intellectual autonomy and academic freedom, which have formally, if not always substantively, shaped the quest for knowledge and truth. Although this history has hardly been unproblematic, the institutional constellation of higher education offers an existing framework within which individuals can work toward thinking, debating, and implementing a *praxis* of democratic public knowledge to inform a much larger, and ongoing, process of recognizing and extending the range of social, economic, and political possibilities and choices. . . .
>
> If public knowledge is a right available to all citizens rather than a privilege, and if the university is a place where such knowledge is produced and promulgated, then the struggle over the curriculum truly becomes a battle for democracy. What this entails, first of all, is the recognition that elitist conceptions of what it means to be an intellectual, whether articulated by the Left or the Right, are antithetical to democracy itself. Beyond that, where questions of intellectual identity and responsibility are concerned, this struggle for democracy involves linking the

utopian impulses of the "not yet" to what Vaclav Havel has eloquently described as "living in truth." This entails consistently and courageously taking "the side of truth against lies, the side of sense against nonsense, the side of justice against injustice," wherever and whenever possible.[1]

If liberal education is ideally about being-in-the-world, then this statement makes a good deal of sense. The fallacy of some of our thinking about liberal education is that we assume that the idea of the university has to be a real philosophy of the university, a set of beliefs or truths, all expressed in a narrative that nails it all down. For one thing, Newman's *Idea* nails little down; for another, the idea of a liberal general education is itself a work in progress, a discovery process amid knotty cultural, scientific, and social dilemmas, working with material that is rich and intellectually challenging but always open to argument, as our pre-Enlightenment and Enlightenment worlds knew well. What students need to learn is to make convincing argument. The idea of the university can just as easily be that we will dramatize and explore large issues of how we know anything at all, how the cultures we live in shape our viewpoints, values, and morality, and why it is interesting to find out why.

In fact, our recent culture wars have missed a crucial point altogether. Our problem is not so much that we have disregarded the great books or ignored important but marginalized voices or collected insufficient data about American culture, but that we have avoided teaching the great issues that affect society at large, no matter what culture has shaped us. The traditional liberal education curriculum has problems before it even gets to the classroom because its construction is deeply influenced by ways of seeing in the disciplines. It is clear that there is no easy definition of culture, for example, beyond its function as a set of social practices of groups, if one is an anthropologist; or if one is an English professor, culture is just about everything people do at any time and in any place. We know to be wary, though, of falling into the trap of keeping culture neatly defined, off to one side as the repository of blame or praise. We know to dramatize how the disciplines see culture differently, how it has always been in a deeply complex relation to society. If one thing has clearly emerged from the culture wars and from our recent concern for globalization it is that this relationship is certainly not getting any simpler. We often feel we cannot adequately define culture or democracy or any other term we hold dear except in the most perspectivist terms.

Thus our problems with the role of culture in defining a liberal education, for example, are not going to go away if we insist, as Daniel Bell does (and I refer to him only for his clear influence on conservative analysis), that culture is "a continual process of sustaining an identity through the coherence gained by a consistent aesthetic point of view, a moral conception of the self, and a style of life which exhibits those conceptions in the objects that adorn one's home and oneself and in the taste which expresses those points of view."[2] This is, of course, a little extreme. But Bell's neo-Arnoldian definition of culture, like that of many contemporary conservative humanists, is not uncommon in general education programs, without the home decorating lesson, of course, but certainly in terms of assuming that culture denotes "the realm of sensibility, of emotion and moral temper, and of intelligence, which seeks to order these feelings." Such a view is both mystifying and elitist. It mystifies the business of culture and it tends to take it off in directions that leave most of society, who presumably do not have adequately developed sensibilities and tastefully decorated homes, in the dust.

Instead, the culture students are more likely to relate to today is the culture we all live in, postmodern culture, the culture of our continuing obsession with modernity—which is itself hundreds of years old: complex and provocative in its protean nature, from the commercial to the aesthetically arcane, multilingual, from business practices to ghetto politics to styles of poetry writing. The more protean it is, happily the less chance we have of oversimplifying culture as a moral or aesthetic depository. But the issue is less a matter of how we construct a semiotics of culture, or how we define taste, and more a matter of asking, How do cultural events and texts serve to shape cultural behavior? How do we know what we like? and why do we like it? To what extent is the aesthetic ideological? What, if anything, makes a culture democratic? These are some of the questions that undergird the field of cultural studies, for example, and they do have a place in any thoroughgoing liberal education. They are also the kinds of questions I have tried to ask in this book concerning the nature of liberal education and its cultural context, steeped in corporate terminology. Indeed, one could make a strong argument that it is only through the study of academic culture as itself inherently contradictory that we can fashion an integrated liberal arts curriculum that will reflect the complex synergies between interpretations of culture and society. This means that the arts, humanities, and social and natural sciences (and professional schools too) all need to have a deeply symbiotic relation in defining a general education program, for all of them, not only the arts and humanities, have a role in defining culture at large.

Truth and Rhetoric

At this point the Democratic Educators must enter the argument: How can an education for culture be a democratic education? How do we achieve our social mission through this approach? That is what I want to explore in this chapter, for nothing is more precious than democratic freedoms, and no issue is closer to the university's mission. But few would assume that an overarching truth about democracy exists to make things easy. The question of truth itself is indeed a stubborn one, as we know. What helped propel the educational controversy among the ancient academies was the most basic philosophical question of all: the relation of knowledge to truth and how both shape the power of the state.

I have not been suggesting that general education merely return to epicurean pleasures. But sooner or later, we do run into people like Vaclav Havel talking about the truth, and we wonder—or should wonder—what he means. Academics have widely varying philosophical axes to grind on this subject, since for ancient wisdom, knowledge—based as it was on a combination of religious myth, a growing scientific empiricism, rhetorical strategies of argument, and propositional logic—seemed to take some precedence over culture if only because its concerns are so foundational. We might want to let this happen again, with or without the religious mythologizing, remembering that the most egregious acts of human genocide this century (not to mention any number of other examples of grotesquely inhuman behavior) have resulted from privileging culture over truth. On the other hand, truth has had its serious problems too. But related to the curriculum, it need not refer to a body of knowledge we might deem truthful. As Dewey pointed out, and Richard Rorty reinforces, truth, like moral values, arises out of situations. It is not a transcendent form. It is always contingent and a work in progress, always open to interpretation. We may know that murder is bad, but we have always to establish the truth of a particular murder. That is the law. Truth cannot be a priori a full or an empty term any more than *corporate responsibility* can; it is a term that fills and empties itself in varying social contexts. As Rorty puts it, "Dewey thought that . . . the pragmatic theory of truth was 'true in the pragmatic sense of truth: it works, it clears up difficulties, removes obscurities, puts individuals into more experimental, less dogmatic, and less arbitrarily skeptical relations to life.' "[3]

Dewey's definition of truth would make an excellent definition of liberal education, which, I have been arguing, is about the contingent conditions of truth in relation to key topics or to social issues: an international situation, the ethics of cloning, the meaning of *The Waste Land*, or even why Rembrandt's eyes have such allure. Students may make their own pragmatic discovery of what could be true and what is not; they would learn to develop habits of mind that stand them in good stead as responsible citizens. All of this goes on in many a classroom, of course, and my aim is to be anything but patronizing of those for whom these ideas are already well known. But it is worth emphasizing the cultural conditions of truth and its place in the curriculum as a particular concern. In interesting ways, theories of culture and society are narratives tested by theories of truth. For example, the issue of whether President Bill Clinton lied under oath or not about his relationship with Monica Lewinsky has been argued publicly by matching accounts of presidential behavior with definitions of *sex*. This was not simply the devious workings of the law or the especially devious workings of the presidential lawyers. This was the inevitable result of the social convention that in a court of law truth has to be argued for and not simply discovered.

Rhetoric, therefore, is inevitably part of the liberal education curriculum. Whether one agrees with the president's definition of sex or not because one finds his argument convincing or not becomes the whole point, not whether he is telling the truth in some kind of absolute sense. Truth is not an ideal, even if the need to tell the truth is idealistic in an important way. Truth is what appears to be the final step we reach in a process of inquiry, something we believe has credibility. Truth is what is left after all objections have been answered. Or, as Rorty once noted, truth "is what will be believed once the alienating and repressive forces of society are removed."

My aim is not to preach about the nature of truth but to suggest that a genuine liberal education can be quite literally about understanding the process of telling the truth: how truths are told in narratives, how those narratives work, how we can read and interpret them. It is about placing truths in their cultural contexts as much as it is a process of helping students argue for new truths. It is about the social forces that formulate and even alienate truth in that process; the cultural contradictions that condition truth itself. It is, therefore, the process of liberal learning that we need to preserve in the curriculum, not necessarily the received truths of the disciplines themselves or even a list of unexamined social virtues. Education is about the pursuit of truth, not for cynical or nihilistic ends, but as a hunt for meaning, the search for reliable evidence, a sound argument. Thus truth and rhetoric go hand in hand, not for sophistic motives, but to validate knowledge through argument.

The reliability of knowledge, then, has something to do with its rhetorical context, its staying power in argument, the art of writing and speech in the service of argument, not to mention the detailed use of evidence: historical context, ends, applications, data, known functions, and so on. For our skeptical age, there may not be such a thing as knowledge for its own sake, but many academics who embrace the need for a liberal education speak affectionately of the power of ideas not simply to construct or deconstruct themselves but to have a certain argumentative resilience. In a liberal general education we offer to school students in the art of rhetoric, joining with them in the arguments that are produced to see if we can form a community of authorship. Rhetoric trains us to produce knowledge that will democratize through argument. This makes it imperative, at the very least, that the university be in the business of developing useful knowledge for the common good and not merely for individual gain or the gain of the disciplines. The definition of the common good that we propose so readily in our university missions is not merely a matter of doing good to others or even just being good, but also of arguing for the good. That is the difference between the democratic agenda for knowledge that is the outcome of liberal learning and professionalized knowledge that simply has exchange value.

Educating for Democracy

The possible transformation of liberal education into what has been called a democratic education is a topic that grows out of the many demands that have been made on higher education over the past century, demands that have followed dramatic social and economic changes, challenges to teach responsible citizenship, the increased scope of mass education, the universalism proffered by new technologies, the remarkable development of the global economy. One cannot help but revisit again the means and ends of liberal learning as somehow related to the means and ends of democracy itself.

As the political philosopher Giovanni Sartori has put it,

> Political systems are all human-made, but only "modern" politics can be meaningfully said to be intentful, that is, driven by the deliberate pursuit of a better life (in common). It is notoriously true that outcomes seldom are as intended. Indeed the inherent risk of the "willed politics" is to backfire on themselves, to result in the very reverse of what was intended. But this has not been the case with liberal democracies. Our democracies disappoint but do not betray. This is so because the theory of liberal democracy is the one theory of politics that includes a theory of its practice, that comprises ends *and* means. Still, ends can always devour their means. Surely, liberal democracy cannot be taken for granted."[4]

Neither can a purposeful education for liberal democracy be taken for granted, for social and economic ends will otherwise surely devour its means. We need to define the relevance of the liberal arts as an education for responsible citizenship and not simply a political battlefield for cultural values and tables of literary contents. There is some controversy about this, though. Not surprisingly, liberal studies have been associated in the minds of some with the politics of late-sixties radicals teaching gender and cultural studies and clinging to theories of social engineering through endless entitlement programs. And the Left today tells us that the most important challenge we face in higher education is to "perform a noble public service, to undertake teaching as a form of social criticism, to . . . play a major role in animating a democratic public culture."[5] But the Right wants clear values that sustain a liberal-democratic, capitalist culture. It considers the academic world the heart of the moral problem, thanks to its championing of postmodernism and a curriculum that supposedly confirms the death of truth, beauty, and family values. So the academy is often ridiculed for replacing classic literary texts with autobiographical polemics, and sociology with leadership courses in which, it is rumored, one can even read T. S. Eliot's verse drama *Murder in the Cathedral* as a study in contrasting management styles.

Relatively few teachers go to any extremes, and specifically leftist or rightist curricula are not as widespread as some would like us to believe. Most academics like to keep their options—and their course outcomes—open. But the academy is vulnerable to criticism that faculty have balkanized the campus into minidepartments, largely to make it ungovernable, so that we can return to our whiskies without fear of interference, listen to each other groan, and watch youth, starved of moral and cultural nourishment, grow pale and specter-thin and die.

It is not surprising, then, that the word *liberal*—especially when attached to *education*—is politically ambiguous because it connotes a mind so open its brains have fled. The liberal mind is not one of those hard-edged, ascetic, neocon minds that decide quickly and clearly what is needed in an incisive way; or so we must assume from the writing of journalists who delight in publishing at regular intervals examples of the absurd preciosity of academic life in English departments.

At the same time, though, some (if not all) of the energy driving the humanities today derives from a social science imperative, as it were, for increasing the impact of liberal education as a democratic education. Led by such scholars as Amy Gutmann, Denis Thompson, Benjamin Barber, Elizabeth Kelly, Henry Giroux, and David Steiner,[6] we are once again awakening to the call for democratic education and citizenship training, first outlined by John Dewey in 1916 in *Democracy and Education*. Indeed, a democratic education is a key part of the foundational liberal education I have been describing. One could argue, for example, that a democratic education demands some formal study at the undergraduate level of the basics of how the law, the economy, and government relate to organize culture and society. It demands some knowledge of how each are formed, transmitted, celebrated, interpreted, and shared. Democracy, after all, is a conscious cultural choice.

Thus, in addition to a number of the topics I have outlined, the undergraduate curriculum could be directly concerned with the nature of civic responsibilities within a liberal democracy; with the historical development of social institutions and capitalism, along with alternative systems; with the social construction of power; with the impact of new international economies and information systems on national identity; with the nature of global interdependency; even with the history of how and why knowledge in the university is organized the way it is and the effects that has on democratic learning. Most students leave college and university without a single course that explains the development and organization of higher education in the United States and why they are studying subjects the way they do and how that course of study has a social mission.

We impart little sense of how and why our culture, society, and polity are organized as they are, and how the organization of knowledge affects what we learn.

Yet if we had to choose one aspect of the mission of the modern university that a majority might agree on I suspect it would be to support the American way of life: namely, liberal democracy, its knowledge economy, and its financial systems. Strange, then, that we so easily gloss over the fact that terms like the *common good* or the *good society* or *civility* or *freedom* are indeed loaded terms and require an education in democracy to ensure their safety. A democratic education is not about politics as such—partisanship in the classroom—but about inquiry and debate that create the condition for politics, which is the condition of our everyday lives. It is, therefore, philosophical, cultural, and even aesthetic in the broadest sense of the terms.

Any theory of a democratic education implies several things at once: an education for democracy, an education that derives from democratic values, and an education that democratizes learning itself. The first option is widely accepted; it is the theory that informs most university mission statements. We know what democracy is, so we educate for it—democracy being, of course, the guarantee of basic freedoms we enjoy or hope to enjoy in the United States. But theories of democracy itself are rather more complex than this, as scholars are careful to point out. We know that to talk about democracy is to talk about efforts to pursue an egalitarian political and social system that is just and individually empowering. But we have many issues to encounter along the way, such as the question of the extent of democracy: How much democracy do we need and how much can we tolerate? How does democracy account for freedom and individuality? inequality? liberalism? the market? And so on. The continual chatter about education as a public good tends to assume that we do not have to theorize the democracy we want because the market will define it for us. But that is very dangerous, as I have shown, because the current market is anything but conducive to a truly democratic system of higher education. If democracy is the one political system that by definition *is* its own process, then that process is by no means self-evident. Democratic education is apparently based on open inquiry and argument, but how far do we go in analyzing democracy before we can promote it? Are democracy's discontents part of the packet? Of course they are, but the more politicized democracy gets, the more we seem to prefer concepts of leadership skills and cocurricular activities dedicated to empowerment, mainly because they tell us how to succeed in a democracy, even without the theory of what a democracy actually is.

It is easier to talk of the second option as having more catholic scope: a democratic education is one that derives from democratic values—from constitutional values, especially. This is controversial too, of course, because the Constitution itself is controversial, as the law makes clear. Furthermore, choosing democratic values can be quite selective. Do we include free-market thinking? unlimited debate? liberal capitalism? civil disobedience? Amy Gutmann has put it wisely: "Since the democratic ideal of education is that of *conscious* social reproduction . . . [e]ducation may be more broadly defined to include every social influence that makes us who we are."[7] So we should look at all our values, controversial or not, which makes way for Henry Giroux and some of the more progressive theorists in higher education today. Giroux explains the educational mission with more rhetorical bite: higher education should clearly deny that "profit-making is the sole purpose of democracy and accumulating material goods the essence of the good life. . . . By focusing on how authority and power shape knowledge, how the teaching of broader social values provides safeguards against turning citizenship skills into training places for the workplace, and how culture works to put into place particular forms of agency . . . [we can] reaffirm the importance of the curriculum as a site of critique, critical exchange, and social struggle."[8]

The problem with the social mission of the university, of course, is that it is the one most laden with value judgments even while it is reluctant to hammer home the message of how those judgments should be made. How far is curiosity supposed to go in establishing social values? How much of a democratic education should be about social struggle? And I ask these questions knowing that few if any campuses will advertise that the rhetoric of their best intent is social change. Indeed, a bare 27 percent of faculty answering the survey mentioned in chapter 1 believe it is a high priority "to help students learn how to bring about change in American society."

The concept of a democratic education has come to the fore in recent years primarily through the multiculturalism promoted by faculty who insist that the university community should reflect the pluralism not only of all its constituents but of American society at large. As we all know, this has produced considerable controversy, raising questions of whether all cultural practices should receive equal exposure in the curriculum and whether students and faculty should automatically gain privileges determined by gender, sexual preference, or color. Even more frequently today, though, we hear of concern for a definition of democratic education that emphasizes not simply accurate social reproduction but the terms of a common global citizenship. To speak of the common good requires us to place in the foreground of general education not only the deep controversies of cultural formation but a broad sense of what it means to live in a world of dramatically shrinking boundaries.

That is the message of Gutmann's *Democratic Education*. She explains things this way: A democratic education

> supports a "politics of recognition" based on respect for indi-
> viduals and their equal rights as citizens, not on deference to
> tradition, proportional representation of groups, or the survival

rights of cultures. . . . Democratic education, therefore, should not limit its vision to a single society. It should encourage students to consider the rights and responsibilities of both a shared citizenship and a shared humanity with all people, regardless of citizenship. Cultivating mutual respect entails understanding people not merely as abstractions, upon which teachers and students project their own conception of what constitutes a good life, but understanding people in their own particularity, with their own lives to lead and their own conceptions of what constitutes a good life."[9]

The irony here, though, is that the more inclusively particular we try to be, the more abstract we become. One can indeed argue with good reason that an enlightened and politically defused definition of a democratic education begins with the recognition of individuality. It includes respect for individual talent, regardless of whether it is large or small. It ends with recognition, too, of a global civil society, a pilgrimage not uncommon in the history of American ideas.

But recognition alone will not do it. Broad concepts of a democratic education have their place but are easily coopted by the rhetoric of sentiment, even if they are not in Gutmann's own work. How many campuses actually teach the dialectics of social struggle and serious cultural critique as part of a general education, as Giroux has been asking? How many ask students, as part of their general education, to critique the nature of capital and liberal democracy, to attempt to understand its contradictions? True, we can, I suppose, always blame postmodernism for the fact that critique with predictable ideological outcomes itself seems rather old. It worked for Socrates to wander about questioning students on the basic principles of their civic responsibility because he knew what the answers were, and a specific answer, rather than an open-ended learning process, was perhaps uppermost in Socrates' mind. There is no one answer anymore given the shifting perspectivism of our times. But answers still have to be argued for in today's classrooms, or else the subtlety of debate implicit in theories of democratic education easily gives way to what Benjamin Barber has memorably called the "aristocracy of everyone":[10] the teaching of privatized ethical mandates designed to make us feel better about ourselves and justify any means of getting rich. The public nature of democratic education is not about the contemplative life alone, with its theoretically cosmopolitan and aesthetic values. So it is not about teaching goodness. And it is not simply about community learning experiences and civic engagement that do not actively examine how cultures are formed and evolve. It is about teaching students, especially in undergraduate general education, to actively engage in the debate over democracy's discontents as well as its delights.

So we come to the third and most controversial definition of democratic education: an education that democratizes learning itself. Democratizing learning means doing a lot of work with open access to college, open treatment of social themes, open acceptance of cultural critique as a primary function of education, and open discussion of the pedagogy of political education. Higher education, if it is to be a democratic education, is by its very nature political. It means that to democratize learning is to focus on what makes learning truly important for all. How, then, do we define such inclusiveness, along with its accountability? How do we measure the dialectical process of a political education, which in a democratic education is every bit as important as the outcomes? What are important pedagogies for democratic learning? After all, if learning and some kind of training for the mind is the key to all aspects of our multifoliate mission, properly integrated with our social mission, then what is it about that training for the mind—for we cannot take "mind" for granted—that ensures success? What specific habits of mind drive thinking to create values and not merely buy into what is there?

A possible answer is that critical thinking amounts to habits of inquiry that have been learned the hard way, by fact finding and working through the protocols of academic debate, carefully reading between the lines, tentatively drawing conclusions or finding it impossible to do so because certain conditions prevail that must first be mediated. But one important reason for the halfhearted efforts by the modern university to theorize itself in clear public statements is that it is more interested in depoliticizing education and creating a set of watered-down democratic (and patriotic) virtues as learning outcomes. At least as far as undergraduate education is concerned, the ideological mainstream in higher education theory has often been so vacuumed clean of any hint of the natural subversiveness of thought and of any social agenda short of making students and parents feel comfortable with the status quo that we tend to talk today about democratic education using the rhetoric of mission statements.

A democratic education must in fact do all three things I have listed above. First, it must be an education for democracy, for the greater good of a just society—but it cannot assume that society is, a priori, just. Second, it must argue for its means as well as its ends. It must derive from the history of ideas, from long-standing democratic values and practices, which include the ability to argue and critique but also to tolerate ambiguity. And third, it must participate in the democratic social process, displaying not only a moral preference for recognizing the rights of others and accepting them, too, but for encouraging argument and cultural critique. In short, a university education is a democratic education because it mediates liberal democracy and the cultural contradictions of capitalism. That definition, I think, is the middle ground between the spokespeople for modest reform, those who focus on the language of common decency and those who focus on education as mainly about social struggle and change. Higher education, if it really is the place where we reproduce society, which even relatively conservative scholars agree is the case, must be the place where a democratic education itself is vigorously debated.

Of course, few if any universities are going to announce as their mission that they stand against crass commercial values, the accumulation of wealth, and social oppression, though that might be refreshingly honest. Neither will they say that they promote a kind of four-year boot camp for the mind where, by God, you'll learn to see the real value of living in a democracy by learning how to argue through its contradictions. Few universities if any will tell us that a democratic society thrives only on open debate that could very well compromise our strongly held values and maybe even make us feel uncomfortable. Nor will they seek to define the power that shapes knowledge and culture, or say that mere training for the workplace is not good enough, that the curriculum is indeed "the site of critique, critical exchange, and social struggle." Realistically, however enticing, this is rather too political a slogan for a university mission statement. Many will even have trouble saying what Gutmann says of political education, that it has "moral primacy over other purposes of public education in a moral society."[11] Yet until some basic democratic values that do have to do with the importance of informed but vigorous debate, problem solving, critique, and an awareness of knowledge as power are part of the missionary agenda—and an appropriately inclusive rhetoric is found for them— the university is not going to be able to explain how it gets from engaging students in the business of education to the creation of democratic values themselves.

Notes

Preface

1. See, for example, Lewis M. Branscomb, Fumio Kodama, and Richard Florida, eds., *Industrializing Knowledge: University-Industry Linkages in Japan and the United States* (Cambridge: MIT Press, 1999); James S. Fairweather, *Entrepreneurship and Higher Education* (Washington, D.C.: Association for the Study of Higher Education, 1988); Roger L. Geiger, *To Advance Knowledge: The Growth of American Research Universities, 1900–1940* (New York: Oxford University Press, 1986); Roger L. Geiger, *Research and Relevant Knowledge: American Research Universities Since World War II* (New York: Oxford University Press, 1993); Hugh Davis Graham and Nancy Diamond, *The Rise of American Research Universities: Elites and Challenges in the Postwar Era* (Baltimore: Johns Hopkins University Press, 1997); Merle Jacob and Tomas Hellstrom, *The Future of Knowledge Production in the Academy* (Buckingham, U.K.: Society for Research into Higher Education & Open University Press, 2000); Martin Kenney, *Biotechnology: The University-Industrial Complex* (New Haven: Yale University Press, 1986); William Massy, *Leveraged Learning: Technology's Role in Restructuring Higher Education* (Stanford: Stanford Forum for Higher Education Futures, 1995); Sheila Slaughter and Larry L. Leslie, *Academic Capitalism: Politics, Policies, and the Entrepreneurial University* (Baltimore: Johns Hopkins University Press, 1997); John Wilson, *Academic Science, Higher Education, and the Federal Government, 1950–1983* (Chicago: University of Chicago Press, 1983).

2. Two works in particular, published just as I was completing this book, are useful: Henry A. Giroux and Kostas Myrsiades, eds., *Beyond the Corporate University: Culture and Pedagogy in the New Millennium* (Lanham, Md.: Rowman and Littlefield, 2001); Stanley Aronowitz, *The Knowledge Factory: Dismantling the Corporate University and Creating True Higher Learning* (New York: Beacon Press, 2001).

3. There are many books that have examined the supposed moral collapse, decadent curriculum, and general malaise of the American university. I am

referring specifically to one of the more scholarly analyses of the contemporary American university, Bill Reading's *The University in Ruins* (Cambridge: Harvard University Press, 1996).

Chapter 1. A Complex Mission in a Market Culture

1. Useful histories of American higher education include Laurence R. Veysey, *The Emergence of the American University* (Chicago: University of Chicago Press, 1965); Frederick Rudolph, *The American College and University: A History* (Athens: University of Georgia Press); Christopher J. Lucas, *American Higher Education: A History* (New York: St. Martin's Press, 1994); Michael B. Katz, *Reconstructing American Education* (Cambridge: Harvard University Press, 1987).

2. Quoted in Lucas, *American Higher Education*, 181.

3. See Roger L. Geiger, *To Advance Knowledge: The Growth of American Research Universities, 1900–1940* (New York: Oxford University Press, 1986), 2.

4. Source: National Science Foundation, quoted in *Chronicle of Higher Education*, March 1, 2002.

5. The mission statement is that of the University of Denver.

6. Mission statements from the following universities: Vanderbilt, Rice, Drexel, Penn State, Cincinnati, the Maryland system, Cal Poly Pomona, Western Michigan, Wayne State, North Texas, Central Florida, Utah, Middle Tennessee State, University of Massachusetts at Boston, Southern Methodist, the Georgia State system, Washington University in Saint Louis, Colorado at Boulder, Nevada at Las Vegas, San Diego, Alfred, Iowa, the Wisconsin state system, Saint Joseph's, Cal State Fullerton, San Francisco State, South Arkansas, Clemson, and Oregon State.

7. James J. Duderstadt, *A University for the 21st Century* (Ann Arbor: University of Michigan Press, 2000), 333–34.

8. Ibid., 51–52.

9. Survey results by Richard Hersh published in *Change*, March/April, 1997, 16–23.

10. Denise K. Magner, "Faculty Highlights Drift from Western Canon," *Chronicle of Higher Education*, September 13, 1996, and Denise K. Magner, "A New Report Details the Graying of America's Professoriate," *Chronicle of Higher Education*, August 30, 1999.

11. Pierre Bourdieu, "The Market of Symbolic Goods," *Poetics* 14 (1985).

12. Christopher Lucas, *Crisis in the Academy* (New York: St. Martin's, 1996), 88.

13. Lester Thurow, *The Future of Capitalism* (New York: William Morrow, 1996), 276–77.

14. See Benjamin Barber, *Strong Democracy: Participatory Politics for a New Age* (Berkeley: University of California Press, 1984).

15. Source for statistics: U.S.Department of Education, *Digest of Educational Statistics, 1977,* tables 241, 244.

16. *Digest of Educational Statistics, 2000,* Introduction (U.S. Government National Center for Education Statistics, http://nces.ed.gov/pubs2001/digest).

17. "Evaluation and the Academy: Are We Doing the Right Thing?: Grade Inflation and Letters of Recommendation," 10, a report from the American Academy of Arts and Sciences by Henry Rosovsky and Matthew Hartley, available on-line at www.amacad.org.

18. Quoted in Thomas Bender, "Politics, Intellect, and the American University," in Thomas Bender and Carl Schorske, eds., *American Academic Culture in Transformation* (Princeton: Princeton University Press, 1998), 21.

19. Giovanni Sartori, *The Theory of Democracy Revisited—Part Two: The Classical Issues,* (Chatham, N.J.: Chatham House, 1987), 410.

20. Daniel Bell, *The Cultural Contradictions of Capitalism* (New York: Basic Books, 1996), 14–15.

Chapter 2. The Consumerist Culture of the University

1. Amy Wu, "Scrimping on College Has Its Own Price," *New York Times,* March 3, 1996, 12.

2. U.S. Department of Education, *Digest of Educational Statistics, 1997,* 324.

3. *Digest of Educational Statistics, 2000,* chapter 3, "Postsecondary Education."

4. *Wall Street Journal,* October 10, 1994.

5. Peter David, "Inside the Knowledge Factory," *The Economist,* October 4, 1997.

6. Stephen Burd, "Report Finds Most Private Colleges Out of Reach for Needy Students; Lobbyists Disagree," *Chronicle of Higher Education,* on-line edition, Monday, January 7, 2002. The report, from the Lumina Foundation, has been disputed by David L. Warren, president of the National Association of Independent Colleges and Universities, who claims that in 1999–2000 private institutions provided $8 billion in student aid to offset costs, "more than their students received from all federal and state grant aid combined." The Lumina Foundation has expressed doubt about this claim, saying that "data provided by colleges and universities to the College Board and the U.S. Department of Education indicate that institutional aid awards at the vast majority of independent colleges would have to be more than double, and in many cases triple, the average award to make the schools affordable to low-income students. Given the trends in packaging of student aid, it is very unlikely that many made such high awards to their low-income students." The quote is from the article by Burd. The report is entitled "Unequal Opportunity: Disparities in College Access Among the 50 States" and is available at www.luminafoundation.org.

7. Arthur Levine, "How the Academic Profession Is Changing," *Daedalus*, Fall 1997 (*The American Academic Profession*), 6.

8. *Digest of Educational Statistics, 2000*, table 175.

9. Ibid., table 184.

10. Arthur Levine and Jeanette S. Cureton, "Collegiate Life: An Obituary," *Change: The Magazine of Higher Learning*, May/June 1998, 15. See also their book, *When Hope and Fear Collide: A Portrait of Today's College Student* (San Francisco: Jossey-Bass, 1998).

11. Levine and Cureton, "Collegiate Life: An Obituary," 7–8.

12. Ibid., 15.

13. Leslie Berger, "The Therapy Generation," *New York Times*, January 13, 2002, on-line edition of Education Life.

14. Levine and Cureton, "College Life: An Obituary," 9.

15. Ted Marchese, "Disengaged Students II," *Change*, March/April 1998, 4 and May/June, 1998, 4.

16. See "The Burden of Borrowing" a report from the Higher Education Project of the State Public Interest Research Groups, March 2002. Also Alex P. Kellogg, "New Report on Student-Loan Data Finds Debt Loads Burdensome for Many Graduates," *Chronicle of Higher Education*, on-line edition, Friday, March 8, 2002; and Diana Jean Schemo, "More Graduates Mired in Debt, Survey Finds," *New York Times*, March 8, 2002, on-line edition.

17. See Richard Light, *Making the Most of College: Students Speak Their Minds* (Cambridge: Harvard University Press, 2001)

18. Donald N. Langenberg, "Diplomas and Degrees Are Obsolescent," *Chronicle of Higher Education*, September 12, 1997, A64.

19. Ibid., 175.

20. Lisa Guernsey, "Tuition Costs Continue to Outpace Median Incomes, Report Says," *Chronicle of Higher Education*, September 6, 1996, A59.

21. The College Board, *Trends in College Pricing 2000*, table 5 and figure 6.

22. Yilu Zhao, "As College Endowments Dwindle, Big Tuition Increases Fill the Void," *New York Times*, February 22, 2002, on-line edition.

23. Andrew Brownstein, "Tuition Rises Faster than Inflation, and Faster than in Previous Year, *Chronicle of Higher Education*, October 27, 2000.

24. At the time of writing, Congress is considering raising the Pell grant to $5,000, but that is unlikely to make much difference to students seeking private school education.

25. The College Board, *Trends in College Pricing 2000*, table 6 and figure 5.

26. Julianne Basinger, "Two Studies Describe Growth in Student-Loan Debt since 1992," *Chronicle of Higher Education*, November 14, 1997.

27. Ibid.

28. Schemo, "More Graduates Mired in Debt."

29. Quoted from Kellogg, "New Report on Student-Loan Data" (see note 16), an article reporting on "The Burden of Borrowing."

30. *Chronicle of Higher Education*, "Daily News," August 28, 1997: "Recent College Graduates Are Deep in Debt but Have Good Job Prospects, Study Finds," on-line edition. Summary from report "Now What? Life After College for Recent Graduates" by the Institute for Higher Education Policy.

31. Schemo, "More Graduates Mired in Debt."

32. Source: Jacqueline E. King, "Too Many Students Are Holding Jobs for Too Many Hours," *Chronicle of Higher Education*, May 1, 1998, A72. King is director of federal policy analysis at the American Council of Education.

33. Terry W. Hartle, "How People Pay for College: A Dramatic Shift," *Chronicle of Higher Education*, November 9, 1994, A52.

34. Mary Geraghty, "More Students Quitting College Before Sophomore Year, Data Show," *Chronicle of Higher Education*, July 19, 1996, A35.

35. David Labaree, *How to Succeed in School Without Really Learning: The Credentials Race in American Higher Education* (New Haven: Yale University Press, 1997), 1–13.

36. The College Board, *Trends in College Pricing 2000*, figure 1.

37. *Digest of Educational Statistics 1997*, 173 and tables 172, 181.

38. Arthur M. Hauptman and Jamie P. Merisotis, "The College Tuition Spiral: An Examination of Why Charges Are Increasing," American Council on Education (New York: Macmillan, 1990).

39. The College Board, *Trends in College Pricing 2000*, Introduction.

40. Leo Reisberg, "Survey Finds Growth in Tuition 'Discounting' by Private Colleges," *Chronicle of Higher Education*, March 13, 1998.

41. See, for example, Michele N-K. Collison, "Private Colleges Unveil Tuition Discounts and Loans to Woo Middle-Income Students," *Chronicle of Higher Education*, June 24, 1992; Steve Stecklow, "Colleges Manipulate Financial-Aid Offers, Shortchanging Many," *Wall Street Journal*, April 1, 1996; Christopher Shea, "Sweetening the Pot for the Best Students," *Chronicle of Higher Education*, May 17, 1996; Andrew Delbanco, "Scholarships for the Rich," *New York Times Magazine*, September 1, 1996; Ben Gose, "Colleges Turn to 'Leveraging' to Attract Well-Off Students," *Chronicle of Higher Education*, September 13, 1996; Peter Passell, "Rise in Merit-Based Aid Alters College Market Landscape," *New York Times*, April 9, 1997; Ben Gose, "Recent Shifts on Aid by Elite Colleges Signal New Push to Help the Middle Class," *Chronicle of Higher Education*, March 6, 1998; Ethan Bronner, "Universities Giving Less Financial Aid on Basis of Need," *New York Times*, June 21, 1998. The definitive accounts of financial aid in American colleges and universities are in two books by the economist/administrators Michael S. McPherson and Morton Owen Schapiro, *Keeping College Affordable: Government and Educational Opportunity* (Washington: Brookings Institution, 1991), and *The Student Aid Game: Meeting Need and Rewarding Talent in American Higher Education* (Princeton: Princeton University Press, 1998). The latter deals in some detail with the newly developing trend toward merit-based aid.

42. See Eric Hoover, "28 Private Colleges Agree to Use Common Approaches to Student Aid," *Chronicle of Higher Education,* July 20, 2001.

43. Allegation by Michael S. McPherson, president of Macalaster College, cited in ibid."

44. Ibid.

45. Peter Carstensen, "Colleges and Student Aid: Collusion or Competition?" *Chronicle of Higher Education,* August 10, 2001.

46. Source: *Chronicle of Higher Education* Website infobank, 6/25/98. The top ten college endowments totaled nearly $50 billion in 1997.

47. John L. Pulley, "No Gain, Slight Pain," *Chronicle of Higher Education,* March 16, 2001.

48. See McPherson and Schapiro, *The Student Aid Game.* According to their study, affluent students have chosen big-name private universities rather than small colleges.

49. "The Halls of Ivy Imitate Halls of Commerce," *Wall Street Journal,* October 10, 1994.

50. See Aaron Donovan, "Education as Investment, Really" in *New York Times,* January 6, 2002.

51. Gordon C. Winston, "Why Can't a College Be More Like a Firm?" *Change,* September/October, 1997, and George Winston, "New Dangers in Old Traditions: The Reporting of Economic Performance in Colleges and Universities," *Change,* January/February, 1993.

52. This quote and others from Winston are from "Why Can't a College?"

Chapter 3. A Corporate Ethos

1. Thorstein Veblen, *The Higher Learning in America* (New York: Sagamore Press, 1918, 1957), 62–64.

2. James F. Slevin, "Keeping the University Occupied and Out of Trouble" in "The University of Excellence," *The ADE Bulletin* (Bulletin of the Association of Departments of English, a subsidiary of the Modern Language Association), Number 130, Winter 2002, 51.

3. Bill Readings, *The University in Ruins* (Cambridge: Harvard University Press, 1996).

4. Readings, *The University in Ruins,* 24.

5. Alexander Astin, *Assessment for Excellence: The Philosophy and Practice of Assessment and Evaluation in Higher Education* (New York: American Council on Education and Macmillan, 1991), 199.

6. Thomas Bender, "Politics, Intellect, and the American University," in Thomas Bender and Carl Schorske, eds., *American Academic Culture in Transformation* (Princeton: Princeton University Press, 1998), 9, 47.

7. Clyde Barrow, *Universities and the Capitalist State: Corporate Liberalism*

and the Reconstruction of American higher Education, 1894–1928 (Madison: University of Wisconsin Press, 1990), 14.

8. For an important discussion of the issue, one that argues for a definition of "dominant ideology" as carried by mass communication media, again see John B. Thompson's *Ideology and Modern Culture* (Stanford University Press, 1990), 92–96.

9. Ibid., 19

10. Ibid., 26.

11. John Guillory, *Cultural Capital: The Problem of Literary Canon Formation* (Chicago: University of Chicago Press, 1993).

12. Thompson, *Ideology and Modern Culture,* 11.

Chapter 4. Faculty and the Division of Labor

1. Louis Menand, "The Limits of Academic Freedom," in Louis Menand, ed., *The Future of Academic Freedom* (Chicago: University of Chicago Press, 1996), 4.

2. Quoted in "Education Life," *New York Times,* Sunday, January 4, 1998, 33.

3. Catherine R. Stimpson, "Activist Trustees Wield Power Gone Awry," *Chronicle of Higher Education,* January 16, 1998, B4–B5.

4. Marvin Lazerson, "Who Owns Higher Education? The Changing Face of Governance," *Change,* March/April 1997, 12.

5. David Harvey, *The Condition of Postmodernity* (Oxford: Basil Blackwell, 1989, 1990), 101–03.

6. Michael Katz, *Reconstructing American Education* (Cambridge: Harvard University Press, 1989), 164.

7. Ibid., 37.

8. Ibid., 165–66.

9. Ibid., 167.

10. Ibid., 178.

11. Clyde Barrow, *Universities and the Capitalist State* (Madison: University of Wisconsin Press, 1990), 10–11.

12. John B. Thompson, *Ideology and Modern Culture* (Palo Alto: Stanford University Press, 1990), 10.

13. Daniel Bell, *The Cultural Contradictions of Capitalism* (New York: Basic Books, 1996), 14.

14. Ibid., 283–84

15. U.S. Department of Education, *Digest of Education Statistics, 1977,* table 250.

16. Alan Ryan, *Liberal Anxieties and Liberal Education* (New York: Hill and Wang, 1998), 183–84.

17. Michael Sandel, *Democracy's Discontent: America In Search of a Public Philosophy* (Cambridge: Harvard University Press, 1996), 4.

Chapter 5. The Ideal of a Liberal Education

1. Bruce Kimball, *Orators and Philosophers: A History of the Idea of Liberal Education* (New York: College Entrance Examination Board, 1995), 4.

2. Ibid., 4.

3. Ibid., 6.

4. Ibid., 7.

5. For an excellent discussion of related issues, see Richard A. Lanham, *The Electronic Word: Democracy, Technology, and the Arts* (Chicago: University of Chicago Press, 1993. The quotation from Richard McKeon's *Rhetoric: Essays in Invention and Discovery,* ed. Mark Backman (Woodbridge, Conn.: Ox Bow, 1987), 18, is on p. 166 of Lanham's book.

6. John Henry Cardinal Newman, *The Idea of a University* (1852; New York: Doubleday, 1959), 195.

7. Ibid., 145−46.

8. Ibid., 191−92.

9. Ibid., 137.

10. Ibid., 146.

11. Ibid., 192.

12. John Dewey, "Logical Conditions of a Scientific Treatment of Morality," in Reginald D. Archambault, ed., *John Dewey on Education: Selected Writings* (Chicago: University of Chicago Press, 1974), 52.

13. Cotton Mather, *History of Harvard* (1702), in Richard Hofstadter and Wilson Smith, eds., *American Higher Education: A Documentary History* (Chicago: University of Chicago Press, 1961) 1:13−19.

14. See Hofstadter and Smith, *American Higher Education,* 275−91.

15. Gerald Graff, *Professing Literature: An Institutional History* (Chicago: University of Chicago Press, 1987).

16. Thomas Bender, "Politics, Intellect, and the American University," in Thomas Bender and Carl Schorske, eds., *American Academic Culture in Transformation* (Princeton: Princeton University Press, 1998), 17.

17. Ibid., 22.

18. Ibid., 46.

Chapter 6. Knowledge, Modernity, and Pragmatism

1. See, for example, Ernest L. Boyer, *College: The Undergraduate Experience in America* (New York: Harper and Row, 1987); id., *Scholarship Reconsidered: Priorities of the Professoriate* (Princeton: Carnegie Foundation for the Advancement of Teaching, 1990); W. B. Carnochan, *The Battleground of the Curriculum: Liberal Education and American Experience* (Stanford: Stanford University Press, 1993); Jerry G. Gaff, *General Education Today: A Critical Analysis of Controversies, Practices, and Reforms* (San Francisco: Jossey-Bass, 1983); id., *New Life*

for the College Curriculum: Assessing Achievements and Furthering Progress in the Reform of General Education (San Francisco: Jossey-Bass, 1991); Darryl J. Gless and Barbara Herrnstein Smith, eds., *The Politics of Liberal Education* (Durham: Duke University Press, 1992); Gerald Graff, *Beyond the Culture Wars: How Teaching the Conflicts Can Revitalize American Education* (New York: W. W. Norton, 1992); Bruce Kimball, *Orators and Philosophers: A History of the Idea of Liberal Education,* 2d ed. (New York: College Entrance Examination Board, 1995); id., *The Condition of American Liberal Education: Pragmatism and a Changing Tradition,* Robert Orrill, exec. ed. (New York: College Entrance Examination Board, 1995); The *Challenge of Connecting Learning* from the Project on Liberal Learning, Study-in-Depth, and the Arts and Sciences Major (Washington, D.C.: Association of American Colleges, 1991).

2. In 1995, Bruce Kimball assembled a list "seven developments . . . becoming prominent in liberal education . . . that have conceptual and historical roots or find principled rationale in pragmatism . . . multiculturalism, values and service, community and citizenship, general education, commonality and cooperation between college and other levels of the education system, teaching interpreted as learning and inquiry, assessment" (Kimball, *The Condition of American Liberal Education,* 97).

3. Ibid.

4. Stanley Aronowitz, *The Knowledge Factory: Dismantling the Corporate University and Creating True Higher Learning* (New York: Beacon Press, 2001).

5. "Washington to Congress on a National University, 1790, 1796" in Richard Hofstadter and Wilson Smith, eds., *American Higher Education: A Documentary History* (Chicago: University of Chicago Press, 1961) 1:157–58.

6. Frederick Rudolph, "Consumerism in Higher Education," *Liberal Education* (published by the Association of American Colleges), Summer 1993, 6.

7. Martha Nussbaum, *Cultivating Humanity: A Classical Defense of Reform in Liberal Education* (Cambridge: Harvard University Press, 1997), 9–11.

8. Dale Neef, *The Knowledge Economy* (Boston: Butterworth-Heinemann, 1998), 2–3.

9. Peter F. Drucker, *Post-Capitalist Society* (New York: HarperBusiness, 1993), 211–16

10. Ibid., 46.

11. Ibid., 216–18.

12. Ibid., 214.

13. See Kimball et al., *The Condition of American Liberal Education.*

14. John Dewey, "School Conditions and the Training of Thought," in Reginald D. Archambault, ed., *John Dewey on Education: Selected Writings* (Chicago: University of Chicago Press, 1974), 52.

15. In *John Dewey on Education,* 427–39.

16. John Dewey, *Human Nature and Conduct* (1922; New York: Random House, 1950), 205–06.

17. John M. Ellis, "Poisoning the Wells of Knowledge," *New York Times,* Saturday, March 28, 1998, A25. See also Ellis's *Literature Lost: Social Agendas and the Corruption of the Humanities* (New Haven: Yale University Press, 1999).

18. Daniel Bell, *The Cultural Contradictions of Capitalism* (New York: Basic Books, 1976, 1996), 37.

19. Frank Rich, "Lord of the Flies," *New York Times,* Saturday, March 28, 1998: A25.

Chapter 7. Democratic Education

1. Elizabeth A. Kelly, *Education, Democracy, and Public Knowledge* (Boulder: Westview Press, 1995), 88–89, 95–96. The quotation from Vaclav Havel is from his "I Take the Side of Truth: An Interview with Antoine Spire," in *Open Letters: Selected Writings, 1965–1990* (New York: Vintage Books, 1992), 248.

2. Daniel Bell, *The Cultural Contradictions of Capitalism* (New York: Basic Books, 1996), 36.

3. Richard Rorty, "Does Academic Freedom Have Philosophical Presuppositions?" in Louis Menand, ed., *The Future of Academic Freedom* (Chicago: University of Chicago Press, 1996), 34.

4. Giovanni Sartori, *The Theory of Democracy Revisited: Part Two—The Classical Issues* (Chatham, N.J., Chatham House, 1987), 506.

5. Henry Giroux, "Liberal Arts Education and the Struggle for Public Life: Dreaming About Democracy," in Darryl J. Gless and Barbara Herrnstein Smith, eds. *The Politics of Liberal Education* ((Durham: Duke University Press, 1992), 39.

6. See, for example, Amy Gutmann, *Democratic Education* (Princeton: Princeton University Press, 1987); Michael B. Katz, *Reconstructing American Education* (Cambridge: Harvard University Press, 1987); James Tarrant, *Democracy and Education* (Aldershot, U.K.: Gower, 1989); Elizabeth Kelly, *Education, Democracy, and Public Knowledge* (Boulder: Westview, 1995); Stanley Aronowitz and Henry A. Giroux, *Postmodern Education: Politics, Culture, and Social Criticism* (Minneapolis: University of Minnesota Press, 1991); Benjamin Barber, *An Aristocracy of Everyone* (New York: Ballantine Books, 1992); Ira Shor, *Empowering Education* (Chicago: University of Chicago Press, 1992); David Steiner, *Rethinking Democratic Education* (Baltimore: Johns Hopkins University Press, 1994); Bruce Kimball, *Orators and Philosophers: A History of the Idea of Liberal Education* (New York: College Board, 1995); Bruce Kimball et al., *The Condition of American Liberal Education: Pragmatism and Changing Tradition* (New York: College Board, 1995); Robert Orrill, exec. editor, *Education and Democracy: Reimagining Liberal Learning in America* (New York: College Board, 1997); Martha C. Nussbaum, *Cultivating Humanity: A Classical Defense of Reform in Liberal Education* (Cambridge: Harvard University Press, 1997).

7. Gutmann, *Democratic Education,* 14.

8. Henry Giroux, "Introduction: Critical Education or Training: Beyond the Commodification of Higher Education," in Henry A. Giroux and Kostas Myrsiades, eds, *Beyond the Corporate University: Culture and Pedagogy in the New Millennium* (Lanham, Md.: Rowan and Littlefield, 2001), 6.

9. Gutmann, *Democratic Education,* 306, 309.

10. Barber, *Aristocracy of Everyone.*

11. Gutmann, *Democratic Education,* 287.

Index

academic freedom. *See* faculty
Althusser, Louis, 97–98
American Association of University
  Professors, 133
Aristotle, 145, 149–51, 160, 162; *Rhetoric*,
  162
Arkansas high school killings, 201–05
Arnold, Matthew, 159, 212; *Culture and
  Anarchy*, 154
Aronowitz, Stanley, 175, 176
assessment, 93–95, 192
Astin, Alexander, 93–94

Barber, Benjamin, 24–25, 219, 224
Barrow, Clyde, 96–100, 134–36, 138
Baudrillard, Jean, 178
Bell, Daniel, 35–36, 139, 157, 201, *See also*
  cultural contradictions
Bender, Thomas, 95–96, 171, 173
Berlin, University of, 92
Bourdieu, Pierre, 19
Boyer, Ernest, 134
"Breaking the Social Contract"
  (report), 51–53
business major, 3, 140

capital: human, 125–26; intellectual, 92–
  93, 102–12
capitalism, and the university, xiii, xv,

9–10, 22–23, 35–36, 101, 111–12, 123,
  132, 140. *See also* corporations;
  corporatization, of the university;
  cultural contradictions; faculty, division of labor
capitalization, of universities, 58–59,
  76–77, 100
Carlin, James E., 116
Carstensen, Peter, 66–67
citizenship, responsible, 21, 193, 217,
  210–11. *See also* democratic education; mission, of university
colonial colleges. *See* liberal education,
  American
Columbine High School killings, 201,
  205
common good, 4, 216–17, 220, 222–23.
  See also, mission, of university
community colleges, 70–71
consumerism, 6, 38–78. *See also*
  corporatization, of university; students, university
Cornell University, 167
corporations: interests in academe, 84–
  85, 96–102; liberalism of, 166; of
  learning, vii, 79–80, 115; philanthropy
  of , 98–100; voluntarism of, 131
corporatization, of the university, 31–
  32, 58, 72–78, 89, 96–103, 173–79;

corporatization (*continued*)
  effects on faculty, 130–38; management styles, 80–83, 109–10
critical thinking, 224–25
cultural contradictions, of the university, xi–xii, xvi, 5, 77–78, 95–96, 125–
  26, 134–42, 204; and their mediation,
  xiii, xvi, 23, 142, 144. *See also* Bell,
  Daniel; curriculum; faculty, division
  of labor; liberal anxieties; market,
  contradictions; university
cultural studies, 198–99
culture: and the humanities, 206; concepts of, 197–206, 210–13; and critique, xii–xvii, 94–95, 119, 204, 217–
  18; and society, 201–09; and truth,
  196–207; University of, 89. *See also*
  liberal education, modernity
culture wars, 37, 102, 108, 133, 147, 200,
  211–12
Cureton, Jeanette, 42–45
curriculum, 20, 47–48, 77, 94, 101, 128;
  and the "big issues," 186, 197, 200,
  207, 213, 219–21, 224; faculty ownership of, 116–20; and power, 196, 198–
  99; and truth, 199, 214–15

Dartmouth College ruling (1819), 114,
  125, 131
deconstruction theory, 172–73, 184
degrees, university, 29, 123–24, 140; as
  credential, 23, 48–50, 56–57; value of,
  48–50, 74–75
democracy, 191, 210, 217; and its discontents, 142, 221; educating for, 217–25.
  See also capitalism; Dewey, John;
  learning; liberal education
democratic education, viii, x–xii, 36–
  37, 143–44, 162, 176, 196; and culture,
  210–13; definition of, 210–26. *See also*
  general education; liberal education
DeMott, Benjamin, 113
Derrida, Jacques, 172, 198, 200

Dewey, John, xiii, 143, 164, 174, 188–94,
  209, 214–15; *Human Nature and Conduct*, 191. *See also* democratic education; pragmatism
digital communications, 111, 136–38, 155;
  and knowledge, 105, 115. *See also*
  Thompson, John B.
disciplines, academic, 11–12, 27, 89–91,
  121, 124–25, 130, 138, 176, 207, 212;
  professionalization of, 170, 172–73,
  176. *See also* interdisciplinary learning; knowledge
division of labor. *See* faculty
Drucker, Peter, 182–88, 190
Duderstadt, James J., *A University for
  the 21ˢᵗ Century*, 7–9, 28

Eliot, T. S., 215, 218
Ellis, John, 197, 200, 206
Enlightenment, the, 195, 211
English departments, 86–87, 149, 157,
  170. *See also* faculty; literary studies
entrepreneurism, academic, xiv, ix, 8–
  10, 24, 28, 41–42, 88
Epicureanism, 146–47
ethics, 200, 205
excellence: rhetoric of, 5, 24, 33–34, 86–
  97, 160; University of, 89

faculty: adjunct, 71, 127; alienation, 124–
  25, 135–38; challenges to, 121; collegiality of, 115, 116, 119, 142; diversity
  of, 222; division of labor, 122–30, 132,
  134, 137–38; English department, 86–
  87; freedom of, 82–83, 114–16, 129–
  30; as knowledge workers, 41–42; and
  power, 83–86, 103, 113–22; professionalization of 90–91; productivity of,
  129; proletarianization of, 89; salaries
  of, 70, 128; subjectivity of, 103, 123;
  and tenure, 113, 128–29, 133. *See also*
  corporatization, of the university;
  disciplines; English departments

federal aid, 32, 52–54, 59, 84. *See also* financial aid; tuition costs

finances, university, 57–72

financial aid, 62–70. *See also* federal aid; tuition costs

for-profit universities, 34–35

Foucault, Michel, 25, 198

Geertz, Clifford, 26, 140

general education, viii, 1, 36–37, 75, 144, 171, 174–76, 207, 210. See *also* curriculum; liberal education

Giroux, Henry, 175, 219, 221–23

Golding, William, 204–05

grade inflation, 32

Graff, Gerald, 119; *Professing Literature*, 170

Guillory, John, 102

Gutmann, Amy, 219, 222–23, 226

Habermas, Jürgen, 195, 198

Hansmann, Henry, 73

Hartle, Terry, 55

Harvard College, 152, 165, 167

Harvard "Red Book" Report, 17–18, 170–71

Harvey, David, *The Condition of Postmodernity*, 122–23, 126

Havel, Vaclav, 211, 214

Hersh, Richard, 13–15

humanism, xii, xvi; Christian, 151–52, 169; pragmatic, xi, 164, 188–93; Renaissance, 152–56, 166, 173, 187. *See also* liberal education; Nussbaum, Martha; pragmatism; Snow, C. P.

humanities, 103, 150–54, 169, 173, 206, 219; and the liberal arts, 151, 172; and the sciences, 154–55, 171–72

idea of the university. *See* university

ideology, 113, 135–38

interdisciplinary learning, 20, 104–05, 173, 208–11, 219–21. *See also* curriculum, and the "great issues"; disciplines; knowledge

Islam, 202–04

Isocrates, 170

Jameson, Fredric, 198

Johns Hopkins University, 168

Kant, Immanuel, 92, 94, 136

Katz, Michael, 130–34, 136

Kelly, Elizabeth, 210–11, 219

Kimball, Bruce, 149–51, 174–75, 192

knowledge: and aesthetics, 162–63, 190; and critique, 94–95; discourses of, 104–05; and the economy, 23–24, 34–35, 41–42, 49–50, 181–86; and emotional intelligence, 191; and enlightenment, 177–79, 193–96; exchange value of, ix, 9–10, 19–23, 34–35, 88, 102–07, 123, 163; for own sake, 26–27, 149, 158–64; and happiness, 177–78, 190; and modernization, 179–88; overaccumulated in the university, 110–11; as power, 102–03, 162, 210; pragmatic, 188–94; and reason, 145–46, 162, 187; and rhetoric, 215–17; and society, 120, 182–88; and symbolic value, ix, 19–23, 92, 107–08, 131, 147, 163; theories of, 144–49, 200, 209–10; utilitarian, 162–63, 183–84, 188; and worldview, 11–12. *See also* capital; curriculum; disciplines; faculty; interdisciplinary learning; modernity; philosophy; pragmatism; truth

Labaree, David, 56–57

land grant universities, 1–2

Langenberg, Donald, 48–50

Lazerson, Marvin, 117, 120

learning: disconnected, 175; and reason, 158–59, 161–63, 168; social power of, 4–5. *See also* assessment; Dewey, John; interdisciplinary learning;

learning (*continued*)
liberal education; knowledge; philosophy; students
Left and Right, politics of, xv–xvi, 200, 208
Levine, Arthur, 42–45
Levine, David O., 101
liberal: anxieties, 138–42; definition of, 12–13, 218; and liberalism, 96, 101. *See also* Ryan, Alan
liberal arts. *See* humanities
liberal arts colleges, 15, 149, 166, 169–70
liberal education, vii, x, 3–6, 107, 143–44; American, 152, 164–73; *artes liberales*, 151, 165; British, 149, 152, 154, 157, 159; Christian, 151–52, 165–67, 169–70; classical, 144–51, 156–57, 165, 187–88; and culture, 208–13; definition of, 12–18; and democratic education, viii, x–xii, 122, 208–26; discontents of, 10–19, 217–18; and the economy, 185–86; faculty views of, 16–17; and general education, 157–58, 163, 174–77; and humanism, 150–53; as key to university mission, 3–6, 9, 88, 116, 176; and modernity, 193–96, 212; and modernization, 179–88; neoclassical, 169; and power, 149, 172–73, 186–87; and pragmatism, 174–75, 192; specialization in, 172; traditional, 26–27, 185–87. *See also* liberal; Newman, John Henry
literary studies, 150–54, 156–58, 166–69. *See also* English departments; power and aesthetics
logos, 149–50
Lucas, Christopher, 21–22

McKeon, Richard, 154
Malcolm Baldridge National Quality Award, 33
Marchese, Ted, 45–46
market, 3, 27, 143, 182; contradictions of, 33–37; culture of, 23–37; educational, vii–ix, 22–27, 75–77, 84, 94, 100–01; forces of, 7–9, 21–22, 29–31, 106, 221
Marx, Karl, 122, 124, 200
massification, of higher education, 178
Mather, Cotton, 165
Menand, Louis, 114–15
metaphysics, 36, 88, 144–48, 164, 189, 199–200, 209. *See also* liberal education, Christian, classical; Newman, John Henry; Plato
mission, of university: complexity of, viii, xv, 1–6, 21, 88, 93–95; cultural, 206–07; and liberal education, 176; social, 21, 27, 121, 160–61, 175, 196, 206–07, 216–17, 219, 221–22. *See also* citizenship; culture; democratic education; liberal education
modernity, 89, 140, 191, 193–96, 211. *See also* Enlightenment; knowledge
modernization of American higher education. *See* knowledge; university
Morrill Acts. *See* land grant universities

nature and nurture, 205–06
Neef, Dale, 181–82
Newman, John Henry, 92, 144, 149, 154, 188–90, 192; *The Idea of a University*, 154, 158–64, 211
Nussbaum, Martha, 179–81, 188

philosophy, 143, 148, 153, 160–61, 189. *See also* knowledge; learning
Plato, 145, 150, 155, 160–61; the *Laws*, 158
power: and aesthetics, 168–69; in the Renaissance, 152–53; in the university, 25–26, 83–86, 96–102, 113–15, 152–56, 185–87, 226. *See also* curriculum; knowledge; students
pragmatism, 174, 188–93. *See also* Dewey, John; humanism; knowledge, pragmatic; Rorty, Richard

President's Commission for Higher
Education Report (1947), 171
professional education, 71, 183. *See also*
knowledge
public intellectuals, xiii

Ramist logic, 153, 156
Readings, Bill, 89, 91
Renaissance humanism. *See* humanism
research, vii, 2–3, 171; universities, 167–
68, 170. *See also* science
rhetoric, 148–58, 161, 168, 213–17. *See
also* knowledge; truth
Rich, Frank, 201–02, 204–05
Rorty, Richard, 214, 215
Rudolph, Frederick, 178
Ryan, Alan, 141

Sandel, Michael, 142
Sartori, Giovanni, 33, 217
science, 150, 152, 168–70, 172, 181, 206–
07; social, 219–20; technoscience, vii,
181. *See also* humanities; research
Slevin, James, 86–88
Snow, C. P., 154–55
Socrates, 144, 223
Sophism, 144, 153
standards, academic, 91–92
Starr, S. Frederick, 41
Steiner, David, 219
Stimpson, Catherine R., 116–20
Stoicism, 146
students, university: admissions, 29–30;
borrowing and debt of, 46–47, 52–55;
consumerism of, 6, 38–41, 44; demographics of, 42–44, 71; enrollments
of, 42–43, 58; and learning, 8, 47–48,
158; and power, 83–86; psychological
issues of, 44–45; quality of, 46–47;
study habits of, 45–46; talent development of, 93–94. *See also* assessment; curriculum; general education;
knowledge; learning

tenure. *See* faculty
Thompson, Denis, 219
Thompson, John B., 107, 136–37
Thurow, Lester, 22–23, 125
trustees, 82–83; activist, 113–20, 133
truth: and beauty, 163–64; and curriculum, 199–200; and epistemology,
144–49, 209; and language, 153–57;
and rhetoric, 213–17. *See also* culture;
Dewey, John
tuition costs, 51–57; and democratic
practices, 66–67; and income levels,
60–61; and price-fixing, 64–66. *See
also* financial aid

university: antitrust issues, 64–66;
bureaucracy of, 25, 132; as business,
57–58, 79; challenges to, ix–x; cultural mediation of, 142; idea of, ix,
92, 94, 158–64; modernization of, 98–
101, 130–35, 167; politics of, xv–xvii;
power of American, ix, 28, 191–92;
power in, 113–14; professionalism of,
30–31; quality of, 32; revenues of, 59–
60; "in ruins," xiii, 89, 91; social value
of, xiii, 92–93; as text, 26–27. *See also*
capitalization; corporations; corporatization; cultural contradictions;
market; mission

values, 200–07, 219, 221, 225–26
Vassar College, 167
Veblen, Thorstein, 79–80; *Higher
Learning in America*, 179
Veysey, Laurence, 132, 134
Von Humboldt, Alexander, 92

Washington, George, 177
Western civilization, 16–17
Winston, Gordon, 72–76
Wu, Amy, 38–41, 47, 50

Yale Report (1828), 166–67

.